COOK for HIRE

COOK *for* HIRE

OR HOW TO CASH IN ON YOUR COOKING

MICHELLE BERRIEDALE-JOHNSON

Macdonald Orbis

For Pat and Susie
— fellow labourers in an entertaining cause

A *Macdonald Orbis* BOOK
© Michelle Berriedale-Johnson 1987

First published in Great Britain in 1987
by Macdonald & Co (Publishers) Ltd
London & Sydney

A member of BPCC plc

British Library Cataloguing in Publication Data

Berriedale——Johnson, Michelle
    Cook for hire.
    1. Food service management——Great
    Britain   2. Small business——Great
    Britain——Management
    I. Title
    647'.95'068   TX911.3.M27
    ISBN 0-356-12568-8

Filmset by Tradespools Ltd, Frome, Somerset

Printed and bound in Great Britain by
Purnell Book Production Limited
Member of the BPCC Group

Editor: Julie Dufour
Designer: Dave Goodman
Production: Julia Mather
Indexer: Dorothy Frame

Illustrations by Ellis Nadler
Diagrams on page 21 by Michael Hodson Designs

Photographs on pages 65, 66, 67 and 68 from *Table
Decoration*, Malcolm Robertson/Macdonald Orbis;
pages 93, 94, 95 and 96, The Anthony Blake Photo
Library.

Acknowledgements
With many thanks to Pat Harbottle, ex-partner, ex-co-
director of Catercall and now, as owner/director of
Winecall, successful wine merchant, for advice,
corrections, bright ideas, general inspiration – and for
having got me into catering in the first place!

Macdonald & Co (Publishers) Ltd
Greater London House
Hampstead Road
London NW1 7QX

CONTENTS

INTRODUCTION

Women and men, both married and single, have been cooking to feed themselves and their families since time immemorial, but it is only relatively recently that amateurs have scented the chance of making some money out of it. A full-time career as a cook or chef has always been a possibility for anyone, but the flexibility of work patterns in modern society has enormously increased the openings for part-time or freelance cooking, especially for the unqualified or marginally qualified cook.

However, no one should assume that this blossoming of opportunity is a golden road to an early retirement. Cooking is hard physical work, labour intensive and, relatively speaking, badly paid. It *is* possible to make a fortune, but you will need to be very talented, very lucky, and extremely hard working. And, you will eventually have to standardize, mechanize and depersonalize, which to many people will take much of the pleasure out of the game. This is not to say that it is not worth doing – just that you should be aware of what you are letting yourself in for before you do it.

So before the enthusiasm engendered by good company, an excellent dinner and better wines gets you into trouble, sit down and seriously assess yourself, your talents, your aspirations and your family situation.

First of all, what are you looking for? Do you want some pin money and an interest, a reasonable part-time job, or a full-time career? Although the first can always turn into the last, it is probably as well to try to decide at the start what is your goal; if for no other reason than to help you decide how you are going to set about it. The range of possibilities is enormous and these are set out in detail on pages 9–19.

How keen are you on cooking? Are you happy to do it from 8 am to 8 pm six or even seven days a week? Or is it the idea of organizing glamorous parties that appeals? The answer to that question will determine whether you should be a cook or a caterer (for further discussion of what each of these entails, see pages 9 and 12). Not that I am suggesting that you should attempt to run a catering business without being a competent cook, but if you are successful, the cooking will eventually take a secondary role.

Assuming that you genuinely enjoy cooking, how good a cook are you? You do not have to have had specialist training to make a good living out of cookery, although such a background can often be valuable, but you must be competent. You cannot afford too many gaping holes in your knowledge or skills, although you should certainly try to concentrate on the kind of food that you are happy with and cook well.

Are you a consistent cook? Can you guarantee that your Bœuf Bourgignon will taste as good on the 178th portion as it did on the first?

Are you imaginative about dishes? You will need some originality if you are going to be competitive.

Can you work fast? Speed is absolutely essential if you are going to cook commercially.

Can you present and decorate your dishes attractively? This skill is vital if you hope to sell your food to someone else.

Assuming that you pass these tests, move on to the next stage of evaluation.

How much physical strength and stamina do you have? Cooking itself is hard work, and you may find yourself humping crockery and cutlery up four floors to your client's dining room as well! What is more, the nature of freelance work means that you will be snowed under with work one week and have nothing to do at all the next. Will you be able to cope with this imbalance?

If you live with other people, are they going to be able to deal with the ups and downs of your 'other life'? Given the high element of risk involved, you would be ill advised to launch yourself on a freelance cooking career with a family who were not prepared to put up with other people's gourmet meals all over the house while they ate Chinese take-away; to help you roll smoked salmon in the early hours of the morning when you have miscalculated how long a party will take to do; or to answer the phone and smooth ruffled clients while you rescue the wedding cake from the cat. Partners, mothers, children and friends can be invaluable, free (or cheap!) assistants in the early years but you do need them on your side.

If you are still on line and eager to go, a little more personal assessment is in order.

A small business, especially if it is essentially a one-person business, requires an enormous range of talents of its owner. You must not only be able to cook, assuming that is what your business is, but you must know how to price your product and market it, deal with your customers, keep track of your supplies and do your books. Above all, and this applies to catering for functions on outside premises in particular, you must be able to organize. Failure in any one of these areas can spell disaster for a small enterprise, especially when its funding is slender. If you are nervous about any of these jobs, you would be wise to try and involve someone else who can make up your deficiencies. Alternatively, try to specialize in an area that will maximize your own strengths and not require you to do too much of what you feel you are not good at; you could, for example, just concentrate on decorating cakes or making pâtés or sweets if you feel that is where your forte lies.

Moreover, remember that as soon as you start to sell the product of your hard work you are subject to a whole series of rules and regulations that may complicate your venture beyond your wildest dreams.

The most important of these, if you are involved in a food business, are those drawn up by the Department of Environmental Health. With good reason, their standards are high and their regulations strict, and without their approval you are not legally entitled to sell a grain of home-roasted popcorn. If you are proposing to cook from your own kitchen, the health officers may insist on all kinds of changes to your kitchen that would make the venture entirely unacceptable, either financially or in terms of comfort and convenience, so get yourself inspected before you spend too much effort on other planning.

Another necessity is insurance. I am sure that you would have no intention of poisoning your clients, and it is very unlikely that you would, but if you did, they could sue you and you could be forced to sell house and home to settle the claim.

Consider also the question of staff. If you decide to employ anyone other than freelance or casual help, you will get involved in PAYE, personal taxation, national insurance and all the complications of the employment and unfair dismissal legislation.

Finally, having swallowed all that, you also need to be sure that you will be happy working alone. Freelance cooks who hire out their skills to prepare food for others either at their customers' homes or their own can lead fairly solitary lives. This is especially so in the early days when there may not be much work around and you cannot afford to employ anyone to help – and keep you company. If this bothers you, it might be wiser to look for a job within an existing organization or try to find a partner or group similarly inclined into which you could slot.

Decisions as to where and with whom you choose to work will also be governed by your home and family circumstances. If the other members of your household want nothing to do with your operation, you will obviously have to base yourself, and seek moral and physical support, elsewhere. The shape and size of your home, and especially your kitchen, are also of vital importance. It is amazing what can be done in a remarkably small space, but be realistic – you cannot seriously run even a small cooking business with two rings and a counter-top fridge. If those are all the facilities you have, then you will have to operate away from home.

A final but relevant consideration: can you drive? And do you have fairly regular access to a car? If not, you will probably be restricted to cooking in other people's kitchens as carrying dinner party dishes to their destination on the bus is not very satisfactory – although there are successful caterers who began this way.

If you have got this far and still feel that semi-professional or professional cooking is for you, it is time to look in more detail at precisely what you could do, where, how, and for how much.

What Sort of Cooking To Do?

The opportunities for freelance cooks are legion, but they do depend greatly on where you live, your facilities, and your own particular skills. How much you want to earn from your labours is also a relevant consideration! Not, of course, that you should necessarily stick rigidly to your chosen market – businesses have a way of evolving almost despite their owners – but some sort of targeting is necessary to get you off the ground.

The first thing is to decide in broad terms where your culinary interests lie. First, what kind of fare should you offer: gourmet food or 'plain but simple old-fashioned cooking', healthfoods, ethnic cuisines, children's food, freezer cooking, cake decorating, petits fours and confectionery, sandwiches and picnics, soups and pâtés? Secondly, what type of function can you cope with best: small and select groups or large numbers, private parties or business functions, weekend shooting parties, or the over-sixties' Christmas lunch? To a certain extent, your choice will be governed by whether you live in the country (plenty of openings for private dinner parties and freezer filling) or a large city (business lunches and corporate entertaining). It will also be influenced by what facilities you have for cooking at home and whether you want to be based at home or not. How much you want or need to earn is also important, so bear the cash potential of each option in mind when you consider it. To spur your imagination, I am listing as many possibilities as I can think of below, although I am sure that there are many more just waiting to be discovered.

Freelance Cooking
As a freelance cook, as opposed to a caterer, you can hire out your services to restaurants, hotels, wine bars, sandwich bars, catering companies, institutional caterers, cake makers, etc. You will only get paid by the hour so there will be no security, but you could gain a wide range of experience at someone else's expense. If you make a total hash of it, the worst that can happen is that they refuse to have you back for a second day! It is worth trying to establish contacts with several establishments, because catering is such a variable business that you never know when they may get particularly busy – or their chef may slice his thumb off with the Sabatier – and they will be in desperate need of a competent freelancer to fill the gap for a few days.

If you are thinking of running a catering business at any point, you would be wise to accept related jobs, such as waiting on tables, as you will need to know about this side of the business later – and anyhow you might get tipped!

Jobs can usually be found through agencies or by plodding round and banging on doors. This can be done literally or, with a lot less effort, on the telephone. In either case, you will need a fairly tough hide as some potential employers can be quite unpleasant. It is also worth scanning pages of local or specialist papers as you never know when you will see an advertisement for freelance cooks – or an advertisement or write up about an organization that might be able to use your skills – or at least enthusiasm!

The rate of pay varies enormously depending on where you live, your skill and experience. Try ringing up several potential employers and asking them what they *would* pay you *if* they had an opening. That will give you some idea of what fee you should be charging.

Directors' Lunches This covers a wide range of jobs, both freelance and permanent. It normally involves cooking for relatively small numbers (four to fifteen); sometimes in the firm's kitchen and sometimes at home, but this will mean you have to deliver the food to the company. You can try and get yourself a contract with one or two small companies who may only want a meal once a week or even once a month, or you can get yourself on the books of several companies who may have more irregular needs. If you have very limited facilities at home, it may be invaluable to be able to use someone else's kitchen to prepare their food. Indeed, many freelance or part-time cooks use their employers' kitchens to prepare food for quite different functions – often with the employers' blessing! Most employers have no use for their kitchens except to prepare their own meals so, if being able to use it for other functions keeps a good cook happy and in their employ, they are not bothered.

Cooks dealing with directors' lunches are either paid a salary or fee based on the time that they spend on the job and are reimbursed for the food they buy, or they quote an 'all-in' price for their work. The subject of pricing is gone into in much greater detail in the final chapter. However, if you are starting off and need to be able to quote an all-in price, try to work out what the food will cost and how long it will take you to buy, prepare and deliver. Charge your time at whatever seems to be the going rate in your area, add the cost of the food and, hey presto, you have a price.

Cooking for Institutions If you would feel happier with simpler cooking, you could also establish relationships with the canteens in local schools, hospitals, meals on wheels, sporting or social clubs, factories, and so on. Some larger institutions may have problems employing too many casual staff, but most of them go through crisis periods when a reliable freelance cook could,

literally, save their bacon. If you choose to work for a larger institution, you will probably have to accept whatever rate of pay they offer, which may not be very high. Nevertheless, it is always worth at least asking for more – they can only refuse.

Holiday Cooking Many freelance cooks find this a good way of gaining experience, although it is usually pretty hard work. It involves travelling with a family or group on holiday and providing for them while there. The risk is that you are stuck with the family for the length of the holiday, so you need to be very sure that you are going to get on before you take the job. You should also establish beforehand exactly what your duties entail so that you do not find yourself working twenty hours a day to keep a family of ten satisfied. However, the saving grace, as with all freelance work, is that you do not have to stick with it. If they are really terrible, you can just walk out; if it is grim but bearable, it is not for ever.

Pay for this type of work is on the whole poor, the theory being that you too are getting a holiday. However, since you are probably going to have to work pretty hard, even if the holiday is in the one place in the world you have always wanted to visit, you would be wise to insist on a reasonable rate. If you get a job through an agency, they will advise you about pay, but even if you are thinking of taking a job privately, it would be worth making a call to an agency to establish the 'going rate'. If you cannot find an agency to talk to, answer lots of advertisements, even if you don't want the jobs, just to get some idea of what fee is being offered for what work.

An extremely popular version of this holiday cooking – ladies only! – is 'chalet girling'. This is a splendid way to gain experience and have fun, if you have no ties, and like skiing. Most of the travel companies organize chalet parties and are always on the look out for good cooks. Again, the pay is not marvellous, but most chalet girls are quite happy to put up with low pay for the chance of spending a whole winter on the slopes – and meeting the ski instructor of their dreams! But remember that you do have to make the beds, do the shopping, cook the food and be nice to the guests before you can head for the slopes.

Another alternative along the same lines is 'expedition cooking'. There are a variety of teams and groups, from archaeologists to pop musicians, who spend their time on tours or expeditions and usually need someone to tend to their needs. If you have a particular hobby or interest, you might well be able to squeeze yourself onto an otherwise barred expedition by offering to cook for them! Again, pay will probably be minimal since few expeditions have money to spare for frivolities like food, but if it is something you are really keen to do, the pay will not be so relevant.

Dinner Party Cooking This is one of the most traditional areas of freelance cookery. It usually involves going to a private house to prepare a breakfast, lunch, supper or dinner party for anything from two to twenty people; it is also the way that many cooks start in the business. From the cook's point of view, it means that all the preparation can be done in someone else's house, using someone else's light, heat and equipment. This is invaluable if you do not have the space to cope at home or are anxious not to increase your domestic bills. However, it does mean that your employer may be standing over you while you work, which, if you are at all nervous about your skills, could be devastating. You may be expected to serve the food, so you should be prepared for this. You should also have some idea about pricing

before you go to your first interview – for this, see the final chapter, and opposite under Directors' Lunches.

You can earn quite a decent 'wage' doing dinner party cooking, but you will find it impossible to expand (see below). However, this sort of arrangement works particularly well for people who are only looking for a fixed income and do not want their 'career' to intrude into their home or upset the other inhabitants.

Barbecues These are becoming increasingly popular, but as a barbecue cook you may have to invest in the equipment necessary to deal with large numbers so as to avoid endless queues. You may, however, be able to establish a relationship with a barbecue shop who would supply you with relatively cheap equipment and recommend you to their clients – in return, of course, for your encouraging *your* clients to buy a barbecue. However, you will also be so reliant on the season and the weather that, if you need to make a regular income, it might be wise to use barbecues only as a speciality within a wider catering business.

You may find that your clients want to provide the food themselves – on the basis that they will get it cheaper. This is fine provided you liaise with them to make sure they are getting enough of the right thing – if they don't and the party is a disaster, inevitably you will get the blame! In this case, you will only charge for your time and the use of your equipment.

Freezer Filling Another cooking job that is sometimes done in the employer's kitchen is preparing food for the freezer, although this can also be cooked perfectly well at home and then delivered to the client. Freezer filling is fine if you already do a lot of freezer cooking for yourself and are merely 'mopping up excess capacity'. The problem with doing it on a commercial basis is that there is so much top-quality, commercially frozen food on the market at really quite reasonable prices that it is very hard to compete. Large companies have all the advantage of economy of scale, so unless you can produce something really quite outstanding, people will not be prepared to pay substantially more for it – which they will have to if it is going to pay you to make it. Remember also that you will have to stock a wide range of packaging materials. If you want to buy these at competitive prices, you will have to buy in bulk which will both tie up capital and require a lot of precious storage space (see also page 18).

This basically completes the list of job options open to freelance cooks with nothing but their skill (and their favourite knife) to offer. For cooks with skill, a favourite knife *and* a base to work from the range increases enormously and you start to move into the realms of catering.

Catering

Once you start to cook from home or from some independent premises, you are into a totally different 'ball game'. As long as you cook in other people's kitchens, you are limited both by the size of their kitchen and by the fact that, most of the time, you can only cook their particular order. Once you cook in independent premises, you will have control over the size and equipment of your kitchen and can improve or extend it to cope with an extra work load. But, much more important, you can prepare two, three, four or many more orders at the same time, thus saving time. It is a recognized fact that twenty portions of any dish take proportionately far less time to cook than four. You can also save money by buying in bulk to fulfil several orders where just one would not have justified it. You can save more time by delivering two or three orders together, and you can bring in extra people to help you if you need them. If you have the work to do or make a major miscalculation on time, you can even work until three in the morning, which you certainly could not do in someone else's kitchen! In other words, you can expand.

Of course, expansion will bring its own headaches and, although you may be making more money, you will also have higher overheads and more responsibility. So before following this course you must first decide whether you are really interested in expansion and can cope with all the extra problems this entails, or whether the hopefully fat fee that you would get from hiring out your skills alone would do you very nicely, thank you.

If you do decide to be independent, you need to at least start off with some idea of the area of cooking you want to aim for. There is much to be said both for and against specialization at an early stage. Since there are so many people nowadays offering cooking services, it may help you stand out from the crowd if you can offer something really unusual. This can just be a variant on general cooking – a Caribbean or 'low calorie' theme to a standard range of starters, main course and dessert dishes for general entertaining. Alternatively, you can go for something quite exclusive – wedding or gimmick cakes, petits fours and confectionery, picnics and hampers. If your skills only run to one type of cooking, then you will not have much choice in the matter. But, assuming that you are capable of a wider scope, the dangers in specializing too early are either that you may choose a speciality that no one wants, or that you may get 'type cast' so that no one will come to you for anything other than your 'speciality'. The best compromise may be to offer a general range but with particular emphasis on one specific area. In any case, it would be wise to aim for an area of cooking that you do at least enjoy and feel confident about.

'Social' Catering

This covers an enormously wide variety of functions – up and down market, large and small – but essentially it involves providing food for specific social gatherings. These can be purely social – family or friends – or they can be 'official' – clubs, civic receptions, etc. The parties may meet up for breakfast, lunch, tea, drinks or dinner; they may get together to celebrate a particular event or merely for a reunion. But whatever it is, they want to eat, drink and be merry.

You will be governed in your choice of client to a certain extent by where you live. Civic receptions are a bit thin on the ground in the depths of the country, whereas people giving dinner parties are quite easy to come by. Similarly, dinner parties or buffet suppers will be more frequent than drinks parties in the country where guests may have to travel some distance and will not be bothered to go if all there is on offer is a drink and a tired asparagus roll.

The aspiring caterer will obviously be anxious to lay hands on as much business as possible no matter what category it may fall into, but the main areas range from dinner parties or lunches to weddings.

Private clients will normally pay by return, although if you are at all dubious about them, you would be wise to get a deposit to cover your outlay.

Private Dinner or Lunch Parties   These are normally for quite small groups (they could also be dealt with by the freelance cook – see above), but will require relatively sophisticated food. If the hosts or hostesses are going to pay someone else to do their cooking, they will want something that they cannot do themselves. You should have all the normal range of 'cordon bleu' type dishes available, but have some unusual specialities to offer and be prepared to accommodate whatever bizarre ideas the client may have!

If you are to do a lot of this type of catering, it would pay you to develop a few – but not too many or your client will suspect that you do not *really* know much about any of them – 'specials' of your own. Experiment with ethnic cuisine – try not to offer just French and Italian, but don't get too carried away: not everyone will want to give Eskimo dinner parties all winter – even if the weather may warrant it! Historic food has a certain appeal – the 1930s, 1950s, Elizabethan, Roman – or offer vegetarian, low calorie or slimming menus, or even 'colour coordinated' meals. Once you put your mind to it, you can come up with all kinds of possibilities. You will also need to plan menus to tempt clients who have no idea what they want – or want something that you know will be disgusting in practice. For more information on menu planning and dealing with clients, see pages 46 and 105.

Pricing can either be split into the cost of the food plus your time, or you can quote an 'all-in' fee. You will very rapidly discover that the larger number you cater for, the more economical it proves; so that a dinner for eight will be appreciably more profitable than a dinner for four. You can 'penalize' the small numbers by charging them relatively more, although the danger is, of course, that you will price yourself out of a job. In the early days, you are probably wise to do anything that comes your way, but you will need to keep a close eye on the situation as your business develops. You will be surprised how quickly you will find it is literally 'costing you money' to do very small functions.

'Sit Down' Dinners for Large Numbers These are seldom private parties as few people have houses large enough to seat more than eight to ten people. If private individuals do want to seat large numbers (weddings and so on), they normally go to a hotel, although you may find yourself doing the odd 'sit down' job in a marquee. The majority of 'social sit downs' will either be civic celebrations of some kind – normally sited in the town hall or a similar venue – or 'club' functions. 'Clubs' in this context could cover everything from Masonic or Round Table dinners, through sporting clubs and church groups to over-sixties' outings and youth clubs.

Obviously, each group will require entirely different menus, but you should keep in mind that, since the guests will have no choice of meal, you may be restricted to relatively boring but generally acceptable food. In many cases, you may also have dietary or cash restrictions on what you can provide. Remember that 'sit down' meals need to be served so you will have to be equipped with efficient waiting staff (for staffing, see pages 124–8). You may also be expected to deal with pre-dinner drinks, wines and liqueurs – and their service (see pages 120–3).

This sort of catering can be very lucrative, but you do have to take great care over your pricing and costing; once you start dealing in larger figures, it is all too easy to miscalculate and find yourself losing money where you should be making it! You will also frequently find yourself being asked to cut your costs to a minimum to squeeze within someone's budget; the danger is that in your eagerness to get the work you will cut your price to the point that you are making no money on the function at all. For further information on pricing, see pages 142–5.

Buffet Parties This is the alternative that most private individuals wanting to give a large party opt for; they can be either 'fork' or 'finger'. A buffet meal can be for almost any number and allows you more freedom in the choice of food. However, you are restricted by the fact that all the food has to be easy to eat with a fork or with the fingers and, on the whole, should benefit from being prepared in advance. It also needs to look good and, hopefully, not to make too much of a mess of the house or hall in which it is eaten (see menu planning, pages 54–60).

Many experienced caterers will try to guide their clients towards 'finger buffets' which gets rid of the need for forks and a lot of extra clutter. With a little bit of imagination, you can plan wonderful 'finger-sized' dishes that will provide the guests with a more than ample meal (see menu planning, pages 52–4).

Buffet parties, like sit down dinners, can be very lucrative, but again, you must take great care over your costing and pricing (see pages 142–5).

Cocktail Parties Cocktail parties are invaluable for people wanting to return hospitality to a large number of friends or acquaintances without having to talk to any of them! They nearly always take place in overcrowded rooms where it is all too easy to drop your soggy vol-au-vent down your neighbour's new silk shirt, so choice of 'cocktail bits' is vitally important. Since it is a very popular form of entertaining, and on the whole the food normally offered is uninspiring, not to say actually disgusting – drooping 'canapés' with tired olives – a reputation for producing really delicious cocktail titbits will guarantee you a lot of work. This is especially true of business entertaining where the clients are out to make an impression (see cocktail party menus, pages 48–51).

You could build yourself up quite a nice little business just providing the food for cocktail parties, since most private hosts are anxious to handle their own drinks. As long as you can devise a way of arranging your food attractively on your clients' dishes so that their family or friends can be hi-jacked into taking them round, you avoid all complications of staff, collection of dirty dishes, and all the other jobs such parties entail.

As the cost of the food for cocktail 'bits' is usually quite low, you can make a good deal of money on them. However, 'canapés' are also very fiddly, so the profit you made on the food can all too easily be lost in the extra time taken. Reasonably speedy but effective decoration is the name of the game. For ideas on menus and pricing, see pages 46–69 and 142–5.

14

Weddings Many cooks and caterers make an excellent living by doing nothing but weddings, with the occasional christening or funeral thrown in. However, it is a branch of catering that stands entirely on its own, not because the food, drink or service required is that different from any other, but because the wedding is an extremely important day in your client's life. If you are to make a success of catering for weddings, it is essential that you can deal with all the stresses and strains that the occasion creates. For further details, see pages 132–3.

Catering for Kids There is a continual need for children's party food both in towns and in the country, but it is not easy to hit the right balance.

The food must be fairly simple, fun, and well packaged. Now that everyone is so additive conscious, especially as far as children's food is concerned, it should be as 'pure' and 'healthy' as possible and you should avoid any ingredients that are likely to cause upset stomachs, hyperactivity, etc. (see pages 61–2 for suggestions). From the parents' point of view, it should create as little mess as possible and the food should also be reasonably cheap, since parents are unwilling to fork out nearly as much for their children's food as they are for their own! This means that your profit margins may have to be fairly slender, but if you plan carefully, you should be able to make a reasonable income. However, if you enjoy cooking for and working with children, it could be worth your while.

Incidentally, if you are going to do children's parties, you would be well advised to provide yourself with a list of children's entertainers and cake makers (if you cannot do them yourself) to offer your potential clients (for 'ancillary services', see page 131).

There is also a market for children's lunch boxes, but the problem of producing these within reasonable financial limits makes it impractical as a serious way of making money.

Business Catering

Business catering differs from private only in the nature of the clients and the kind of service they need. Some caterers find it a far more satisfactory atmosphere to work in, others prefer the more personalized nature of private catering.

A business client requires good service, just as much as a private client, but although he or she will usually take a close interest in the event, especially if it is an important one, the nature of the interest is professional rather than personal. This may sound as though I am playing with words, but in effect it means that business people, as long as they have faith in your ability, will leave you to get on and organize their food or their function; the host of a private dinner party will want to have a more personal involvement. It is also true that business clients often have more money to spend and, since it is not their money, they are not quite so concerned where every penny goes! 'Business lunches' (see page 10) fall slightly between the two stools as they are usually provided for the in-house staff and the occasional guest on a fairly regular basis. The cook or caterer therefore gets to know his or her client far better than in a 'one-off' situation and will develop more of a 'family' or personal relationship with him or her as time progresses.

The types of meal that you may be required to prepare for business clients will fall into the same general categories as in private catering. However, you will normally find that business clients will be delighted if you take the whole organization of the function off their shoulders. So, thinking that you were organizing a simple dinner, you could also find yourself arranging staff, cloakrooms, entertainers, chauffeurs, menus, place cards, gifts for the guests, and dancing girls! This can provide a quite substantial extra income as you should, and will be expected to, charge for your time and contacts in organizing these extra services.

Over the last ten years, business entertaining has also come to be seen in a much sharper 'commercial' light. If a company throws a party, it does so because its managers or members wish to woo, impress or thank potential or existing clients, suppliers or staff – they seldom throw a party merely to have a good time. This means that the party must not only run smoothly, but should be so enjoyable that the guests remember it with positive pleasure if not delight. The unspoken corollary to this is that they will also think better of the hosts and subconsciously be more prepared to fall in with the hosts' plans. As a result, originality in terms of food, location, entertainment and whatever else may be laid on to improve the party and make it 'truly memorable' is of vital importance.

Although business clients usually have more money to spend than private ones, they tend not to pay so fast. This is not necessarily through bloody-mindedness, but because large companies' accounts are organized in monthly, or two-monthly, cycles and, if your bill happens to arrive at the end of one cycle, you may have to wait for the full period to go round before you get paid. It is also true that some of the biggest companies are notoriously bad payers and will delay payment for two, three or even four months, thus causing considerable hardship to their smaller suppliers. If you are relatively small and you are dealing with a large company, make it quite clear at the start that you cannot afford to wait for your money; most companies have ways of circumventing the system.

Although companies do entertain in the evening and at weekends, they prefer to do so between 9 am and 5 pm, Monday to Friday, whereas most private entertaining is done on Friday evenings and at weekends – for obvious reasons. Your choice will be influenced by what fits in better with your personal life style.

Specialist Catering

If you do not want to get involved in the general hurly burly of party catering and there is one particular area of cookery that interests you, or if you think you see a wonderful commercial opening that no one else has spotted, you may want to concentrate on a specific product. The advantages are, of course, the expertise and speed gained by practice, savings in costs through bulk buying of your fairly limited raw materials, and the possibility of 'sewing up' a specific market. The disadvantages could be boredom and staleness, plus the increased difficulty in building up a retail market for a very specific product than for a more generalized service. You might find yourself having to sell your wares to other retailers (shops, restaurants, delicatessens or other caterers) who have wider outlets. Since they also have to make a living, you will have to accept a lower price to cover their 'mark up' (see below).

Successful specialization usually depends on spotting a gap in the market – and filling it – no matter how trivial it might appear to be. On a recent canal trip, as I was struggling with the fourteenth lock gate that day, the keeper stuck his head round his front door and asked whether I would be interested in buying in some home-made pasties and apple pie – how could I resist! In fact, they were frozen, but none the less excellent. His good lady no doubt did a monthly bake up and I am sure they did a roaring trade. I am listing a few other examples below, but some serious research into the needs and habits of your local community could throw up all kinds of possibilities.

Specialist Cakes A growing area for the freelance cook is speciality cakes, which, of course, includes wedding cakes. Cake decorating is an art in its own right – any competent cook can make the cakes – but if you enjoy cake decorating and are good at it, it can be lucrative. Many cooks who are artistically inclined just adore decorating wedding cakes and for them the pleasure may outweigh the profit motive, so they will be able to produce them reasonably cheaply – and will always have a queue of people waiting for them. However, even for a skilled and practised decorator, it is a very slow business – you will be horrified at just how many hours you can spend on one cake. So if you intend to make any money, you will have to grit your teeth and charge almost as much as the shops.

Speciality, fun or gimmick cakes – tennis rackets, telephones, computers, horseshoes, cars, tractors, teddy bears, pianos, space rockets, etc. – are in increasing demand, not just for children's parties but for celebrations, anniversaries, business product launches and so on. These require a flair that may come quite easily to those who could not ice a wedding cake to save their life. It is also a skill that will improve as you go along, so if you fancy yourself as a decorator, do not be put off by a couple of failures. With a little practice, you will be surprised what you can produce. However, it is very time-consuming, even for the expert. So be careful when you are costing your masterpiece that you do not find yourself working for slave wages because you have grossly underestimated the time Pooh Bear will take to create. This can cause problems when doing cakes for children's parties, as hard-pressed parents may flinch at a realistic price for creating a realistic Pooh Bear. If you want to make cakes for children, it would be worth working on some relatively simple, but effective, designs that will not take too much time to do. For techniques of cake decorating, see pages 44-5.

If you do not want to deal direct with the public to sell your cakes (and it can be quite hard to get going and get your name about), you can make them for shops, restaurants or catering companies, although you will, of course, get less money for them. If you want to make wedding cakes, it is worth contacting local wedding photographers and showing them some of your wares, either 'live' or *good* photographs, as they often get asked to recommend wedding cake makers.

Petits Fours and Confectionery This is another area that has little to do with general cooking but that has proved very profitable for those who do it well. However, home-made petits fours and 'sweets' are very much in the luxury class, so you will need to ensure that you will have access to sufficiently wealthy clientèle or else be prepared to sell through retail outlets with the consequent drop in selling price. You will also need to have a flair for packaging and decoration as up-market confectionery has to 'look its price'. And will you be able to stand all that chocolate?

Sandwiches Several people have started successful sandwich delivery services, taking orders the night before or even early in the morning and delivering to offices, shops and small factories. This will, obviously, only work if you live in a town. You can start with a minimal investment – and could even do your deliveries without a car – but there is enormous room for expansion if things go well for you. Since many sandwiches freeze successfully, you can work ahead of yourself, although a strong selling point could be that the sandwiches are made fresh daily. You could also 'diversify' by offering Thermos flasks of home-made soup in the winter to go with your sandwiches – each office supplying its own Thermos.

Picnics, Hampers and Packed Lunches On the whole, this is the luxury end of the trade, since the numbers are normally so small that you have to charge a great deal for your food to make it pay. If you are supplying the hampers complete, there is also a considerable investment in equipment, a lot of which may get lost or broken on each outing. It is also both seasonal and heavily dependent on decent weather. However, if you have good contacts with visitors to Ascot, Glydebourne or other society events, you could do quite well.

At the other end of the scale, there is a great need for 'packed lunches' for outings and trips of all kinds: school parties, sports group outings, old people's trips to the seaside, tour buses. The numbers involved in these picnics will be much larger, but your budget, and therefore your profit margin, much smaller. You will also need to make a sizeable investment in disposable packaging, which will not only soak up money, but will require space to store. However, if you could get an entrée with a coach hire company or a tour company, in time you could build up quite a successful business.

Freezer Filling This has already been touched upon (see page 12), but may be worth considering if you do a lot of freezer cooking yourself, or live in an area where there might be a particular call for your services. For example, people who shoot or fish may have quantities of 'sporting trophies' that could well be cooked and frozen. Some housewives would love to save money by buying a whole carcass of meat but cannot face dealing with it – you could butcher and cook it for their freezers. Enthusiastic gardeners with gluts of fruit and vegetables might be only too glad to find someone who would turn them into a year's supply of tarts or gratins. In these cases, you would probably be merely preparing your clients' food for a fee, but you might be able to do a deal by which you got a client's 'glut' at a knock-down price in return for cooking a proportion of it for them. You would then be able to prepare the rest and sell it elsewhere. Remember, however, that the competition from commercially frozen foods will be very stiff.

Jams, Pickles, Preserves or Mustards Pots of home-made jams, marmalades or pickles can always be guaranteed a good sale to those too lazy to make their own! They can also be made in relative bulk when the raw materials are cheap, and stored, so they do not involve you in working every day if you don't want to. The possible disadvantage is that they are difficult to sell except through retail outlets; they are too delicate to seriously consider selling them through mail order. This means that your profit margin may be low. It would be worth approaching tea shops, whose

main income comes from their restaurant trade rather than from selling things, or the gift shops of stately homes, neither of whom might be looking for as a high a mark-up as a regular shop.

Supplying Retail Outlets

As I have pointed out several times, selling your product to a retailer rather than direct to the public means that you cannot charge so much for it – which is not necessarily a reason for not doing it. A wide range of shops, delicatessens, restaurants, tea shops, wine bars and catering companies 'buy in' much of what they sell and are always on the look out for good suppliers of quiches, pâtés, desserts, cakes, ice creams, home-made biscuits, petits fours, or anything else they think they can sell profitably.

If you have a particular talent for making any of these things, it may suit you very well to supply them to a retail outlet, especially if they have a fairly long shelf life so that you can supply them in weekly or fortnightly batches. A contract or agreement with one or two outlets will give you a certain amount of security, allow you to plan and organize your cooking when it is most convenient for you, and indulge yourself in cooking your favourite dishes. However, you should remember that a favourite dish, once it has been cooked five hundred times, may lose a little of its charm. This kind of cooking is also rather lonely since your only contact with the consumers of your wonderful pâté is probably the cleaner who takes in this week's batch when you deliver it. And, to

allow the retailers to put on the 100 per cent plus mark-up that they need to make their own businesses pay, you will not get paid all that much for your goods.

When pricing your food, you will be governed to a large extent by what the pub, delicatessen, or whatever will pay for it. It would certainly be worth trying several different outlets before settling for the pittance that the first one offers – a few hints to the effect that the pub down the road had quoted a higher price per 450 g/1 lb of pâté might not go amiss either. In any case, you must be sure that you cover the cost of your ingredients and your overheads, even if it is worth selling your labour a bit cheap to get off the ground. Do not sell it too cheap; when the time comes for putting up your prices, your clients will be very upset if the rise is too large.

None the less, a couple of small contracts of this kind are invaluable for the cook just starting out as they at least keep some cash flowing in. Just be careful not to allow them to push more lucrative jobs out of the way; the time will probably come when you should resign them to another newcomer and concentrate on the better profit made by selling direct to your client.

Of course, should you want to go into this kind of cooking seriously, there is money to be made in supplying retail outlets, but to make it you need to be able to produce in bulk. This means a considerable degree of standardization, mechanization and automation which may not appeal to the person who really wants to cook – and which will require a large investment in equipment, staff, marketing, etc.

THE PRACTICAL SIDE

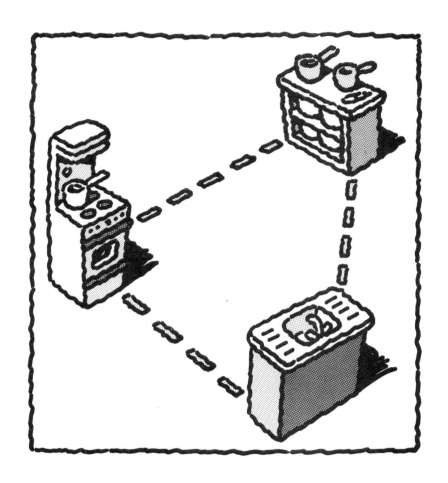

Designing and Equipping a Catering Kitchen

Layout and Major Equipment

Ideally, every catering kitchen should be situated on the ground floor and be large and square, with easy access to shelves and cupboards from wherever you are standing. It should be light and well ventilated, with a convenient opening onto the street, and have a soft but easy-to-clean floor. However, as we all know, ideals are seldom found in this life, so you are probably going to have to make the best of something long, thin, dark, in the basement, with a stone floor and with no windows at all!

A vast amount of research has gone into the planning of domestic kitchens over the last fifty years and most of it can be equally well applied to a commercial kitchen – or a domestic kitchen that is going to have to serve time as a commercial kitchen. The main consideration is to reduce the amount of walking that the cook has to do by positioning the various working areas and pieces of equipment in the most convenient way. This is known as the 'work triangle' and is based on a triangular route between the sink, the cooker and the storage space – the three most used parts of any kitchen.

A commercial or semi-commercial kitchen will have to handle a good deal more than the average domestic one, so you will have to increase the scale of your plans somewhat – that is, of course, if you are in the happy position of being able to plan your kitchen rather than make do with what is there. The two diagrams below illustrate larger commercial kitchens, both with islands, but still attempting to keep the walking to a minimum.

If you do have the chance to choose, a ground floor location is infinitely preferable to any other, both for the delivery of goods to you and for loading your cooked food for delivery to your customers. This becomes even more relevant if you start to supply crockery and cutlery, which is surprisingly heavy and has to be lugged to and from your delivery van – often while still dirty!

However, the chances are that you will be adapting an existing kitchen rather than starting from scratch. The suggestions that I am making below assume that you are either working from home or on a strictly limited budget in separate premises. If and when you move on to a 'dedicated' commercial kitchen, the principles will be the same, but the scale and the cash involvement will be quite different. By that time, you will have a pretty good idea yourself of how you want your kitchen to be! Meanwhile, here are some areas on which to concentrate.

Sinks and Washing Up You will accumulate an enormous number of dirty dishes, pans, etc., so if at all possible, you need a large double sink – one bowl can be used for stacking and washing the dirties, the other can be kept for washing foods, etc. Ideally, both bowls should have some counter space on either side and be as far as possible from

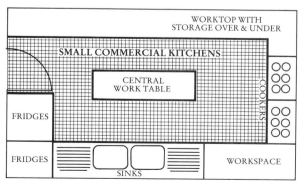

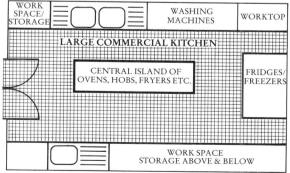

the cooking area. If pans 'back up' on you and have to be stacked on the floor, you want to minimize the risk of falling over them when you are carrying heavy pans of boiling soup.

A high, old-fashioned mixer tap is useful – the smart, low, modern ones prevent you getting any decent-sized pan underneath. And you must make sure that you have *plenty* of hot water. Nothing is worse than trying to clean greasy pans with cold water. A disposal unit in a relatively small kitchen where you may not have too much space for rubbish is useful but not essential.

Whether or not you should have a dishwasher is debatable. They are wonderful in domestic terms and useful for stacking equipment that you are not going to need again soon, but in a busy kitchen the average domestic dishwasher is too small and takes too long to be much use for the cooking equipment. Proper commercial dishwashers are quite another thing, but they are large, very expensive, and require constant attention.

If you are supplying a lot of crockery and cutlery, that is a totally different matter and you will definitely need at least one machine. However, if you possibly can, you should set it up in a separate area so that you are not falling over piles of filthy plates all day. The Environmental Health officer will also insist on a separate sink or basin for washing your hands.

Cookers, Hobs and Ovens Even if you are operating in quite a small way, you are going to be cooking relatively large quantities in relatively large pans. You will, therefore, need the largest hob top that you can get. Four burners will be essential – if you could run to six, or to two separate hobs, so much the better. Whether you use gas or electricity will be a matter of personal choice and where you live (gas is not always available). Modern, radiant electric rings are practically as speedy as gas, although electricity may be rather more expensive to run.

If you have the space, it is better to keep the hob and oven apart, so that if two of you are working in the kitchen you are not constantly shoving each other out of the way. What is more, the person who is working at the hob will not get baked along with the profiteroles in the oven. However,

separation is not essential; most commercial cookers have ovens below their hobs.

What is essential is two ovens, even if the second oven is only small. One oven is terribly limiting as you will only be able to cook one set of things at the same time. If you really do not have space for a second or a double oven, it might be worth investing in a small portable oven or cooker – there are several around – that could be brought out and put on a work top when you were desperate. Another alternative would be to have a dual convection/microwave oven as your back up – as far as I know, there are none manufactured at the moment that would be big enough to use to the exclusion of a conventional oven but new models are constantly appearing on the market.

Whether the ovens are to be on the floor or at eye level is a matter of personal choice. Many people would rather not lift heavy pans from floor level, but you may find that you are running out of counter and eye level space so have no alternative. Again, most commercial cookers have ovens on the floor, so maybe you should just get used to it.

Microwaves People have very different views about microwaves, but I feel that they are an invaluable aid to a serious commercial cook. They are not necessarily useful for what you will cook in them (they are usually too small for more than around eight portions), but are ideal for softening butter, melting gelatine or chocolate, defrosting stocks, sauces and soups, and so on. If you have the space and can afford the cost, I would definitely recommend one, but don't spend a lot of money on fancy pre-timer clocks and gadgetry – concentrate rather on a good turntable, an accurate timer, and a high wattage.

Storage Space Storage space will always be at a premium in any kitchen and, since one of the most successful ways of wasting time is looking for small pots of spices hidden behind tons of flour and baked beans, it will pay you to organize your storage space as efficiently as you can. Whenever possible, frequently used equipment or food should be stored within arm's reach; kitchens are dangerous enough places at the best of times without teetering on wobbly stools to get a fish kettle down from a top shelf. In fact, avoid standing on stools at all costs; a small expenditure either on small folding steps or one of those wheeled stools that you can kick around would prove a good investment.

Dry Goods You will be horrified how many of these you accumulate, especially once you start buying in bulk to save money. In convenience

terms, there is much to be said for storing all dry goods on relatively narrow open shelves. They are easy to see and easy to get at and, as long as the shelf is not too deep, things cannot get lost at the back. You can shelve right up to the ceiling using the higher, less accessible shelves for the spare goods. You can also shelve every little nook and cranny where no cupboard would fit – it is amazing how useful those extra bits of shelving can be. The disadvantage of open shelves is that they get dirty quicker than shelves closed in cupboards, but since you are going to have to clean your new 'commercial' kitchen pretty frequently anyhow, I feel that the extra cleaning is amply compensated for by the extra convenience – not to mention the fact that they are relatively cheap and easy to put up. If you use laminated chipboard, you can buy it in a wide range of widths and it can be installed with minimal disruption on any of the shelf-support systems that are available in all DIY shops. Do remember to paint the ends to keep the Environmental Health officer happy. Cupboards are no easier to install and a great deal more expensive.

If you do go for open shelves, grade them in depth terms, giving yourself long, narrow shelves for spices and herbs just above the counter top level, then deeper ones for small packets, etc.

Refrigerators and Freezers You will certainly need as large a refrigerator as you can possibly squeeze in – two would be preferable if you could run to them. Commercial refrigerators hold a much greater amount than domestic ones, but they are proportionately larger and more expensive. If and when you reach that stage, you will not be able to do without one, but it would be an unwarranted extravagance to start with. If you cannot fit more than one into the kitchen, you can always store a second refrigerator (and freezer) in a basement, back kitchen, garage or even the spare bedroom. Incidentally, you will need to learn to pack it efficiently; you will be astonished how much a domestic refrigerator can take if every single inch is used.

At least one freezer will be essential for most types of catering. One of the best ways to cope with 'flexible' demand is to be able to prepare large orders in advance and to keep 'a stock' of certain regularly used items in your freezers. At Catercall, we normally have six freezers going full time. Chest or upright freezers are equally acceptable; uprights take up less space, but are more expensive to run as you lose so much cold air every time you open the door. Since you will probably not be using them more than a couple of times a day, it might be better to keep the freezers out of the kitchen – saving both space and running costs as they will not be battling with the heat of your steaming pans.

Kitchen Equipment Ideally, equipment needs to be kept as close as possible to both the washing-up and the working area so as to minimize the amount of time spent getting it out and putting it away. However, I realize that this may be a counsel of perfection. Try to at least keep the most used bits within easy reach. I am all for keeping the equipment, along with the dry goods, on open shelves so that you can get at it easily without hitting your head on open cupboard doors. However, the closer you get to the floor, the more of a problem dirt becomes, so you may feel that you would rather not have open shelves under your feet.

Large pots and pans are going to be difficult to store in cupboards – or anywhere. If you do not need them very often, they might be better off in the basement or spare bedroom along with the

freezers and spare refrigerator. Some can also be hung on the wall, although your wall space will be at a premium to allow for your shelves. If you have a tall kitchen, you could also hang them from the ceiling – like hams!

A monster peg board with really long hooks is well worth giving up one bit of wall space for as it will allow you to hang the majority of your smaller bits of equipment out of the way but easy to get at. Even so, you will need drawers somewhere for cutlery and all the bits and pieces that refuse either to hang on a board or lie on a shelf.

Work Space This is the most important part of a commercial kitchen and you cannot have enough of it. In particular, you will need it close to the cooking area (for preparation and somewhere to put the pans as they come off the hob) and close to the sink area (for preparation of vegetables, etc.). Inevitably, it will get cluttered up with the smaller bits of equipment (mixers, processors, etc.) which is another reason to have as much of it as possible. You should also make sure – if you can – that you have a really liberal supply of power points. You will be amazed how many bits of gear you will have and it is dangerous to plug powerful equipment into adaptors. I would estimate that ten power points was an absolute minimum and preferably fifteen to twenty.

Although a central work table is seldom recommended in a domestic kitchen, it can be very useful for commercial cooking as it will give you a decent surface that several people can work around together. A table also allows you to sit at it to work. So many cooking jobs need to be done standing up that any opportunity to sit for a few minutes while you peel the spuds, roll the smoked salmon, or pipe the cream, should be grabbed – especially if you have a hard floor.

Your work tops must be hard and easy to clean. The most hardwearing is aluminium, which is what most commercial tables and equipment are made from. However, it is expensive and not very attractive if your kitchen is also doubling as your home. Any good-quality laminate will do, but try to pick one with a slightly rough surface and a small pattern – it will show the scratches less!

Heating and Ventilation You will need some sort of heating in your kitchen if you do not already have it. You can put up with freezing until the oven has been going long enough to warm the

atmosphere, but it is better to avoid this. However, be careful what sort of heating you use; radiators are ideal, even if they do take up wall space, as they are flat and have no flexes or flames. Whatever you do, do *not* use electric fires with trailing leads or calor gas or paraffin heaters, which you can knock into and overturn. Radiant electric heaters high on the walls are efficient, although they are expensive to run.

Good ventilation in the summer is almost more important than heat in the winter. A heatwave, two ovens and three rings all going full blast would be enough to finish off the hardiest of cooks. Although it is said that the heat in the kitchens of many Chinese restaurants is well over 37°C/100°F, I doubt that many Europeans could stand it! Windows or doors giving a good through draught are obviously best, but a good extractor fan will help to move the air around.

If you are cooking in your own home, a powerful extractor fan would also be a good idea if you do not wish to live 24 hours a day with the cooking smells. On the other hand, if you do not want to blast your neighbours with it either, and the Environmental Health officers will be very anxious that you do not, it might be better to install an internal filter extractor. The health officers prefer a chimney to be used for ventilation, but if that is impossible, they will probably accept a filter, provided the filters are changed frequently.

Lighting If you are going to spend all day in the kitchen, lighting is of vital importance. The best is lots of daylight, but that may not be available.

Warm fluorescent tubes are the most practical alternative, but do make sure that they are placed so as to give good light to all the main work areas. If this is not possible, you can always supplement the lighting with a few small spotlights in dark corners. Spotlighting each work area of the kitchen is another alternative, but although it will produce a more attractive light than fluorescent tubes, it will be substantially more expensive both in running and replacement terms. It will also generate a lot more heat – desirable, possibly, in the winter but not in a heatwave.

General Decoration If you are thinking of decorating as part of your refurbishment, remember that every surface has to be easy to clean, both for your own convenience and to pass the eagle eye of the Environmental Health officer. On the whole, paint (shiny variety) is more hardwearing than vinyl wallpaper, and easier to throw another quick coat over at a weekend.

Flooring also falls under this heading. Whatever you use, it must have no cuts or joins that can secrete bits of food or dirt. It must not be slippery, and has to be quick to clean; there should certainly be no rugs or mats lying around. From your own point of view, it should also be as soft as possible as you are going to spend an awful lot of time on it. Cork tiles over wood are ideal as they are both warm and relatively soft; padded vinyl is next best, although it is not very hard-wearing. After that, linoleum tiles or sheeting or quarry tiles are suitable – both are very hard-wearing but also hard on the feet – and on anything that may get dropped on them!

Location
If you get the chance to choose where you will be, remember that, unless you want to combine your catering business with a retail outlet, a High Street location will be wasted. You will be far better off in a convenient back alley, with fewer parking problems, and no one to complain about you lugging trays of food across the pavements or about your extra generous allowance of overflowing dustbins. Such a location will also be quite a bit cheaper.

Small Equipment

You are, of course, going to need more equipment than you would for purely domestic purposes, but depending on the area you are hoping to work in, you will need a completely different range of gear – a fancy cake maker will have little use for three dozen pâté tins; a supplier of pâtés to the local pub no use for a turntable. What is more, it will be difficult to assess how much you are going to need until you start doing business. Investing in a vast quantity of equipment will eat up money, and valuable storage space. It would be better to set the money aside to buy what you need if and when you find you need it. However, you must have something, so here is a short checklist of what I feel any commercially orientated kitchen ought to have. Incidentally, all these pieces of equipment come in a commercial size which you may want in due course, but since they are large and expensive (unless you can get them secondhand), it would be unwise to invest in them too early.

Electric mixer with basic attachments
Food processor – this will double as a liquidizer and mincer if you do not have these attachments on your mixer
Electric kettle
A decent set of balance scales
Several measuring jugs
A reasonable collection of pans and frying pans, including one really large one of each
Some flan dishes, cake tins, pâté tins, loaf tins, etc., depending on what area you intend to work in – you will need at least a double set so that one lot can be cooking in the oven while the next lot is being prepared
Some casserole dishes, preferably attractive enough to serve from if you are aiming for dinner parties
A good selection of sieves
A good selection of mixing bowls
Piping bags and nozzles for cream cheese, profiteroles and innumerable other things apart from cakes
At least six assorted sharp knives and a steel
Several good chopping boards
Plastic storage containers with lids *that fit tightly* – there is nothing worse than soup slopped all over the back of your van. Try to use square ones rather than round as they are so much easier to pack into refrigerators, freezers and crates

Ample quantities of cling film and foil for packaging
A good selection of plastic bags of various thicknesses and ties
Efficient marking labels, both stick-on and tie – it is most important that you label *everything*, otherwise you risk both mixing up orders and wasting vast amounts of time opening and shutting containers looking for the mayonnaise you were sure you put in the refrigerator
Kitchen paper, kitchen towels and all sorts of cleaning and wiping-up gear – it is so much easier to clean up when things are still warm and not burnt, although not many of us do it
Some ring binders or files for storing your regularly used recipes – although it is a fiddle to type them out, they will be much more convenient stored in one file than in half a dozen different books. Typing them out also means that you can adjust quantities and methods for larger numbers
Some reasonable serving dishes, so that you can arrange and decorate the food at home if necessary
A good selection of wooden spoons, spatulas, etc. – they all have a tendency to disappear when you want them

Buying in Your Raw Materials

Where and how you purchase your raw materials will, of course, depend to a large extent on what you are going to cook. The more specialist your field, the more specialist your suppliers will need to be. Buying, however, is a vitally important part of any caterer's business. Extravagant shopping can play havoc with your costings, as can unreliable suppliers with your quality control and your schedules.

How and where you shop will be governed by the time you have available and where you live and operate. Shopping facilities can include wholesale specialist and general merchants, 'cash and carry's, local supermarkets, wholesale and retail markets, ordinary shops, and home producers. Most people end up by using a combination of suppliers, but it is probably worth reviewing the merits and demerits of each.

Be warned: once you start to buy in bulk, the temptation is to take advantage of reduced prices to 'stock up'. This can be a false economy. With all 'cheap buys' you need to assess carefully how much time and effort (and maybe petrol) you are going to have to expend in order to get however much off the price of the product – and whether you have that money to spare. There is no point in getting 10 per cent off the price of the goods if you are going to have to pay 15 per cent interest on your overdraft to pay for it. It is also all too easy to get carried away with your wonderful bargain only to find that you have spent twice what you have saved in actually getting the wretched thing from its place of production to your kitchen. If in doubt, don't. Apart from anything else, you probably won't have anywhere to store it!

Wholesale Merchants

These can include general wholesale grocers or greengrocers or specific suppliers – butchers, cheese merchants, etc. They will normally deliver to you (a great saving in time and labour) and allow you to run an account with them (which is a help if you anticipate cash flow problems). They do have minimum order restrictions that may, in the early days, be difficult for you to fulfil. On the other hand, they will supply goods in fairly small packs – 'cash and carry's may only sell in large packs. You are limited to what that particular wholesaler will supply both in terms of variety and quality, and you may find the goods relatively expensive. However, this may be worth it for the convenience of having what you need delivered. They are to be found in local trade directories, but recommendations from other people in the business would certainly be worth having as you know these will be reliable.

'Cash and Carry's

All caterers use, and should use, several different 'cash and carry' outlets as their areas of specialization are quite different. Unless you live in the depths of the country, there are normally several branches quite near. As a *bona fide* caterer or cook, you should have no difficulty in getting a card. Again, local directories will give you names, but personal recommendations are better. You will often get good bargains at 'cash and carry's, but take care not to be tempted by wonderful 'special offers' into spending a lot of money

(which could be better used elsewhere) on a load of stuff that you will have difficulty carrying, cannot use, and have no place to store. You will also find that most goods are packed in bulk; this makes it cheaper, but it may be impractical for your needs or your available storage space. Watch out, too, for shelf-life dates; a bulk pack of cream crackers will cease to be a good buy if you fail to use them up before their expiry date. Because of the competitive pricing, credit is seldom given.

Shopping at 'cash and carry's is labour intensive and time-consuming – although it can also be fun – so plan your trip thoroughly before you go and list everything that you think you could need so as to reduce your visits to a minimum.

Local Supermarkets

If you live in a relatively populous area, you will find that many of the local supermarket chains have almost turned themselves into 'cash and carry's, although you are unlikely to be able to buy in bulk in quite the same way. Because of their size and buying power, and the competition among them, their prices are extremely competitive (sometimes even better value than the 'cash and carry') and you could search far before you would buy your food more cheaply.

Supermarkets also specialize to a surprising degree – some are excellent for fresh fruit and vegetables but lousy for frozen goods, some have excellent health food departments but terrible bread, and so on. Some also are very cheap for certain goods but make up for it on others. So it is well worth getting to know your 'locals'.

It is also useful to keep an eye open for the moment when they mark down goods that are just about to go 'out of date'. These are normally fresh foods (fruit and vegetables, meat, fish, cheese, etc.) which, of course, the supermarket will not be able to sell after they have passed their date stamp. They are, however, perfectly good, will be sold at half price or at least with a substantial reduction, and will do you very well indeed. Some supermarkets also sell goods with damaged packs but untouched contents at reduced prices.

A knowledge of the 'quiet' periods will speed up your shopping and keep your nerves untattered –

not to mention those of other customers confronted by your bulging trolleys!

Markets

The wholesale markets (for example, Covent Garden, Smithfield and Billingsgate in London) are really not practical for the relatively small-time caterer unless for a very special order. For a start, you will need to be able to buy in reasonable bulk – quantities that you will only be able to use when you have a large turnover. Secondly, they happen at unearthly hours of the morning – which is fine if you can knock off at lunchtime, but the average cook/caterer has to put in a good 9 am–6 pm day. If you have to do a full day on top of getting up at 3 am to go to market, this is not practical for more than the odd occasion. For the large-scale caterer, they are, of course, invaluable – quite apart from being an experience.

Local retail markets, if they are good, will provide you with the best value you can get, but they are very time-consuming to shop in. Unless you know for sure you can park very close to the market, you will also be restricted in what you buy by what you can carry. If you can develop a relationship with a particular stallholder, you may be able to 'place orders'; otherwise, you will always be at the whim of seasonal shortages and gluts. None the less, if you have the time to spare, a market can be an extremely cheap and fun place to shop in.

Local or Specialist Retail Shops

It is always assumed that a caterer cannot afford to shop in ordinary shops, but you will find few caterers who don't. Obviously, you should try not to buy goods that could be bought cheaper in bulk at the 'cash and carry' or through a wholesaler, but for the occasional packet of biscuits, pint of milk, etc. the local corner shop is invaluable.

Local specialist shops may also be much more use to you than a large and impersonal 'cash and carry'. Butchers, bakers, fishmongers and greengrocers are delighted to develop a relationship with a professional cook who they know is going to bring them regular trade. They will often give you a discount and nearly always buy specially for you. The other advantage from your point of view is that you get to know their strengths and weaknesses and will be able to rely on the quality of your supplies – a very important consideration. Depending also on what you need and in what quantity, it may be advisable to go and buy it in a specialist shop as a member of the retail public rather than attempt to make it or get it cheap from a wholesale producer. If you want really first-class Italian cheeses, for example, you would be better off buying them in a good Italian delicatessen and paying the retail price for them than buying second-rate ones from a cheese wholesaler who only stocks the ordinary run of Italian cheeses along with Gouda and Wensleydale. Petit fours and chocolates are also items that it would probably be worth paying the going rate for in a quality chocolate shop rather than messing around trying to produce some yourself. Yours will no doubt be inferior and, if you cost in the time you will have spent trying to make them, probably have cost you more.

Individual Producers

Nearly all cooks and caterers have a couple of suppliers who produce just one product from base: eggs are often delivered by one person who buys direct from the farm or battery; home-baked and cured hams are a favourite cottage industry. If you live and work fairly close to the country, growers of strawberries, spinach, beans and innumerable other crops will be happy to supply you as a caterer as the sale will be much larger than to the general public – and from your point of view, the price will be appreciably lower. However, unless you live close to such growers, you may have problems of delivery and collection.

Pre-prepared and Convenience Foods

The extent to which you buy in other people's products and sell them on will depend entirely on the type of business you want to run, but it is certainly an area that every cook or caterer should

consider. Indeed there are several extremely high-class foods that can only be bought as 'convenience food' – for example, smoked salmon, caviar, Parma ham.

There is, theoretically, a great bonus in making everything yourself. It is, and should be, used as a good selling point and on the whole you should actually do so. However, smoked salmon and Parma ham aside, no matter how brilliant you are, you cannot cover absolutely every aspect of catering. Unless you are going to restrict yourself to selling foods that you are really expert at producing, you are sometimes going to have to supply items that you have seldom, if ever, cooked before.

There is also the question of how much use you should make of 'convenience' products in terms of frozen vegetables, packet sauce mixes and so forth. This decision will really have to be governed by the kind of business you want to run. Making custard with a custard mix is undoubtedly easier and cheaper than making it with eggs and milk, but, undoubtedly, does not taste as good. There are a few convenience foods that are comparable with the 'real thing', but they are fairly few and far between and relatively expensive. There is no reason why you should not use them, but take care

not to make a big hiss and thump about the genuineness of your home cooking if in fact you are using convenience products. The public is not as stupid as it is sometimes made out to be and nothing will get you a bad reputation faster than serving as 'home-made vegetable soup' what all too obviously came out of a packet.

Even within your normal range of products, if you can find someone who only wants to make pâtés and who will make really good ones for a reasonable price (that is, a price that will still allow you a decent profit – see pricing, page 142–5), it may be more profitable in the long run for you to buy them in. Even if you have to pay twice what you would have paid for the raw materials, the time you will save may be more usefully spent on making something else, planning new menus, working on your publicity, or one of the many things involved in running a small business that you cannot farm out.

Planning Your Cookery

Economies of Scale

If you are going to make the best, and therefore the most profitable, use of your own and your assistants'/partners' time, you must plan. Profit in food production tends to come with volume, since the marginal extra time taken to prepare twenty portions of any dish rather than ten or fifteen is far less than it would be to cook those five or ten portions from scratch. Consequently, the more portions of any dish that you can prepare at the one time, the more money you will make. If you follow this principle to its logical conclusion, you will end up by only making a very limited range of products in large quantities – which is a perfectly acceptable way to run a catering business if you can find the customers to buy what you produce.

However, unless you are going to wholesale your product (see page 19), you may have difficulty in selling nothing but sausagemeat balls, macaroons and stuffed peppers, no matter how delicious and how cheap. So, the average caterer has to be prepared to produce a wide range of different dishes. But the principle remains the same. If you have several beef dishes to cook, do them all on the same day; the basic preparation of the meat will probably be similar even if the finishing touches change. If you anticipate three cocktail parties within two weeks, try to sell them all sausagemeat balls, for example; you will then be able to make one big batch of sausagemeat balls, portion them out and freeze them labelled for each customer. When the time for each party comes, you need only defrost the relevant bag and crisp up the balls in the oven.

Planning

To ensure that you do not waste cooking time, you have to plan ahead. Ideally, you should sit down at least once a week and review all the orders that have been placed for the next two, three or four weeks. The foods will have to be divided into those that have to be prepared at the last minute and those that can either be done a day ahead and stored in the refrigerator, or several weeks ahead and stored in the deep freeze. Foods that can be prepared ahead of time can be fitted into days when there are no orders or very little happening; although you have to remember that they will still need 'finishing off' and decorating before they get sent to the function. You can also use slack periods to 'forward cook' certain fairly standard items. These can be stored in deep freezes for the busy time you hope is about to happen.

Schedules and Timetables

To plan efficiently, you will need to know how long it is going to take you or your minions to make a thousand sausagemeat balls, two hundred macaroons or a hundred stuffed peppers. There is absolutely no rule of thumb for gauging this as different cooks' speeds of working vary from snail's pace to greased lightning. The only thing you can be sure of in the early days is that it will take longer than you reckoned. In an attempt to bring your timing under control, make out a timetable for each day and allocate chunks of time to each job; it will soon become clear how long it takes to do what. Remember also that decoration can take more time than actual making and that loading up vans, looking up the address and writing out the bill to go with you, all have to be fitted into your timetable.

Writing up the day's list of tasks, with their allotted times, on a large pad or board that everyone in the kitchen can easily refer to not only keeps everyone hard at work as they can see how much there is to be done, but gives everyone a great thrill when they are allowed to cross out a job that has been completed – especially if the job has been finished ahead of schedule!

Also, don't forget to plan in time for *shopping and ordering*, *clearing up*, *coffee breaks and a proper lunch* (you will get much more out of yourself and your staff if you treat them right) and, most important, *time to do the planning*.

Organizing Ingredients

No matter how efficient you or your team are, you will not be able to cook anything unless you have the ingredients to hand and you will waste an immense amount of time if you have to break off cooking your two hundred macaroons to go and buy more ground almonds. This means that your planning must include listing and ordering all the ingredients likely to be needed for each day's cooking. These should be divided into the various suppliers so that they can be ordered by telephone or time can be allocated to shop for them. It would help to type out and have photocopied 'order sheets' for each of your suppliers, with their telephone number on the top. As you go through the recipes to be cooked on any given day, you can write down on each relevant pad the goods that you will need from that particular supplier.

A checklist of absolutely *everything* that you could want is invaluable, especially in the early days. It is so easy to forget things such as cocktail sticks which are essential for the putting together of a cocktail party, but which probably do not feature in any of the recipes that you will be checking through for ingredients. Exactly what goes down on your checklist will depend on the type of cooking you are doing, but constant revision over a couple of months will cover most things – you can then type out a 'fair copy' which can be available for your own use or for anyone else who may be trying to plan with or for you.

It would also be useful to keep a list of the general supplies that you need in the kitchen which you can check once a week for major buys – flour, sugar, spices, floor cloths, washing up liquid, loo paper. A blank list stuck up somewhere in the kitchen on which you or anyone else can note things that are running short or have been finished will be a great help when you are making up your shopping lists.

Equipment

A check that you do have the right equipment needed for the jobs in hand should also come into your planning. Attempting to ice a wedding cake without an icing bag and nozzle, for example, is going to be difficult. Even a shortage of loaf, cake or pâté tins, flan dishes or saucepans can slow you down enormously. I am not suggesting that you should immediately go and buy a dozen of everything; if you need them for a once-only job, it may be worth making do rather than spending a lot of money on equipment that will thereafter sit on a shelf gathering dust. If, however, you anticipate more business of that kind, it would be better to invest in enough gear to allow a quick 'turn around' or a more efficient use of oven or hob space. One really large saucepan, for example, can save endless frustration and solve the problem of having three overflowing pans cluttering up the hob.

Portion Control and Cooking in Quantity

'Portion control' is one of those technical-sounding expressions that instil fear and trepidation in the heart of every aspiring cook. All it actually means is that you must keep tabs on the quantities of food that you sell for your stated price. This may sound very obvious, but it is surprising how easy it is, when cooking for large numbers, to throw an extra handful of this or that into the pot – each handful costs money and, if it was not allowed for in your pricing, will eat large holes in your profits.

The quantity of each ingredient that you use in each recipe, although not the only consideration, is one of the major factors in deciding how much you can charge for that dish. It is therefore important that the amount should be accurate if you want your costs to remain in line with what you feel you can charge. Without wishing to labour the point, a teaspoon more of ground almonds than you have costed in each macaroon will mount up to an awful lot of ground almonds – and a surprising dent in the profit on your macaroons – so portion control is important. Obviously, you do not want to become a Scrooge with your cooks or assistants, but it is worth keeping an eye on them – and yourself – to make sure that portions are not slipping and food being given away.

Portion Sizes

Although you may wish to give particularly generous helpings to your clients, there is agreement on standard-sized portions, deduced from years of catering experience, which is extremely useful as a guideline. I have provided a list of the most basic foodstuffs (see pages 34–5). However, these should not be taken as gospel in all circumstances. You will also need to assess how frugal or greedy your particular clients are, whether they wish to be seen as particularly lavish hosts (among some groups it would be considered impolite for the tables not still to be groaning when everyone had eaten), how much they can afford to spend, and how rich or filling the food you are giving them is.

Too much is obviously preferable to too little, so most cooks or caterers tend to give too large portions rather than too small. At least you avoid that moment of panic at buffet parties when the first (and usually the greediest) people in the queue appear to have scoffed three-quarters of the food.

However, oversupplying is wasteful from everyone's point of view, so careful, even if slightly generous, portioning of the food is well worth the cook's or caterer's effort.

Quantity Cooking

As a rough rule of thumb, it can be assumed that twenty people will eat slightly less per head than two, and two hundred slightly less than twenty – but the saving is not very noticeable. How much your twenty or two hundred eat will also depend on whether they are sitting down to their meal or eating buffet style (the latter is less conducive to a major stuff), what time of day they are eating, whether they are mainly male or female, whether they are young or old, and what part of the world or country they come from.

To confuse matters, certain elements of a meal 'go further' when cooked in large quantities than others; for example, you will not need ten times the quantity of sauce you supplied for two, but you will need ten times the amount of meat or fish. And certain foods behave differently when they are used in large concentrations: spices, seasonings and herbs, for example, do not multiply in strength in exact proportion to the quantity in which they are used. Again, the rules are not set in concrete. However, I have tried to give some indication in the portion guidelines overleaf.

Other Hazards of Cooking in Quantity It is not only the actual quantities you have to worry about when cooking for large numbers, you also have to remember that food heats up and cools down more slowly and that certain foods react to being used in quantity in different ways.

1 When planning your cooking, you need to take account of the fact that a pan containing 20 kg (40 lb) of potatoes is going to take a great deal longer to heat up and cook than a pan containing 1 kg (2 lb).
2 Delicate ingredients will be more likely to disintegrate when they are cooked in a large pan and constantly stirred around.
3 Sheer weight of food may cause the bottom layer to burn.

4 When a large pan of sauce, stew or soup is cooling, it will take a great deal longer than a small one, which means that it stands a far greater chance of going off in hot or humid weather. Wherever possible, it should be split up into smaller containers or poured into a large, flat tray for cooling and storage.
5 The sheer weight of a large saucepan containing 20 kg (40 lb) of potatoes covered with boiling water will be very great – you need to take particular care when handling it so that you do not tip boiling potatoes and water all over your feet.

Quality Control

It may seem obvious, but quality control, or making sure that your food is up to snuff, is of vital importance to the successful cook or caterer. And it does not only become necessary when you have staff cooking for you – you can easily become stale or tired and let a dish slip through that 'will do' without really being up to your initial, high standard. As with all things, your clients will be quick to notice a 'falling off' in your standards of flavour or decoration and all too easily abandon you in favour of someone else. Of course, when you do start to employ other people, quality control becomes even more important, but do try to do your overseeing tactfully. Your employees should be aware that you are keeping an eye on them, but they will not be happy if they feel that you are constantly leaning over their shoulders. And do give praise when a dish is particularly delicious as well as criticizing when it is not – it will certainly be appreciated.

Serving Quantities

	per head	for 20	for 100
Cocktail snacks (assuming variety of 5–8 bits)	1½ bits	20 × 1½ bits	100 × 1½ bits
Nuts	15 g/½ oz	300 g/10 oz	1.8 kg/4 lb
Finger food (assuming 5–10 bits per head)			
Quiche/flan	50–75 g/2–3 oz	1.8 kg/4 lb	5.75 kg/12½ lb
Mini sandwiches	½ round	10 rounds	50 rounds
Stuffed egg/tomato	½	20 × ½	100 × ½
Mousse/pâté for stuffing profiteroles, etc.	10 g/¼ oz	200 g/7 oz	1 kg/2¼ lb
Pâtés (starters)	50 g/2 oz	1.25 kg/2½ lb	5.5 kg/12 lb
Terrines	75 g/3 oz	1.7 kg/3¾ lb	8 kg/18 lb
Soup	300 ml/½ pint	4.8 litres/8 pints	24 litres/40 pints
Sauces			
Plain – béchamel	60 ml/2 fl oz	1.2 litres/2 pints	5 litres/9 pints
Rich (chocolate)	45 ml/1½ fl oz	900 ml/1½ pints	4.2 litres/7 pints
Mayonnaise	45 ml/1½ fl oz	900 ml/1½ pints	4.2 litres/7 pints
French dressing	30 ml/1 fl oz	450 ml/¾ pint	2 litres/3½ pints
Fish			
Whole salmon	225 g/8 oz	4.5 kg/10 lb	22.5 kg/50 lb
Whole sole, plaice, etc.	200 g/7 oz	3.5 kg/7½ lb	17 kg/37 lb
For mousse, pilaffs, etc.	50–75 g/2–3 oz	1.25 kg/2½ lb	5.75 kg/12½ lb
Meat			
Roast with bone	100–175 g/4–6 oz	2.8 kg/6¼ lb	14.5 kg/32 lb
Roast without bone	75 g/3 oz	1.7 kg/3¾ lb	8 kg/18 lb
Boneless (for casseroles, etc.), depending on vegetables	100–175 g/4–6 oz	2.8 kg/6¼ lb	14.5 kg/32 lb
Poultry			
Whole/chicken, about 1.5 kg/ 3½ lb, or joints (one 1.5 kg/ 3½ lb chicken gives about 675 g/1½ lb meat)	¼ bird	5 birds	25 birds
Poussin (baby)	1 bird	20 birds	100 birds
Poussin (1.25 kg/2½ lb)	½ bird	10 birds	50 birds
Chicken off the bone, depending on vegetables	100–175 g/4–6 oz	2.8 kg/6¼ lb	14.5 kg/32 lb
Duckling (1.8 kg/4 lb)	¼ bird	5 birds	25 birds
Turkey including bones	175 g/6 oz	3 kg/7 lb	15 kg/33½ lb
Turkey off the bone	75 g/3 oz	1.7 kg/3¾ lb	8 kg/18 lb

	per head	for 20	for 100
Game			
Grouse and pigeon	1 bird	20 birds	100 birds
Pheasant and guinea fowl, roast or casseroled	½ bird	7 birds	34 birds
Quail	2 birds	40 birds	200 birds
Venison (steaks)	100–175 g/4–6 oz	2.8 kg/6¼ lb	14.5 kg/32 lb
Finished casseroles	225 g/8 oz	4.5 kg/10 lb	20 kg/45 lb
Vegetables (prepared weight)			
Potatoes	150 g/5 oz	2.8 kg/6¼ lb	14.5 kg/32 lb
Rice for pilaff	40 g/1½ oz	800 g/1¾ lb	4.2 kg/9¼ lb
Rice for vegetable	50 g/2 oz	1.25 kg/2½ lb	5 kg/11 lb
Spinach	225 g/8 oz	4 kg/9 lb	19 kg/42 lb
Other vegetables	100 g/4 oz	2.25 kg/5 lb	8.5 kg/19 lb
Salads	100 g/4 oz	2.25 kg/5 lb	8.5 kg/19 lb
Mousses (sweet and savoury)	100 g/4 oz	2.25 kg/5 lb	8.5 kg/19 lb
Pies			
Meat and vegetable	225 g/8 oz	4.5 kg/10 lb	20 kg/45 lb
Fruit	100 g/4 oz	2.25 kg/5 lb	8.5 kg/19 lb
Pastry	75 g/3 oz	1.7 kg/3¾ lb	8 kg/18 lb
Puddings/desserts			
Milk	200 ml/7 fl oz	4 litres/6½ pints	19.5 litres/32½ pints
Steamed	100 g/4 oz	1.7 kg/3¾ lb	8 kg/18 lb
Jelly	100 ml/3½ fl oz	1.9 litres/3¼ pints	9.5 litres/16 pints
Ice cream, depending on whether served alone	60–120 ml/2–4 fl oz	1.2–2.25 litres/2–4 pints	6–12 litres/10–20 pints
Gâteau	75–100 g/4–6 oz	1.8 kg/4 lb	9 kg/20 lb
Cream			
For desserts	30 ml/1 fl oz	600 ml/1 pint	2.75 litres/5 pints
For coffee	20 ml/¾ fl oz	450 ml/¾ pint	2.25 litres/4 pints
Coffee			
Demitasse	120 ml/4 fl oz	2.25 litres/4 pints	12 litres/20 pints
Morning coffee cup	200 ml/7 fl oz	4 litres/6½ pints	19.5 litres/32½ pints
Tea			
To drink	200 ml/7 fl oz	4 litres/6½ pints	19.5 litres/32½ pints
Milk for	30 ml/1 fl oz	600 ml/1 pint	2.75 litres/5 pints
Sandwiches	½ round	10 rounds	50 rounds
Cake	75–100 g/3–4 oz	1.8 kg/4 lb	9 kg/20 lb
Biscuits	2	40	200

Decoration and Presentation

Almost more important than what food tastes like is what it *looks* like. We are all so gullible that if a dish looks or smells delicious we will take a lot of convincing that it does not taste delicious. Of course, your clients will expect your food to taste delicious too, but they are much more likely to think it does if it looks as though it is going to.

Smells are not necessarily easy to produce in a catering situation, but you can do a lot about appearance. You can also ensure that hot dishes are always served hot (on hot plates), that chilled dishes are served chilled, that condiments, sauces, ice, etc., are available when needed. You can usually also ensure that tables are properly laid, crockery and cutlery clean and polished and, most important, that the food is efficiently and pleasantly served. However, much of this will come into the chapter on organizing functions; for the moment, we will concentrate on the food itself and the various ways of presenting it.

Serving Dishes or Platters

What you serve your food in or on will depend on the type of business you intend to run, but whatever style you choose, you should be aware that your dishes will have a strong influence on how your clients see your food.

Stainless Steel Catering equipment has a hard life and needs to be tough to stand up to it – nothing looks worse than chipped and battered serving dishes. This is why the majority of catering companies use stainless steel 'flats' or platters, vegetable dishes, etc. for serving their food; it is relatively cheap, extremely tough, easy to clean, and easy to store. The only thing that matches it in terms of durability and storability (although not cleanability) is silver or silver plate. However, these days even silver plate is so astronomically expensive that it is totally impractical for general use, although larger caterers and hire companies do sometimes have stocks of silver plate for their 'posher' functions.

In practical terms, stainless steel is the best thing to use, although some companies feel that they would like to have a more individualistic look. If you want to buy in a supply, keep an eye open for sales of bankrupt stock or hotels closing down – you can often get very good bargains. If you are going to buy new, any of the larger catering suppliers will have large stocks.

Silver (Gold, Bronze, etc.) Dishes For certain 'up-market' functions silver dishes are certainly 'the thing'. Even a couple (the 'entrée' dishes that your mother no longer uses?) will lift the tone of your service. Unless you have *a lot* of money to invest, you will not want to buy silver serving ware. However, you can hire relatively plain stuff from most of the larger hire companies. If you want really fancy dishes or platters, theatrical hire companies often have a good selection that is expensive but can look really wonderful.

Enamel, Cast Iron, etc. This is usually only available for casseroles and looks very good if kept clean and in good condition – which is easier said than done if it is also being used to cook in. However, cast iron is *very* heavy, so it should never be used to serve from except in a buffet situation. White enamel does bring back memories of school dinners, but coloured enamels can be decorative. However, enamel chips all too easily when dropped.

Wood Wooden platters, dishes and bowls are cheap and reasonably hard-wearing. However, they can chip and with constant washing will dry out and may crack or break in half. Environmental Health officers look on them with a slightly jaundiced eye as they reckon they are more difficult to clean properly than metal or china. However, they are a good background for food and can look attractive, especially if your food is of the wholefood or generally health-orientated type. Wooden ware can be bought cheaply wholesale – a visit to a trade fair of fancy goods will usually unearth suppliers – or in ones or twos as needed from any kitchen shop.

Pottery Pottery is cheap, comes in lovely colours and shapes, and is a great temptation to use. However, it is not really very practical. It is heavy (which will make you unpopular with your waiting staff) and chips terribly easily. If you decide to use it, you will have to resign yourself to a pretty rapid turnover of dishes which, if you have a cheap source of supply is fine, but otherwise may work out expensive.

If you are buying pottery, remember that dark and plain colours make a much better foil for food than pastel shades and 'busy' patterns. It would also be wise to try and stock up with basically the same shape and colour so as to achieve some sort of 'house style', although you may want some special platters for particular dishes as well. For example, we find that desserts (cheesecakes, chocolate cakes, etc.) look wonderful on dark blue, lightly patterned Spanish platters, whereas savoury food looks better on plain dark green.

China, Stoneware, Earthenware, etc. Most oven-to-table ware, even stuff designed for the domestic market, is pretty tough these days, so you should have no difficulty with the standard range of flan, soufflé dishes, etc. Whether you choose to use white, a colour or a pattern will be up to you, but remember that a 'homely' recipe for a quiche may look very nice in your family flan dish, but it may look a touch amateur when served to a client.

If you are looking for other dishes, be wary of buying ordinary domestic ware no matter how pretty; it has not been designed to stand up to commercial use and will not. There is a huge range of hotel or catering ware made now, much of which is extremely attractive and not remotely like 'hotel crockery'; it is designed for hard wear and is quite staggeringly tough.

Glass Toughened glass or ovenware is indeed tough and is very good for flan dishes and that sort of thing. You can get a wide range of platters, dishes and bowls in it, but although it is practical, it does smack of school dinners, which may not be quite the image you are trying to project.

Cut glass is, of course, an entirely different matter and can be a stunning backdrop for a dish. However, proper cut glass is heavy (think of the staff) and *very* expensive so should only be used on very special occasions. Cheaper 'moulded' or factory-made cut glass looks just that – cheap.

Coloured glass is another possibility; it is a bit cheaper than cut glass and very attractive but still quite expensive and relatively fragile. Again, I would suggest you keep it for special occasions only, unless you have a cheap source of supply.

Mirror glass is another very effective base for foods. You can use plates (expensive) or small squares stuck onto a tray or platter. It is particularly good for a cocktail party or on a buffet table where the guests get the full effect.

Individual Dishes Individual bowls, dishes, ramekins or glasses can be a very effective way of serving all kinds of foods. The classic 'sundae' dish does smack slightly of prunes for breakfast at a seaside boarding house, but ordinary stemmed glasses make excellent containers for a whole range of desserts and starters. They have the added advantage from a caterer's point of view that they are cheap and that they stack easily and safely for carrying in their boxes.

Decoration

'Decoration' covers not only the little twirl on the top of the dish of trifle but the way the food is laid out on the dish, what is served with what, and so on. This can be much more difficult for a caterer than for a restaurateur as a caterer's radish roses and cream twirls will have to wait around for a couple of hours before being eaten, be covered in cling film or foil, be loaded into crates, driven around the countryside, hiked up and down in lifts or on stairs and still emerge looking pristine and divine. Furthermore, a caterer can't just nip back into the kitchen for another bowl of cream or bunch of radishes to repair the damage travel has done because by that time the kitchen is probably fifty miles away, although it is amazing what repair work can be done 'on site' with a piping bag and a small container of whipped cream.

Catering decoration does, therefore, have to be 'tough and hard-wearing' as well as attractive. Exactly what you use will depend on the type of food and business that you run and the type of image that you wish to present: healthy and wholesome with large bunches of crisp fresh watercress everywhere; or dainty and ephemeral with spun sugar and finely piped cream. Whatever you choose, it must look fresh and inviting. Each person will develop their own personal style of decoration, but I am listing some ideas below just to give you inspiration.

Overall Layout To be effective, your decoration needs to be kept simple but striking – especially if the food is laid on a buffet table. Guests will be taking a quick glance rather than a long slow look, so the dishes need to stand out. Simple colour and shape contrasts (dark green spinach leaf salad with a few slithers of bright red pepper or pimiento; swirls of cream with just a single chocolate curl or crystallized flower) are the most effective. Too many colours or shapes on one dish become busy and distracting – which is why on the whole plain serving dishes are more effective than patterned ones and dark colours are a good contrast to predominantly pale foods. Height and texture are also important in the composition of your dishes and decoration, particularly on a buffet table.

Remember also that food that looks marvellous 'en masse' on a platter may look less inviting in individual helpings 'dollopped' onto a plate. This applies particularly to 'silver service' when guests only get the briefest glimpse of the platter before their portion arrives on their plate. It is also most important from the waiting staff's point of view that food that is to be 'silver served' is easy to get off the serving dish and put on the guests' plates without reducing it to a featureless heap.

Decorative 'Beds' Many foods are served on a 'bed' of something – lettuce, watercress, vegetables, etc. 'Beds' have several virtues: they make what could otherwise appear a rather stingy portion look generous by filling up empty plate space; they prevent whatever is laid on them looking 'bare'; they can make a rather unattractive piece of food look quite pretty. A hunk of fillet steak laid on a bed of curly endive is going to look a lot more appetizing than it would sitting by itself in the middle of a white plate.

Green leaves of various kinds are the most popular 'beds', but caterers need to be especially careful that they are not going to droop into a sorry shadow of their former selves by the time they arrive at the table. Watercress, mustard and cress and round lettuces all have a tendency to wilt under the strain, so unless you can be sure that they will have plenty to drink and still be perky by the time they are ready to appear, avoid them. Curlier lettuces (of which there are now a great variety), curly endive, radicchio, some small-leaved spinaches, vigorous parsley and tansy (particularly tansy) are all reliable and will withstand a good deal of heat and strain. The darker leaves may look rather 'heavy' in large quantities; if so, try 'lightening' them with a few sprigs of something pale – celery tops or 'feathered spring onions' are very good stuck among the dark leaves. The large-leaved herbs (rosemary, rue, lovage, fennel tops, etc.) can also make attractive beds, as can neatly overlapping slithers of cucumber, courgette, tomato or any other decorative vegetable. Carefully done, overlapping slices can look like armour and can be used on top of foods (salmon is the classic example) too.

Hot vegetables can be used in the same way, but this becomes impractical when catering for larger numbers as by the time you have arranged the vegetables on the platters or plates with the meat or fish on top the whole lot is going to be cold. When serving game, you can also use slices of fried bread as 'beds' for your birds, or possibly even game chips, although you do risk them going soggy.

Leaves and Herbs Leaves and herbs can, of course, also be used to decorate the top of the food. A generous bunch of fresh watercress or parsley is incredibly simple, but still looks delicious with most meat and fish dishes. If you want to be a little more unusual, celery tops and fennel tops are easy to come by and cheap. Otherwise, there are all kinds of herbs with pretty and unusual leaves that can be used. Take care, however, to choose 'tough' herbs; some, like mint, will wilt away at the breath of a warm plate.

Flowers Whole flowers or flower petals can be used to decorate both sweet and savoury dishes, but do make sure that they are not poisonous before you use them. A really colourful flower like a nasturtium can look wonderful on a salad or with a pâté, while crystallized and sugared flowers are very effective with sweet dishes. You can wax, sugar and crystallize flowers and flower petals yourself (specialist books on garnishing will give you simple instructions), but it is time-consuming; it might be better either to use them fresh or to buy ready-crystallized violets or rose petals.

'Cut Up' Decorations There is a great art to cutting vegetables and fruits for decoration – the Japanese are particularly good at it – but it is a skilled and time-consuming job and therefore impractical for the common run of cooks or caterers. If you do want to make a speciality of it, there are several books on garnishing available. However, here are a few simple techniques that even the most ham-fisted can master.

Spring onion brushes and flowers Trim medium-sized spring onions and slice the green part into long slithers down to where it joins the white. Lay them in a container of chilled water and store them in a refrigerator for a couple of hours – the green bits will frill out and look very pretty with a salad, salmon, etc. (see illustrations).

To make flowers, slice the white parts across until you get a good mottling of green among the white. Slice the green parts into long slithers for the leaves and use the white rounds for the flowers.

Spring onion brushes
1 Trim and then cut each onion into 3 or 4 pieces.
2 Make several cuts down each onion; don't cut all the way through.
3 Put the brushes in iced water to open out.

Chilli flowers Remove the pointed end of a green or red chilli and using scissors cut up towards the stem in long fronds – take care not to rub your eyes and wash your hands well afterwards. Leave the chillies in chilled water until they frill out.

Chilli flowers
1 Cut the ends, then rinse and remove seeds.
2 Cut with scissors to form petals.
3 Leave in iced water until they frill out.

Radish and tomato stars or flowers Stars are used by a lot of restaurants and hotels and are very simple. You merely cut the radish or tomato in half in a series of short diagonal cuts. You usually need to put a little parsley or something similar in the middle. Tomato roses are popular but fiddly and do not withstand waiting very well as they dry up round the edges. They are made by carefully peeling the tomato and forming the skin into the shape of a rose. For radish flowers, simply cut petals in the sides of each radish (see illustrations).

Radish flowers
1 For tulips, cut 5 petals; leave their bases attached.
2 For roses, cut off the root; cut 3 or 4 petals in the sides of each radish.
3 Drop in iced water and leave to open out.

Cucumber, tomato, radish slices, etc. Any suitable vegetable can be cut into very thin slices which are then laid out overlapping each other. If the vegetables are similar sizes, the different slices can be interspersed with each other. This 'armour-plated' effect is very useful for disguising salmon that has got a little battered in the cooking and can hide all kinds of culinary mishaps. The 'plating' can also be painted with aspic if you want it to last a little longer.

Large radishes, with their white middles and red skins, can be thinly sliced and fanned to give a very pretty effect – I often find that just one radish in the corner of a dish of salad will add colour and quite change its look.

Cucumber slices also look pretty when twisted, but you need to take care to get the slice exactly the right thickness to twist gracefully without collapsing.

Another way to make attractive cucumber slices is to 'ridge' the skin first with a cannelle knife.

Citrus fruits Lemons, oranges and limes are all very popular and are a good contrast both in colour and taste to many varieties of food. The simplest way to serve them is to quarter them, but if so, make sure that as much pith as possible is trimmed off. They can also be sliced and the slices turned into butterflies (see illustrations) or twists like the cucumbers above.

Citrus peel can be used in all kinds of ways, but if there is going to be a lot of it, be sure that it is lightly blanched for a couple of minutes to take away some of the bitterness. Alternatives are to peel it very thinly in long thin strips that will curl, to peel it in shorter strips which can then be cut into very fine matchsticks, or to grate it.

Lemon butterflies
1 Cut into fine slices.
2 Cut V-shaped wedges; add strips of red pepper for the feelers.
3 Or cut each slice in half and place the curved halves back to back.

Olives, Gherkins, etc. These used to be *de rigueur* in decorating any cocktail dish – which is probably why they are somewhat out of favour today. I personally find that green olives and gherkins are rather 'dirgy', but black olives, especially if they are firm shiny ones, can look very effective. They can also be chopped very small and used to highlight pale foods such as prawns – this is time-consuming but extremely cheap.

'Sprinkled-on' Decoration Something that can be just 'thrown over' a dish is, of course, the quickest and easiest of all decorations – and accordingly very popular! There are a wide range of alternatives, all of which will enhance your food and look attractive.

Herbs Finely chopped fresh herbs – parsley, dill, etc. – will always look good and will keep their looks much better than the whole leaves. Do not, however, try to get away with dried chopped herbs – they need to be cooked to release their flavours and get rid of their 'dried' taste. Deep-fried herbs – usually small sprigs of parsley – are also effective.

Seeds Most seeds (sunflower, poppy, sesame, pumpkin, etc.) will look pretty when sprinkled over a dish, but you do need to match the size and colour of the seed to the dish. Pumpkin seeds, for example, can look great with a salad but thoroughly agricultural on an individual pâté. Some seeds, such as sesame, usually look better if they are toasted.

Nuts Most nuts look good either whole or chopped, although brazils or macadamias might be rather large whole. Nuts with interesting textures, shapes or colours (walnuts, pecans, pistachios, etc.) should be used either whole or halved. Some, such as slivered or nibbed almonds, hazelnuts, etc., look better toasted and they can all be used on both sweet and savoury dishes. Almonds are particularly good with sweet dishes as they can be arranged in patterns or used with angelica to look like flowers.

Mimosa balls, angelica, cherries, hundreds and thousands, chocolate drops, etc. All of these are useful for sprinkling over almost anything but should be used with discretion as they can make your dish look rather 'shop bought'. Usually one is sufficient – a sweet soufflé with cream ribs piped over it, each one decorated with mimosa balls, will look very 'tasteful', whereas if you were to add a few cherries and bits of angelica it would probably look a mess.

Chocolate Curls, Leaves, etc. Chocolate drops, strands and grated chocolate are the quick and easy way to decorate with chocolate – in each case they need only be sprinkled over the dish concerned. More 'up-market' but also more time-consuming are chocolate curls, leaves and shapes, but since none of them are very difficult, they all look good and keep well you may think it worth the effort. They do freeze but need to be defrosted *very* slowly to avoid sweating and discoloration.

Leaves, curls and shapes will need to be 'arranged' with a little more care, but since one or two are usually quite sufficient, their application will still be speedy.

Puff pastry roses
1 Fold over a strip of pastry to form the centre.
2 Wrap the strip around this, pinching the base to open out the petals.
3 Cut out leaf-shapes. Bake roses and leaves in a hot oven until golden.

Curls Slowly melt some plain dark chocolate in a double saucepan. Pour it onto a cool surface, ideally marble, and spread out with a spatula. Continue to work and spread the chocolate until it firms. Once it is cold and firm, use a very sharp knife or a cheese cutter to pare it off the surface in curls. Store in a box in a refrigerator or freezer until needed (see illustration).

Leaves Slowly melt some dark chocolate in a double saucepan. When it is melted, use a small brush and paint the chocolate on the upper side of a well-washed and dried leaf. Leave until cold and set, then carefully peel away the leaf and store the chocolate in boxes in the refrigerator or freezer.

Shapes Melt the chocolate as before, then, using a small nozzle, pipe whatever shape or decoration you want onto some clean greaseproof paper, making sure that your shapes are not too delicate. When the chocolate is cold and firm, carefully peel off the greaseproof paper and store in a box as above (see illustrations).

Fancy Shapes Almost any food can be made in fancy shapes that themselves provide a good deal of decoration. The most obvious are cakes, biscuits and mousses, and you can get cake tins, cutters and moulds in a wide variety of decorative or fun shapes. If you cannot find the shape you need (I remember needing sweet biscuits in the shape of a cello for one party we did), it is not too difficult to 'remould' a cutter since they are normally made of fairly soft metal. If the mixture is solid and will retain its shape during cooking (shortcrust pastry, for example), you may be able to cut it into shape with a knife; if it is softer (choux paste), you can often pipe it. The other alternative is to carve it into the shape you want when it is cooked – this works especially well with cakes when you can disguise your deficiencies as a sculptor with icing! If you feel energetic enough – and the occasion demands – there is no reason why you should not carve steaks or pork chops into weird shapes before you cook them. Vegetable shapes have also become popular since the advent of nouvelle cuisine; for these you can buy small cutters, which relieves the job of much effort and saves time.

Pastry Apart from baking it in shapes, you can use pastry trimmings to decorate most pastry dishes. Latticework on the top of a flan is easy and effective, either flat or twisted. Pastry balls are also simplicity itself and only need fixing on with a little water or egg. Depending on your artistic skills, you can create any number of decorations with your remains. Roses and leaves are the simplest and most popular, especially since they can be easily persuaded to stand proud of the lid (see illustrations), but there is no reason why you cannot create apples, pears, fish, spears of asparagus, ears of corn or anything else your fancy moves you too. Remember, however, that very fine detail is likely to get lost in the baking, so 'work large'. Finally, a good coating of egg yolk or whole egg will always do great things for pastry; it can be used equally successfully on sweet or savoury dishes, although it is more common on savoury.

Cream, Mayonnaise, etc. Whipped cream, mayonnaise, etc. are often used as decoration and just spread over whatever dishes they are intended to enhance. This is perfectly acceptable, but you may need to use a little 'sprinkled' decoration on top if it is not to look bare – the alternative is to pipe it (see below), but this will create a quite different effect which you may not want. They can

Chocolate shapes
1 Spread melted chocolate on a slab. Use a sharp knife to form curls.
2 Pipe melted chocolate into lattice shapes.
3 Pipe petals around a thick dot of chocolate.

also be used in conjunction with gelatine to create more formal decoration – see below under aspic and jellies.

Aspic and Jellies Decorating with aspic or jelly has rather gone out of fashion except among the traditional, 'international cuisine' type catering companies, but although it is fiddly and time-consuming, it should not be discarded as, when properly done, it can look extremely spectacular.

The easiest way to use either sweet or savoury jellies is to chill them in trays and then to chop them very finely and heap them round whatever you are serving. Even if you are coating your dish, you will need some spare chopped jelly to disguise the little puddle of jelly or aspic that will inevitably form around the bottom of whatever you are coating. However, this is not how they were intended to be used.

If you want to use them for coating your dish, you will need lots of patience and a steady hand. The aspic or jelly should be allowed to cool completely before you start to use it and must then be spooned over the food *very* slowly and *very* carefully in *very* thin layers. If you want to implant decoration in the jelly, it should be laid in place with tweezers, secured by the thinnest layer of jelly and allowed to set totally before the next layer is put on. It sounds, and is, very slow but can be worth it.

If you do not want a clear jelly, you can add gelatine to a sweet or savoury sauce and work in exactly the same way so as to get an opaque coating over your dish.

Piping Piping on decoration is one of the most traditional ways of decorating dishes, both sweet and savoury, and has a lot to be said for it; it is quick to do and can cover a multitude of sins. You need to be equipped with a fairly wide range of piping bags and nozzles and to have a reasonably deft hand. Cream and mayonnaise are the two most usual mediums, but anything that will hold its shape can be used. You can also flavour or colour creams and mayonnaises so as to create patterns – but take care when doing this as you can end up with something that looks spectacular in visual terms but that no one would want to eat! You may also find that you will need a little something to complete piped decoration – nuts, chopped parsley, a lemon twist or a chocolate curl.

Nouvelle cuisine The arrival of nouvelle cuisine has brought a whole new meaning to decoration, but for the average cook or caterer, unless he or she is going to specialize in nouvelle cuisine, it is too time-consuming to get involved in. Much use is made of shapes for vegetables, biscuits, etc. Piped chocolate outlines for sweet dishes, contrasting puddles of sauces, vegetables tied in little bunches with strands of spaghetti, and so on look wonderful on the plate, but you need the resources of a large kitchen and an army of cooks to arrange it all. If you are going to indulge in this kind of decoration, remember to set your prices at a level that will cover the extra work involved.

Butter There are many ways of serving butter and as it is ever present it is worth making it as attractive as possible. Some of the more economic ways are also the prettiest – and the most time-consuming – so you will have to take your pick.

You can merely fill ramekin dishes or larger bowls with butter and stick some parsley on top – which is quick and easy but extravagant. You can cut blocks or squares and lay them on saucers or butter dishes – they can be decorated with parsley, etc. and/or by scraping forks over them in patterns. You can cut the butter into little blocks or cubes which can be piled in a dish and sprinkled with parsley or whatever.

You can roll the butter into little balls with butter rollers. I find this immensely fiddly and rather extravagant since you have to allow at least one ball per person and they do not normally need that much. You can further decorate these by rolling them in chopped herbs, nuts or seeds. Finally, you can make butter curls which look the prettiest, are the most economical, but which do take quite a time to do. Whichever you choose, they can be done in advance and frozen in layers in boxes for your time of need.

Other Decorations I have not attempted here to give more than a pointer towards the kind of things that you can do. All cooks should be as imaginative as possible about their arrangement and decoration, ideally developing a 'house style' of their own. Do not forget also that apart from edible decorations you can always call in ice sculptures, gold and silver epergnes, 'shop-made' decorations, feathers, birds (we have done some wonderful displays with stuffed birds) or anything else that you can think of.

Cake Decorating

Tea Cakes Ordinary tea cakes are relatively easy to decorate with icings, fruits, nuts, etc., and you will find suggestions in most cookery books.

Wedding Cakes These are an art entirely on their own and require a very steady hand, lots of patience, and endless practice on bits of greaseproof paper. You should either buy a book and study the different techniques or attend a class – there are several good evening classes available in most areas. Even the simplest decoration is very time-consuming as not only is the work fiddly, but you have to leave the cake for long periods while the various layers of icing dry. You will need to cost your time carefully if you are going to make any money from them, and don't forget that you will be up against stiff opposition from shops.

Fancy or Fun Cakes Fancy cake decorating is no less of a specialized business than wedding cakes and just as time-consuming, but it is fun to do and becoming increasingly popular. If you really want to get into it, you should buy a book on this subject – there are several now available – and study the various techniques. Meanwhile, here are a few pointers just to give you some ideas.

Cake Materials The easiest cake to work with is a plain but relatively solid sponge; a Victoria sponge or even a Madeira cake but not an eggless sponge which will not hold its shape properly. Fruit cakes or any cakes with 'bits' in them are difficult to work with as they crumble when you cut them. Biscuity cakes also crumble as soon as you try to cut or carve them.

Shapes Try to keep the shapes simple and as close to the original cake shape as possible, especially in the early days. Computers, houses, cars, cheque books, etc. are all relatively simple, rectangular or square shapes. You can carve your sponge into more esoteric shapes – Eiffel Tower, churches, seated teddy bears and violins – if you feel skilful enough, but take care not to embark on any shape that will have a small base – goblet, standing animal, table, etc. – as the sponge will not support

any weight. This is, of course, assuming that you are intending the whole of your cake to be edible. If you are prepared to support it on an inedible 'scaffolding', your range widens enormously – although I must admit that I rather feel that is cheating. You will, of course, be able to 'cement' your construction with icing, but it is better not to put more strain on it than you can help!

Unless you are very skilled or confident, always work with a model – a picture is quite enough – and try to work 'to scale'. You will find that a little time spent with a ruler 'designing' your creation will pay you hands down. When we made a model of St Paul's Cathedral to celebrate the wedding of Prince Charles and Lady Diana, the works department at St Paul's gave us scale drawings of the entire cathedral to work from! The whole thing also took us over eighty hours to make, so be warned.

Icings To a cake 'builder', icing is your cement and thus absolutely vital. Not only will it stick your cake together, but you can dye it different colours to represent your Paddington Bear's coat or hat, the tractor's tyres, or the roof of your building. Everyone has their own favourite, but butter, fondant and royal are the three best. You will find recipes for all three in any standard recipe book or cake decorating book.

Butter icing This is extremely easy to work with, but has the rather major disadvantage that it will melt in hot weather. I remember making an old-fashioned record player for someone's birthday once (very nifty with a little cassette built into the base so that it actually 'played'). The only trouble was that it was in the summer and the stylus arm collapsed into the 'record' if it stayed out of the refrigerator for more than ten minutes! However, butter icing is probably the easiest to deal with for a beginner. If you don't use it all, it can be frozen.

Fondant icing This is the most popular with professional cake makers as it is the quickest to work with and very malleable. My only objection is that it is a little 'thick' so you cannot do really fine work with it. However, that disadvantage can usually be overcome by piped decoration. You can colour and dye it easily and it stores well.

Royal icing This is, of course, what is used for wedding cakes and has the advantages that when it is set it is very strong and that you can work very finely in it. However, it is slow (you have to wait for bits to dry and set) and it is not easy to work with. I found that it was best for architectural cakes (which were our speciality) as you could make pillars and 'statues' separately, then 'cement' them in place with a little fresh icing when they were dry. However, it does not keep unused for more than a few days in the refrigerator, although once set it will last for ever.

Decoration You can, of course, use anything in the way of flowers, fruits (edible or otherwise), feathers, small toys, ribbons, lace, etc. to decorate your creation, but coloured icing and some piping

bags will come in very useful. These will allow you to write or draw on your cake – cartoons, 'happy birthdays', etc. It will also allow you to 'paint in' what you may not have been able to do with different coloured icings. We made a real tennis court for a client on one occasion and all the lines on the court were 'drawn' in with white icing piped from a very thin nozzle. If you really get into the business of cake decorating, you can buy a tiny air brush which allows you to shade and shadow your decoration – bushes and hedges growing up the side of a house, for example.

If you are using royal icing, you can make certain decorations and apply them – icing flowers and leaves are obvious examples, but also the strings of a violin, the fence to go round a house or outline 'drawings' of almost anything. This kind of thing can also be very successfully done with melted chocolate. Again, use a fine nozzle and steady pressure to achieve an unbroken line.

Menu Planning

Menu planning is one of the most vital areas of any professional cook's or caterer's business as the success of the meal or party will hang on it. The trick is to get the food not only tasting good, but looking right and suited to that particular function – you will do your reputation no good at all if you serve rich cream gâteaux, no matter how delicious, to a group who are neurotic about their cholesterol levels, any more than if you serve *nouvelle cuisine* titbits to a sports club after a rugger match! I will go into more detail about specific suggestions for menus later, but first here are a few guiding principles that need to be borne in mind when planning any menu.

Transportability Remember that, when planning meals to be served other than where they are cooked, they have to be got there – very delicate jellies or spun sugar decorations will not survive the rigours of the journey.

Variety Variety is essential in taste, texture, colour and shape.

Taste Unless your client is besotted about one particular flavour, or you are doing a themed party, such as pancakes, you do not want the same flavours to crop up in each course. This might seem obvious, but you would be surprised how easy it is to draw up a delicious-looking menu only to discover that you have got cream or cheese in every single dish. You need also to take care that you do not use ingredients that, although theoretically different, in fact taste very similar.

Texture This is equally important. You do not want four courses of totally smooth, bland textures any more than you want four courses of 'bitty' textures, such as rice, or four courses of chopped raw vegetables – unless you are preparing a diet meal. Any meal, buffet or 'sit down', should combine a selection of as many textures as is realistic.

Colour This is obviously vital on a buffet table where nothing but brown dishes is going to look very boring and dreary. Similarly, a series of courses of all the same colour (often all white) is going to be just as uninspiring. That is not to say that you want a plethora of colours all jammed in with little attention to anything except variety; your meal should be as visually pleasing as it is gastronomically, which means 'designing' your dishes to achieve quite specific visual effects. To do this you can use one or two colours only, but if so, they must be used in such a way as to make the intention obvious – and attractive.

Shape This is just as important to the visual effect of the meal as colour. Six courses all served in ring moulds is going to be boring unless, once again, it is being done to create a quite specific effect. We once did a fashion show where, to match the design of the show, all the food had to be white and have a hole in the middle – so we did have six courses in ring moulds. You should make an effort to get variation in the shapes and heights of the foods as well as the dishes they are served on, especially on a buffet table.

Tailoring the Meal to the Client No matter how delicious or how attractive your menu may be, if it is not what the client wants, it will be a failure.

46

The onus is on you as the experienced caterer to ask the right questions to discover exactly what your client really does want. Here are just a few of the points you should bear in mind.

Try to discover the age range of the group – if they are young, they will tend to be hungry; if elderly, they will eat relatively little.

Will the guests be mainly male or female – women do eat less and on the whole feel less deprived if they do not get their sticky cake or their cheese at the end of their meal?

If it is either a lunch or dinner, find out what they will have been doing beforehand and what they will want to do afterwards. If they have all been for a brisk walk around a development site in February, they are obviously going to be cold and hungry and want a large bowl of sizzling soup followed by a steak and kidney pie – or something similar. If they have sat all morning in a meeting stuffing themselves with coffee and biscuits, they will want a relatively light lunch. If the hosts (your clients) want their guests to work the morning after a dinner, you should not feed them too richly or too heavily (or provide too much drink).

If it is a purely social function, try to find out your clients' attitude to it. Several ethnic groups take it as a matter of pride to produce enormously more food than anyone would ever really eat, so you will need to bear this in mind.

Try to discover what sort of food they really like and what sort of decoration they would best appreciate. You can encourage them to make suggestions if you want, but that may land you in all kinds of problems when they ask for something you don't feel competent to handle. Most people are only too happy to have you provide them with ideas, but do encourage them to at least take an active interest in the decision between various alternatives.

Find out how much money they want to spend. This is absolutely essential and you should discover this before you start talking about food at all. Most people do have some kind of notional budget even if it is rather vague, and at least it will give you somewhere to start even if you have to revise your ideas later.

Try to find out whether they or any of their guests have any phobias, allergies – or passions – about foods. It is no use only discovering on the night that the host cannot eat eggs.

Preparation, Timing and Serving When planning your menus, you must bear in mind the fact that you are going to have to cook them. So take care not to get so enthusiastic that you suggest something that will make your life hell – or be impossible to achieve in the context of that particular party. For example, you cannot prepare hot soufflés for a large party without a proper kitchen, and if you try, you will have a disaster.

Take care not to plan menus where all the dishes require last-minute attention – if you do, you will blow all your profit on employing extra staff to cope with the rush of work at the end. You should be able to achieve a balance between dishes that can be prepared well in advance and frozen, dishes that can be prepared the day before, and dishes that can only be prepared immediately before serving. In the menu suggestions below, I have indicated whether each dish can be safely prepared ahead or be frozen.

Think also of your staff. No matter how delicious the food may look on the platter, if it is very difficult to serve – slices of meat that have not been totally separated from each other – by the time it gets onto the guest's plate it will look like something the dog brought home. Anyhow, it is not fair to your waiting staff (and you will not keep them) if you make their lives any more difficult than they have to be. This point is even more important if the guests are going to serve themselves; being inexperienced, they will probably tip your wonderful bouchées over their new clothes if they cannot get them off the dish.

Set Menus No matter how good you may be at finding out the clients' wants and secret longings, you are going to need some 'set menus' to show them the sort of thing that you can do, and you will certainly need lists for your own reference. Most brochures do contain a certain number of menus as illustration of the sort of thing on offer. If you are going to include them, you need to be sure that they show you off in your best light, so take plenty of time and care in planning them.

It is obviously impossible for me to give specific menus, as the range of cooks and caterers reading this book will be far too wide for me to produce something suitable for all. I am therefore merely going to mention dishes that could be used in the context of each type of meal – and let you take it from there.

Recipes Certain dishes mentioned in the menu section will have an asterisk (*). This will mean that a recipe for it appears in the recipe section. I have not given recipes for dishes that are in common usage and that can be found in any one of half a dozen cook books – unless I have discovered some amazingly speedy, cheap or delicious way of preparing them! What I have provided is recipes for dishes that are unusual or that we have found particularly useful in a catering context. Many dishes can be frozen and are therefore able to be prepared far in advance; others can be prepared a few days or the day before. You will find a key to the symbols on the opposite page.

Cocktail Parties

For even the most meagre of cocktail parties I feel that you need a selection of at least four different nibbles; for the most exotic, you can serve ten or twelve. Remember that all the 'bits' will have to be eaten in the fingers by guests who are already holding a glass, possibly a cigarette and, if they are women, a handbag – and who will probably be wearing relatively good clothes. So try to serve things that will be clean and easy to eat in a single 'lady-like' mouthful, and not ones that drip down their fronts and prevent them from doing more than grunt for three minutes. This also means that, although hot 'bits' should be hot, they should not be so hot as to burn the mouth! Americans always offer a small paper napkin with the drink which does help with the mopping-up operation, but since this seldom happens in the UK, it is even more important that the food should not make a mess and drip everywhere.

Even if the bits have been prepared immediately before the function, if the guests are late or the room is particularly hot, they can wilt or deteriorate rapidly. Take care when planning your dishes that your decorations are not going to look tired, the base to your canapé (toast, pumpernickel, bread, oatcake, etc.) is not going to go soggy, and that your crisp little numbers (deep-fried vegetables, etc.) are not going to go flaccid. I find that pumpernickel and oatcakes are a great deal more tolerant than bread, toast or biscuits – and taste a lot better too. There is a recipe for oatcakes in the recipe section, although you can now buy cocktail-sized ones in some stores.

As for deep-fried 'bits', we only serve ones that can be cooked earlier and reheated in an oven. This means that you can be sure that they will be hot and crisp – and that the guests will not be assailed by the smell of old fat.

An average of one and a half portions or pieces of each 'nibble' per person is usually ample, although if you were only serving three or four things, you might want to increase this slightly. Conversely, if you are serving ten or twelve different snacks, one portion of each will be more than enough; indeed you may want to cut down a bit on the more esoteric of your creations.

KEY TO SYMBOLS

* RECIPES INCLUDED IN THE BOOK

● CAN BE PREPARED IN ADVANCE

△ CAN BE FROZEN

Cheap and Cheerful

CHEESE STRAWS OR SABLÉS △

SEEDY PASTRY SQUARES * △

SAUSAGEMEAT OR ANY SMALL
AND WELL-FLAVOURED MEATBALLS △
(hot or cold, with or without a dip)

CRUDITÉS
(cut one or two raw vegetables into fingers and
serve with a dip – if you restrict the number of
vegetables to one or two, it keeps the price down.
You can make a feature of your restriction by only
using red and white vegetables, or green and
yellow)

DEVILLED WHITEBAIT*
(or any really small fish)

MINIATURE VEGETABLE OR MEAT KEBABS
(these are good with raw peppers as they give
colour)

DEEP-FRIED PLANTAIN SLICES
(these reheat well)

STUFFED RAW VEGETABLES
(cut celery, peppers, chicory leaves, etc. into small
pieces and use cream cheeses, pâtés, etc. for
stuffing)

MUSHROOM CAPS STUFFED WITH BLUE CHEESE
(if you use Danish Blue mixed with a milder cheese
it will be quite cheap)

ANCHOVY PINWHEELS

Posh and Expensive

DEVILLED CASHEW AND MACADAMIA NUTS * ●
(these can be prepared several weeks in advance
but do not need to be frozen – they will keep well
in an airtight tin)

MELON BALLS AND PARMA HAM ●

MUSHROOMS STUFFED WITH SPINACH
AND GORGONZOLA * ●

SEAFOOD PLATTERS * △ WITH MAYONNAISE DIP ●
(the seafood can be mainly frozen so only needs
defrosting)

STEAK TARTARE ON PUMPERNICKEL

SMOKED SALMON, TUNA FISH, BRESSAOLA,
SMOKED REINDEER ROLLS/PLATTER ●

KING PRAWNS OR CRAB CLAWS △ WITH
MAYONNAISE DIP ●
(the prawns and crab claws can normally only be
bought frozen, so this makes for a very easy but
spectacular dish)

CANAPÉS OF FOIE GRAS OR PÂTÉ DE FOIE GRAS

OYSTERS ON THE SHELL, GRATINÉED

Healthy or Vegetarian

CRUDITÉS WITH ASSORTED DIPS

PICKLED OKRA ●

MINIATURE VEGETABLE KEBABS
(including peppers for colour)

SPINACH AND HERB OMELETTE*

MARINATED MUSHROOMS
(or any other vegetables)

MINIATURE HERB SANDWICHES
(use brown and black breads and mix the herbs
with cream cheese, houmous, etc.)

TOMATO SLICES ON OATCAKES * △ WITH
HORSERADISH BUTTER ●

Summery

MINIATURE PROFITEROLES△
(stuff with cream cheese and herbs, smoked haddock mousse or whatever you feel like; freeze uncooked)

CHEESE PIECES ON STICKS WITH VARIOUS FRUITS
(*not* tinned pineapple chunks – try halved strawberries, raspberries, loganberries, halved plums, etc.)

BLANCHED FLORETS OF CAULIFLOWER AND BROCCOLI WITH VARIOUS DIPS

CRUDITÉS WITH VARIOUS DIPS

STUFFED CUCUMBER SLICES
(pipe soft pâté onto each slice)

STUFFED VINE LEAVES
(vegetarian, rice, wholewheat, fish, etc.)

STUFFED ARTICHOKE HEARTS
(pipe cream cheese, pâtés, etc., on top)

SEAFOOD PLATTER*△ WITH MAYONNAISE DIP●

THIN SLICES OF ROAST BEEF ROLLED WITH HORSERADISH

STUFFED SQUID*●

Wintery

SMOKED MACKEREL, KIPPER OR SALMON PÂTÉ ON OATCAKES* OR IN MINI SANDWICHES△

POTATO SKINS AND DIPS

DEVILS ON HORSEBACK△
(or bacon rolled round almost anything – chicken livers, mussels, artichoke hearts, etc.)

DEVILLED MIXED NUTS*●
(these do not need to be frozen for storage)

MELON BALLS WRAPPED IN ANCHOVY FILLETS OR WITH SLITHERS OF STEM GINGER

SPICY MINI KEBABS△
(the vegetables can be added on the day)

CHICKEN SATAY*△ WITH DIPS

ROLLS OF THINLY-SLICED ROAST BEEF WITH HORSERADISH

STUFFED DRIED FRUITS
(prunes, dates, etc. stuffed with spiced cream cheese)

SESAME CHEESE BISCUITS
(cheese straw mixture rolled in sesame seeds)

WINTER CRUDITÉS WITH DIPS
(Brussels sprouts, red cabbage, carrots, parsnips, celery, etc.)

Hot

DEVILS ON HORSEBACK△
(or anything rolled in bacon – see above)

MUSHROOMS STUFFED WITH CHEESE
(cheap or expensive)

TORTELLONI AND TOMATO DIPS

FINGERS OF CHEESE ON TOAST WITH
CHILLI OR ANCHOVY

OYSTERS OR MUSSELS ON THE SHELLS,
GRATINÉED

FILO PASTE PARCELS
(fill with cream cheese, meat, etc.)

FINGERS OF PISSALADIÈRE△

SAUSAGES△

SAUSAGEMEAT OR OTHER MEATBALLS△

Dips Dips should be well flavoured and reasonably firm to prevent them from dripping down everyone's tie or top. A first-class vinaigrette may taste divine, but it is going to be hell to eat and you will not be popular with your guests if you have irretrievably ruined their best clothes.

Yoghurt base with fresh herbs, salt and garlic, lemon, chilli or any other flavouring you fancy

Mayonnaise, plain or as a base for mustard, curry, herbs, tomato, etc.

Cream cheese as a base with chilli, herbs or garlic

Whipped cream as a base with any of the above

Avocado

Taramasalata

Peanut or nut-based dips (see CHICKEN SATAY*)

Theme or Fun Cocktail Menu – Flower Garden If you have a large number of guests, you will have to do a central display table with back-up dishes of all the eats. It would be best to arrange your display on a mirror glass base which will serve as your 'garden pond', then arrange the chosen dishes as you feel inclined (see below).

A greenhouse made from clear savoury jelly, its struts of spring onion stalks set into the jelly – this is tricky but looks spectacular

Garden walls – brick or stone – made from 'bricks' of cheese biscuits

Young trees made from twiglets

Hedges made from young spring onions stuck white end down in a narrow bed of cream cheese or any other firm dip

Lawns made of pieces of pumpernickel spread with cream cheese and very liberally coated with chopped fresh herbs

Flower beds of radish flowers and other raw vegetables chopped small and arranged as a parterre

Strawberry beds made from alpine strawberries

A compost heap of cocktail sausages cooked in chutney with nibbed almonds

Finger Buffets

'Finger buffets' or, as they are known in the States, 'heavy cocktails' are an immensely convenient way of substantially feeding a large number of guests with minimum hassle. The idea is that everything should be able to be picked up in the fingers, thus doing away with forks and possibly plates, although it is sometimes easier to use a plate if you want to make a meal of it. You can now buy small clips that fit on the side of the plates to hold stemmed glasses, which makes the business of tucking into a finger buffet even easier.

You may experience some 'customer resistance' when you try to sell this idea to clients; if they have never been to one, they will fear that no one will get enough to eat, but although they need careful planning, there is no reason why a finger buffet should not be a really satisfying meal. Moreover, you can easily serve sweet things at the end of a finger buffet with the coffee in case anyone feels they will suffer from pudding withdrawal symptoms.

However, as with cocktail parties, you need to make sure that what you are offering is 'clean'. You also need to supply plenty of paper napkins for mopping up, and make sure that you have waiting staff constantly clearing up débris – chewed drumsticks and cutlet bones, crab claws, etc. For a finger buffet, you should allow at least one of each item for each guest; for the smaller and more popular ones, you may choose to supply slightly more – say one and a quarter on average.

Cheap and Filling

SAUSAGES AND SAUSAGE OR ANY OTHER
MEATBALLS △
(with or without dips)

PIECES OF SPANISH OR ARNOLD BENNETT OMELETTE*
(either on their own or on oatcakes)

SMALL HERB, CHEESE, PÂTÉ OR MEAT SANDWICHES
(some can be made in advance and frozen, or use halved or quartered, filled pitta breads, but make sure that the filling is not too messy nor falls out all the time)

BOWLS OF PÂTÉ △
(serve any kind as long as it holds together reasonably well – smoked fish, chicken liver, etc., but not terrine maison – with small crackers. If you stick a few knives in the bowl, people will just help themselves and, hopefully, leave the knife behind! On average you will need to allow approximately 15 g/½ oz of pâté per head)

CHEESEBOARD WITH CRACKERS
(again if you leave several knives on the cheese board with some butter near at hand, people will butter themselves a cracker, put on some cheese and take it away with them on their rounds. You will need to allow about 25 g/1 oz of cheese per head)

CHICKEN DRUMSTICKS △
(these are standard fare at all finger buffets and, although they are not particularly cheap, they are very popular. They are greatly improved if marinated or 'treated' before they are cooked. They are often served in batter or egg and breadcrumbs, neither of which I feel is a particularly good idea – they either turn out greasy or soggy. Given lots of flavour by a marinade and then cooked until they are well browned and tender, they can be good both hot and cold)

BARBECUED SPARE RIBS △
(a bit messy to eat but delicious, particularly hot)

FLANS, QUICHES AND PIZZAS ●
(all of these are good in finger-sized pieces, but take care that your filling is not too runny. You

have to hit a happy medium between too much pastry – a danger if you do individual flans or whatever – and not enough to keep the filling in check. Many can be frozen in advance – BACON AND APPLE FLAN* △, PIZZA △, PISSALADIÈRE △, SMOKED MACKEREL AND COCKLE FLAN* △ – others are better prepared the day before – blue cheese flans, mushroom, etc.; quiches should really be made on the day, but I feel that a quiche, if it is a good one, will be too soft to be eaten successfully in the fingers)

PASTIES △
(various kinds can be served, but they need to be small enough to be eaten in one or at the most two mouthfuls – if it is to be two, then the filling must be fairly solid)

CRUDITÉS AND DIPS
(allow plenty as they are eaten in lieu of salad and vegetables)

TORTELLONI AND DIP
(tomato dip is particularly good. Tortelloni can be bought from any good pasta shop if you don't want to have to make them)

OPEN ROAST BEEF SANDWICHES
(these are always popular and cheap as you can cut the beef very thinly. You can 'butter' your bread or pumpernickel with horseradish)

STUFFED TOMATOES*
(you can use almost any filling, although rice is more difficult to eat than bulgar wheat or breadcrumbs)

STUFFED LEAVES
(many leaves can be stuffed with cream cheese, pâté, etc. – chicory leaves are good because they are firm and fairly large)

Posh and Expensive

LAMB CUTLETS △
(these can be spiced, minted or barbecued and served hot or cold. You can also coat them in mint aspic, which looks good but is very fiddly)

CHEESE BEIGNETS

PROFITEROLES △
(stuff with anything from taramasalata to beluga caviar with soured cream)

FLANS
(some of the more exotic fillings, such as blue cheese and walnut, cashew nuts, spiced mushroom, etc., will make delicious fingers of flan)

POLLO TONNATO FINGERS●
(small pieces of chicken with tuna fish mayonnaise)

SMOKED OR MARINATED MEATS
(bressaolo, Parma ham, smoked reindeer, duck, marinated cooked partridge, pheasant, grouse, etc. are all good. These can either be rolled or cut into fingers and speared on cocktail sticks. They can be served with a dip or a fairly solid dressing or, if they are rolled, 'sandwiched' with a dressing)

SMOKED FISH
(salmon, trout, tuna, etc. can be served as pâtés, rolls, sandwiches or even as a platter with a horseradish dip)

SEAFOOD PLATTERS* △
(any frozen or fresh fish speared on cocktail sticks and served with a mayonnaise dip)

CRAB CLAWS OR KING PRAWNS △ WITH MAYONNAISE DIP●

BELUGA OR SEVRUGA CAVIAR
(serve tubs on ice for dipping into)

STUFFED VINE LEAVES △
(meat or vegetarian)

FILO PASTE PARCELS
(cream cheese, meat or fish)

FINGERS OF HAM ROLLED IN LIGHTLY-BLANCHED SPINACH LEAVES LINED WITH MUSTARD

Hot

SAUSAGES, PLAIN OR BARBECUED, SAUSAGE OR ANY
OTHER MEATBALLS△
(with or without dips)

CHICKEN DRUMSTICKS△
(see above)

LAMB CUTLETS△
(see above)

VOL-AU-VENTS
(take care they are reasonably easy to eat)

GOUJONS OF FISH

BEIGNETS

SAMOSAS AND BAJEES

CHICKEN OR BEEF SATAY*

FILO PASTE PARCELS
(cheese, meat or fish)

DEEP-FRIED MUSHROOMS AND DIPS

POTATO SKINS AND DIPS

FLANS AND PIZZAS
(see above)

Sweet Dishes

ANY SWEET BISCUITS△
(especially chocolate)

MERINGUES AND MACAROONS●

FINGERS OF ANY SOLID CAKE●
(Madeira, gingerbread, seedy cake, fruit cakes,
etc.)

SWEET PROFITEROLES△
(fill with cream or a sweet custard, top with
chocolate, caramel or fresh fruits – strawberries,
raspberries, kiwi, etc. Freeze uncooked)

CHOCOLATE FRUIT FONDUE
(fresh fruits cut into manageable pieces, served
with cocktail sticks and a bowl of hot chocolate
sauce to dip into)

Buffet Parties

Fork or 'running' buffets (a 'running buffet'
always conjures up visions of the salmon in hot
pursuit of the trifle) are the most popular form of
catered entertainment, so be prepared.

Guests at a buffet will either be expected to
stand on one foot perched on the stairs,
manœuvring their plate, fork, glass and other
paraphernalia as well as they can, or, at more

civilized – and more expensive – parties, they will
be provided with tables and chairs to sit at, but
will still have to collect their food from the buffet
table. Obviously, you will not need to be as careful
planning the latter sort of meal as guests will be
able to wield both knife and fork in perfect
comfort and thus be able to cope with large slices
of home-glazed ham or a langoustine in its shell.
The 'stand in a corner and stuff' guest will,
however, need foods that can easily be tackled
with a fork alone so as to minimize the number of
plates of Coronation Chicken upended over the
new carpet!

The advantages of a buffet arrangement is that
it is cheaper on staff – you do not need as many as
you would for a full, sit-down meal – and that you

can offer your guests a much wider choice of food. Since you will be dealing with such a range of dishes, quantities become rather more complicated. Allowing for the fact that people are much greedier when helping themselves from a buffet than they would be if they were being served, you need to provide at least one and a half main courses for each guest with about one and a quarter helpings of salad. What this means is that if you are serving three main dishes for one hundred people you would prepare fifty portions of each, making a total of one hundred and fifty portions. What will actually happen is that almost everyone will take a little bit of everything so as to make up a plateful. The same principle should be applied to puddings, with especially generous quantities of the old favourites, such as Chocolate Roulade.

As the food is all on view, you need to pay particular attention to colour, shape and general looks, and to ease of serving as the guests may well be helping themselves. You also need to give as wide a selection as you can: both light and filling salads – for example, pretty leaves and vegetables and filling beans, rice or pasta; sticky and rich puddings (trifles, chocolate mousses, gâteaux) as well as light and 'slimming' desserts (fresh fruit or frothy soufflés); and maybe cheese for those who don't like either.

Cheap, Cheerful and Filling

FLANS, PIZZAS AND QUICHES●
(the range of these is obviously enormous and many of them can be prepared days or weeks in advance. Apart from the ones you will find in other cookery books – vegetarian cookbooks are particularly good for flans – try the BACON AND APPLE FLAN* and SMOKED MACKEREL AND COCKLE FLAN* already suggested in the finger buffet suggestions. We have found the following flan based on an historic English dish very popular – HERB TART*)

PÂTÉS
(all kinds of pâté are relatively cheap and easy to eat with a fork. If they are to be eaten with salad rather than bread, and the guests will be standing, it is better to use the coarse, less rich pâtés – a terrine maison rather than a chicken liver pâté)

SLICED BEEF, HAM OR SPICED BRISKET●
(*very thinly* sliced meats are economic – each slice weighs under 25 g/1 oz – and easy to eat as the guest can wrap them round a fork. However, you really need a professional slicer to achieve this. Meats such as spiced brisket or silverside, or stuffed and rolled breast of veal, are particularly cheap, tasty and unusual, although you can never go wrong with rare roast beef)

MEAT LOAVES●
(these do not sound very inspiring but can be delicious and, since they only use cheap meat, are very cheap: A VICTORIAN 'BEEF CAKE'* (based on a Victorian recipe); A 'BATTERED' MEAT LOAF*)

RAISED PIES●
(these are not particularly cheap, but are very filling)

SPICED HAM SALAD●
(there is an old Cordon Bleu recipe for ham in a tomato sauce with rice and hard-boiled eggs which is both tasty and filling)

PILAFFS AND RISOTTOS●
(any rice-based dish will be filling and relatively cheap, but do make sure that it has plenty of flavour. We have a standby recipe which my mother took out of a newspaper many years ago (I can't trace whose recipe it was, so I fear I can give no credit). It was originally for prawns but can be adapted for chicken, turkey or sausages: TURKISH PRAWN PILAFF*. Pilaffs and risottos can also be successfully and maybe more interestingly made with bulgar wheat, millet, etc. – try the health food cookbooks for ideas)

SAVOURY MOUSSES●
(egg, fish, chicken or vegetarian)

JELLIED TOMATO OR OTHER VEGETABLE MOULDS OR TERRINES●
(these can all be made in advance, look quite spectacular, and are very cheap, but are not very easy to eat with just a fork: TOMATO RING MOULD*; CHEAP VEGETABLE TERRINE*)

SALADS
(these can include beans, potato, pasta or rice for bulk, but in each case make sure that they are well

dressed and have plenty of flavour. Health food and vegetarian cookbooks are a good source of recipes. One excellent and unusual one we have used is CURRIED LENTIL SALAD*)

BREAD OR BISCUITS

(these are always a good filler up, but if the guests are not going to be able to sit down, it might be better to give them biscuits, which are easy to eat, rather than bread or rolls, which have to be pulled apart and buttered)

Desserts

CARAMELIZED ORANGE SALAD●

(this is always popular, simple, good and cheap)

FRESH FRUIT TARTS●

(these are quite cheap and can look very pretty if the fruits are attractively arranged and you take the trouble to glaze them)

CHEESECAKES●

(always a popular dessert, these are filling and reasonably cheap)

CHOCOLATE ROULADE*●

(this, or any other chocolate gâteau, is rich and filling and relatively cheap if you use a cake base)

SPONGE FRUIT GÂTEAUX

Rich, Luscious and Expensive

COLD FILLET OF BEEF●
(slice thinly)

COLD BEEF STROGANOV*

BONED, STUFFED GROUSE*●

RAISED GAME PIE●
(make sure the meat is cut small enough)

PUPTON OF PIGEONS*●
(this is an unusual recipe based on an old English dish – it makes a change from the usual terrines)

DRESSED SALMON

SMOKED FISH PLATTERS

LOBSTER OR CRAB MAYONNAISE

VITELLO OR POLLO TONNATO●
(the meat should be very thinly cut)

GALANTINE OF SALMON OR SALMON AND SEAFOOD●

EXOTIC MOUSSES
(smoked trout, haddock, avocado, crab, etc. are all suitable)

SMOKED SALMON AND PARMESAN ROULADE

SALADS
(unusual leaves and herbs, artichoke heart and bacon, avocado and strawberry, beanshoot and brazil nut, curried mushroom, etc. are all delicious. Health food and vegetarian cookbooks have excellent salads)

Desserts Almost any luscious dessert will be good on a buffet table – creamy gâteaux and alcoholic rum babas. Serve these with exotic fruit salads or fruit dishes for the calorie conscious. Here are a few of our favourites: LEMON BOODLES FOOL*; RUM AND WALNUT GÂTEAU*; LYCHEE AND BLACK GRAPE SALAD*; PINEAPPLE WITH FRESH GINGER*.

Provide a really expensive and unusual cheeseboard. Go to the best shop and buy the best you can get – don't make do with what your normal supplier has unless you are quite sure that it is the tops.

Summery

Any of the above that seem suitable plus the following suggestions.

COLD SOUPS●
(there are lots of delicious cold soups that, provided they are reasonably thick, will be quite easy to eat from a bowl standing up. Really well chilled, they are also delicious on a hot night. Here are two of our favourites: CHILLED FENNEL WITH GINGER SOUP*; GASPACHO)

COLD FISH DISHES
(apart from salmon, there are many recipes for sole, plaice, mackerel, etc. in mayonnaise or fruit dressings that are delicious cold)

BONED, STUFFED CHICKEN* △
(this is an excellent buffet standby that freezes well)

CORONATION CHICKEN OR CHICKEN IN A CURRY MAYONNAISE●
(this excellent Cordon Bleu recipe was worked to the bone back in the seventies but deserves another outing)

CHICKEN, APPLE AND PARSLEY SALAD*●
(a great favourite based on a recipe by Oliver Cromwell's wife)

BEEF, MUSHROOM AND ASPIC MOULD*●
(this is light, pretty and cheap, although a bit fiddly to make)

AJWAR*●
(this delicious Yugoslavian red pepper pâté looks wonderful on summer buffet tables)

SALADS
(in the summer we are spoilt for choice with salad vegetables, so feel free to indulge – try mixing fresh fruits, *not* tinned pineapple chunks, with some of your salads; a few kiwi fruit or strawberries will go a long way and look pretty)

Desserts Use as many really nice fresh fruits as possible for summer desserts. You can also serve ice creams, but this can be a little dodgy if they are going to have to sit around for too long.

Wintery

One of the troubles with hot winter buffet dishes is that it is difficult to make them look interesting – on the whole you are dependent on the dish in which your casserole is served for decoration. What is more, you have to keep them hot. If possible for your own convenience, serve a couple of hot dishes only – if these appear at the beginning of the meal, the guests will not even notice that the rest is cold.

I have always found that hot soup is a wonderful winter dish and as long as it is fairly thick it will not be a problem to eat. Hot casseroles or pies can be combined with most cold buffet dishes, although I would avoid a dark beef sauce with a mayonnaise.

SOUPS●
(most soups can be made in advance and frozen. Here are a few suggestions: MRS BLENCOWE'S GREEN PEA SOUP*, a great favourite, based on an old English recipe; SAFFRON SOUP*, MULLIGATAWNY (hot in all senses); CURRIED PARSNIP AND APPLE SOUP*; PINK RHUBARB SOUP*; ALMOND SOUP*; CREAM OF MUSHROOM SOUP)

CASSEROLES●
(almost any casserole can be made in advance and frozen or at least left in the refrigerator for a couple of days – it actively improves the flavour. Do remember that if the guests are going to be standing, the meat and vegetables need to be cut fairly small. Two of our old favourites are: CASSEROLED VEAL WITH MUSHROOMS IN SOURED CREAM*; BEEF CASSEROLE WITH PRUNES*)

PIES●
(many pies reheat well and can be made in very large dishes. They are filling and warming, but make sure that you are going to be able to get the dish with your pie into whatever heating equipment you will have on the night. Any of the traditional pies will go down well)

MADE-UP DISHES●
(lasagne, fish pies, moussaka and all such made-up dishes are excellent for buffets as they are very tolerant about being reheated. You can make them with meat, fish or purely vegetarian and you will find recipes in many cookbooks, especially ethnic ones. Two of our favourites are: AUBERGINE AND SAUSAGE CASSEROLE*; PARSNIPS MOLLY PARKIN*)

Vegetables These need to be easy to eat, especially if the guests are going to stand up – baked potatoes are *not* a good buffet dish. The easiest way of all to serve them is to incorporate them in the meat dish, but if you need something else, a made-up vegetable dish such as ratatouille (tarted up by sprinkling crushed crisps mixed with a little Parmesan on the top) will be easy to deal with. Otherwise, serve mashed potatoes or any other puréed vegetable, a simple rice pilaff or a bean dish – on the whole pasta is too difficult to eat to be much use as a vegetable. Our all-time favourite as a potato dish is SHERRIED POTATOES*.

If you want to serve salads for no other reason than to cover a bit more of your buffet tables, try to serve something other than flaccid winter lettuce. Two tasty winter salads are: A CHRISTMAS SALAD* (excellent for Christmas dinner); CABBAGE AND CAPER SALAD*.

Desserts Winter desserts can afford to be a little richer to stoke up the inner man. Any of the normal range of 'sticky puds' will be fine, including the following: TREACLE TART●; UPSIDE DOWN CAKES (pineapple or ginger); RICH CHOCOLATE OR OTHER MOUSSES● – CHOCOLATE AND ORANGE MOUSSE*●; TRIFLES AND GINGER TRIFLES●; CHOCOLATE OR OTHER GÂTEAUX● – 'FROG' SACHERTORTE*●.

You will be pushed to find good fruit at a reasonable price, so if you do not want to be too extravagant, stick with: ORANGE SALAD (caramelized or plain); APPLE PIES OR FLANS.

More expensive but seasonal would be the LYCHEE AND BLACK GRAPE SALAD*.

Themes or Exotic Buffet Menus
Buffet meals are ideal for 'theming', especially if you can tie in the decoration, drinks entertainment, and so on.

'Ethnic' Themes These have always been popular – a pasta party, a Greek party, a Scandinavian party. It is particularly easy to organize if there is one traditional dish, such as COUSCOUS* for a North African party.

Date Themes You can also tie into a particular date: Guy Fawkes' night, pancake Tuesday, Thanksgiving dinners, and so on. These can be easy to devise – Thanksgiving, for example, where there is a traditional menu – or more challenging – Guy Fawkes, where there is no obvious food analogy at all. For interest here is a Guy Fawkes menu that we served last year. The guests sat at tables but had to collect their food from a buffet table. As you will see, in these circumstances the trick lies in thinking up fun names for relatively traditional dishes.

FIREWATER SOUP△
(a hot mulligatawny)

FLAMING VENISON STEAKS

FIREBALL CHILLI CHICKEN△

THUNDERFLASH (STEAK AND KIDNEY) PIE●

GREEK FIRE CELERY●

BLAZING RED CABBAGE●

'SCORCHED' POTATOES●

BOMBE SURPRISE●

FIZGIG (CABINET) PUDDING●

ST CATHERINE'S BURNT CREAM (CRÈME BRULÉE)●

CHEESE AND 'CRACKERS'

The table decorations were miniature bonfires made of twigs and cones, painted red, silver and gold, with candles and sparklets in the middle.

Colour Themes These are fun but need to be tied into the general decor to be really effective. Be careful too what colours you choose: greens, reds, oranges, and so forth are easy; black and blue are definitely tricky. We once had to provide food for a series of fashion shows with a blue and white colour scheme; this was almost impossible as blue food on the whole looks thoroughly unattractive. We compromised by using blue and white ripple ice cream (stirring blue colouring into white yoghurt ice cream) but for the rest of the menu sticking to white food with blue napkins, table decorations, etc.

Black and white is not quite so bad and looks effective for a Hallowe'en party – for example:

ALMOND SOUP * △
(decorate with chopped black olives and serve hot)

BLACK FIELD MUSHROOM SOUP●
(decorate with white sesame seeds and serve hot)

WHOLE TURBOT
(poach and serve whole like a salmon, decorated
with slithers of black (purple) peppers, olives,
black peppercorns, etc.)

TURKEY OR CAPON (WHITE) ROASTED IN HONEY *●
(this gives it a black and shiny skin)

PEPPERONATA●
(made with black and white peppers only)

ITALIAN AUBERGINE AND SESAME SALAD●
(this could also be served hot. It will be well
toasted so it is almost entirely black)

BLACK AND WHITE RICE SALAD●
(you can dye half the rice black with food
colouring and then arrange the two halves in a
geometrical pattern)

BLACK RYE AND PURE WHITE BREADS

PRUNE AND PORT WHIP
(prunes soaked in port and puréed, topped with
whipped cream)

BLACK AND WHITE RIBBON JELLIES *●
(these are very effective for other parties too)

Any creamy dessert can be served – soufflé,
mousse, trifle, etc. – decorated with black
chocolate curls, leaves, flowers, etc.

Historic This can cover any period from any
country. My particular interest has always been in
historic English food, so we have done a great
number of 'period' English parties, both buffet
and 'sit down'. However, to do the job properly
will involve a good deal of research, so be warned.

Food Theme A client may wish to emphasize one
particular food in the menu which can be quite
fun, but you need to take care not to overdo it. No
matter how besotted the host may be with prunes,
not all the guests will share this passion. A couple
of years ago we did a dinner for a medical
conference on fatty acids and heart disease which
was taking place in the Museum of London. Since
London is on the Thames and for many centuries
lived on the fish from the river, and since fish is
good for all kinds of heart complaints, we had a
wonderful time with a menu that combined both
fish and history. As the guests arrived they were
greeted by a cockney shellfish stall offering them
cockles, whelks, jellied eels and such like. They
then explored the museum until they reached the
buffet.

ROMAN
A DISH OF SOUSED ROMAN FISHES●
POACHED MUSSELS WITH LIQUAMEN DIP●

MEDIEVAL
A BLACK AND WHITE FISH PIE WITH SALT FISH AND FRUITS●
A FISH BLANCMANGER●

TUDOR AND STUART
JOHN FARLEY'S FILLETS OF PICKLED MACKEREL△
ROBERT MAY'S FISH PIE WITH EEL AND ARTICHOKES△

GEORGIAN
A PUPTON OF SPINACH AND SOLE●
FILLETS OF MACKEREL WITH GOOSEBERRY SAUCE●

VICTORIAN
FILLETS OF COD IN A CAPER MAYONNAISE●
SMOKED MACKEREL AND COCKLE TARTS△
DEVILLED WHITEBAIT

EDWARDIAN
ARNOLD BENNET OMELETTE* ON HOME-MADE OATCAKES*△
WHOLE DRESSED CRABS
CRAB CLAWS△ WITH A MAYONNAISE DIP
COLD POACHED FRESH SCALLOPS WITH A LEMON MAYONNAISE
SMOKED COD'S ROE PÂTÉ●
LARGE POT OF FISH SOUP●

VEGETARIAN
MUSHROOM, SPINACH AND WALNUT PÂTÉ●
LENTIL, SPROUT AND PUMPKIN SEED PÂTÉ●
WHOLEWHEAT OPEN MUSHROOM FLAN
WHOLEWHEAT LEEK AND TOMATO FLAN
MIXED MUNG BEAN AND OTHER BEAN SALAD
CHINESE LEAF, BEANSHOOT AND RED PEPPER SALAD
GREEN SALAD OF SPINACH, HERBS AND CRESSES

Breakfasts
In 'social' catering, breakfast parties nearly always take place after a ball, so you will find yourself working in the early hours of the morning, probably in a soggy marquee. What you will be able to provide will depend entirely on how much equipment you have been able to ship in – in other words, edible bacon and eggs do depend on you having a proper cooker, although adequate (just) versions can be produced by the use of *bain-maries*. For your own comfort and convenience, it would be better to concentrate on dishes that can be successfully precooked:

KEDGEREE
(hot)

OMELETTES
(ARNOLD BENNET OMELETTE* for example, tastes excellent cold or warm)

COLD MEATS
(side of ham, beef, tongue, game (very Edwardian) or salamis)

SMOKED SALMON OR ANY OTHER SMOKED FISH

SAUSAGES
(hot)

BLACK PUDDING
(hot)

DEVILLED KIDNEYS
(hot)

If you do have proper cooking facilities, you can enlarge your range to cover:

BACON AND EGG

FRENCH TOAST

KIPPERS, BLOATERS OR 'FINNAN HADDIE'

POTATO CAKES

MUSHROOMS ON TOAST

PANCAKES AND WAFFLES

Obviously you would not want to serve all of these, but you would be surprised how hungry people can be at five in the morning. You would also need to have a back up of fruits, fruit juices, breads, croissants, coffees and teas, although at this kind of party it is the hot, cooked dishes that go down best.

The other sort of breakfast party is the 'business breakfast', sometimes for a quite small group meeting but often for a fashion show or an exhibition. In this case, the guests are feeling somewhat more fragile, having only just dug themselves out of bed, so rather less vigorous menus go down better. Plenty of fruits and interesting breads and maybe just one or two cooked things, but keep these healthy as most guests will be going on to a day's work and will not want to load themselves down with too much food. Here are some suggestions from which to pick:

DRIED FRUIT COMPÔTE*●

FRESH FRUIT SALAD

INTERESTING FRESH FRUITS
(melon, peaches, mangos, etc.)

FRESH FRUIT JUICES

CEREALS
(muesli, porridge or hot oatmeal with a choice of yoghurt, honey, various milks, etc.)

PLATTERS OF COLD MEATS AND THINLY-SLICED CHEESES●

SMOKED SALMON●

KEDGEREE●

ARNOLD BENNET OMELETTE*

POTATO CAKES WITH CRISP BACON

PANCAKES OR WAFFLES WITH CRISP BACON

Serve brown and white rolls, breads, croissants, brioches, oatcakes, toasts and toast (all *very* fresh) with butter and low fat spreads, and offer marmalade, honey and a selection of jams, and, perhaps, patum peperum and anchovy spread.

Coffee (caffeinated and decaffeinated but in either case real unless you are on a very tight budget), tea (Indian and China if possible), herb teas and hot chocolate should cover most tastes, or serve alcoholic drinks – Bucks Fizz always goes down well, but you might want to add a Bloody Mary or a Ramoz Fizz.

Small Children's Parties

'Large' children are usually so busy being 'adult' that a simple version of a grown-up buffet will be the most popular. However, the annual round of young children's parties strikes dread into the hearts of most grown ups, so anything to keep the little dears quiet and happy is good news. Since most children are less interested in the actual food than the event, the more fun the food can be, the better it will be liked. One of the most successful

parties we ever did involved packing a picnic into a whole lot of boxes, one for each child, and tying them with rubber bands. By the time the kids had sorted out their boxes (you could even put a name on for each child and pull them out of a sack), opened them, explored the contents and eaten them, they were almost ready to go home!

Fun cakes always go down well, but may cost more than the hard-pressed parent can face; remember that children will not be supercritical as long as it gives the right impression. It might be more economic to make small biscuits cut into fun shapes or decorated with faces. On the whole, children have less sweet teeth than adults expect, so remember to provide plenty of savoury nibbles, and in these days of healthy eating, try to steer clear of additive-laden drinks or foods that may send little Johnny, who has a tendency to hyperactivity anyway, right over the top.

A barbecue is always fun as long as it is well supervised by an adult.

Savoury

SAUSAGES●
(preferably small – hot or cold)

CHEESY BISCUITS OR STRAWS●
(these could be stamped out in fun shapes)

CHICKEN PIECES OR DRUMSTICKS●

SANDWICHES
(these are not so popular nowadays, but fill a few with savoury pastes and cut out in fun shapes. They can also be threaded onto a kebab stick, although this would be dangerous with young children)

PINWHEELS●
(made with any kind of paste or well-coloured filling to look good)

PIZZAS AND FLANS●
(make individual ones if possible. You can make good individual pizzas on muffins. Quiches will probably be too messy for younger children)

CHEESE AND FRUIT PIECES
(pineapple chunks are particularly good – for younger children they should go in a bowl to be 'dipped for'; for older children they can go on sticks)

CRISPS OF VARIOUS KINDS
(the round ones are particularly popular as they can be fitted on fingers)

Sweet

TEA BREADS OF VARIOUS KINDS●

SWEET BISCUITS●
(cut ginger or chocolate biscuits into fun shapes and/or decorate them on top with icing – faces, numbers, even the children's names so that they all have to find their own)

CHOCOLATE FINGERS

FLAPJACKS△

CHOCOLATE CRISPIES●
(make with whichever breakfast cereal you favour)

INDIVIDUAL 'CUP CAKES'●
(ice like the biscuits above – individual shapes or numbers will be more fun than large ones)

JELLY WHIPS*

ICE CREAM
(if you can provide an ice cream maker so that a continual supply of home-made ice cream will be constantly on tap, you will be very successful; otherwise buy pre-prepared. Most flavours will go down well, especially fresh fruit ice cream made with half yoghurt and half cream)

'SPECIAL' BIRTHDAY CAKE

Drinks Try to avoid saccarine-sweetened drinks. Fresh juices, carbonated water, milk and HOME-MADE LEMONADE* would all be good.

Sit-Down Meals

There is such an enormous range of dishes that can be served for 'sit-down' formal meals that I feel all I can do is to list some of the menus that we have served successfully over the years – and hope that they will give you inspiration. In each case, I have indicated how many the meal was for and what sort of facilities we had available, since this obviously affected the menu we served.

1 A sixtieth birthday party for 100 guests in an eighteenth-century mansion. No facilities apart from imported hot cupboards and hot rings – limited electricity supply; we fused the lot at one point!

COLD STUFFED FILLETS OF SOLE
LEMON SPINACH SOUP● (hot)
POUSSIN FORESTIÈRE● (hot)
SHERRIED POTATOES*● AND GREEN BEANS (hot)
PRALINE SOUFFLÉ●
COFFEE AND PETITS FOURS

2 Light, cold, summer lunch for a group of 40 fashion journalists prior to a site visit.
COLD STUFFED TROUT WITH A HERB AND
CREAM SAUCE
BROWN RICE SALAD●
SALAD OF HERBS AND CRESSES
WHOLEMEAL ROLLS AND BUTTER
CIDER SYLLABUB*
COFFEE

3 Vegetarian dinner for an eating club – 50 guests. Very basic kitchen facilities.
AVOCADO AND STRAWBERRY SALAD
ALMOND SOUP*● WITH BROWN ROLLS (hot)
RICE, CHILLI AND BAMBOO SHOOT CASSEROLE●
(hot)
TOMATOES STUFFED WITH HERBS AND LENTILS●
(hot)
CELERIAC AND SPINACH BAKE● (hot)
CHILLED GINGER AND FIG SOUFFLÉ WITH SESAME
BISCUITS
FARMHOUSE CHEESE AND BISCUITS
COFFEE AND SWEETMEATS

4 A Burns' Night party – 25 guests. Domestic Aga, electric cooker and small electric hot cupboard.
SCOTCH BROTH● (hot)
HAGGIS, NEEPS AND CHAMPIT TATTIES△ (hot)
THISTLE SALAD OF THE ISLES
ATHOLL BROSE
BANNOCK AN' KEBBUCK
COFFEE

5 Promotional dinner for oil company to launch a gallery guide in the Victoria and Albert Museum – 110 guests. No facilities at all – water in the Ladies' loo and one electric point on a long extension.

CREAMED MUSHROOMS WITH PRAWNS
PINK RHUBARB SOUP*● (hot)
BONED, STUFFED GROUSE*● (cold)
CHICORY, ORANGE AND WATERCRESS SALAD
GAME STICKS (hot)
HOT CHERRY PROFITEROLES
COFFEE

6 Medieval dinner in the Great Hall at Penshurst Place – 100 Americans on up-market tour. No facilities apart from cold water and electric rings.

MEDIEVAL BLANCMANGER OF FISH●
SAFFRON SOUP△ (hot)
RARE RIBS OF BEEF WITH RELISHES●
NEW POTATOES (hot)
HERB AND CRESS SALAD
PENSHURST PLACE CURD CHEESE AND STRAWBERRY TARTS●
COFFEE AND SWEETMEATS

7 Lunch for 40 French ambassadorial guests. Full kitchen facilities.

TARTES DE TOMATES À FARINE D'AVOINE
FILETS DE SOLE FARCIES D'EPINARDS SAUCE BLANC
LÉGUMES DE SAISON
PÊCHES À L'EAU DE VIE●
CAFÉ

8 Annual dinner of the Hampton Court Royal Tennis Club – 80 guests. A very limited budget but ample hot cupboards, hot water and space.

SMOKED MACKEREL AND COCKLE FLAN*△ (warm)
BALONS OF THE BREASTS OF FOWLES● (hot)
SEASONAL VEGETABLES (hot)
STILTON, DIGESTIVES AND CELERY
COFFEE AND SWEETMEATS

9 Dinner at Osterley Park (eighteenth-century stately home) for cosmetic company – 150 guests. No facilities at all. One room in which to store hot cupboards about 200 metres/220 yards away and down spiral stairs from 'dining' room; one cold tap about 200 metres/220 yards in opposite direction. The only way you can cope with a hot meal in this sort of situation is to use a dish that will benefit by reheating; we find that small birds or game birds can be successfully casseroled but still look 'up-market' enough to fit the style of the evening.

OGEN MELON
SCOTCH SMOKED SALMON
WILD PHEASANT WITH CELERIAC AND APPLE● (hot)
SHERRIED POTATOES*● AND FRENCH BEANS (hot)
CHEESES
ENGLISH SYLLABUB*●
COFFEE AND PETITS FOURS

10 Dinner at the Banqueting House, Whitehall, for an Italian Bank – 'A Mantuan Banquet in the early seventeenth century' – 200 guests. Space to plug in hot cupboards and electric rings. Plenty of hot water.

ANTIPASTO
ZUPPA DI PISELLI DI BARTOLOMEO STEFANI●
BIANCA MANGIARE DI POLPA DI PESCE●
FRICANDO CON CONTORNO DI SPINACI DI BARTOLOMEO SCAPPI●
DOLCI E FRUTTA

Make the most of fresh spring flowers for an Easter
Sunday breakfast. Surround each place setting with
garlands of daffodils, irises and narcissi, and choose
simple china and napkins in matching colours.

For a wedding buffet, place netting over a white tablecloth and decorate with satin bows and flowers to match the bride's bouquet. Provide plain white plates and silver forks for the guests to help themselves, and strew confetti over the table for the final touch.

A formal dinner will require crystal glasses, fine bone china and silver cutlery. White napkins can be decorated with silk flowers, and ivy and flowers can be trailed down the centre of the table. To complete the decoration, place matching candles in a glass candlestick.

Create a traditional Christmas atmosphere with a
combination of red, green and white. Drape lace
over a white cloth and decorate with scarlet ribbons
and bows. The centrepiece can be made with holly
and Christmas roses, red silk flowers and white
candles. Place cards and small gifts can also be
provided for the guests.

For a special Sunday lunch, choose simple earthenware crockery and glassware and wooden-handled cutlery. Keep the background white and add colour with flowers – a nice idea is to place a flower head in each bowl.

11 Livery Hall dinner for stockbrokers' annual conference – 80 guests. Full kitchen facilities.
SEAFOOD PLATTER* WITH HOME-MADE MAYONNAISE
WHOLEMEAL BROWN ROLLS
CREAM OF FENNEL AND GINGER SOUP*● (hot)
LOIN OF LAMB ON A BED OF HERBS AND SPINACH (hot)
SEASONAL VEGETABLES (hot)
TRADITIONAL ENGLISH TRIFLE WITH WHIPPED SYLLABUB●
FARMHOUSE ENGLISH CHEESE WITH BISCUITS
COFFEE AND SWEETMEATS

12 Nouvelle cuisine wedding lunch – 30 guests. Private house kitchen.
PARMA HAM WITH THINLY-SLICED FRESH FIG
POACHED SALMON CUTLETS WITH YOGHURT AND GREEN PEPPER SAUCE
GREEN BEAN AND CELERY MATCHSTICK BOUQUETS, TIED WITH WHOLEWHEAT TAGLIATELLE
RADICCHIO AND CORIANDER SALAD WITH WALNUT OIL DRESSING
STRAWBERRY SHORTCAKE HEARTS
COFFEE

13 A seventeenth-century 'Pepys' dinner for 40 European conference delegates. Domestic Aga, electric cooker and small hot cupboard.
PATRICK LAMB'S WHITE MALGRÉ SOUP● (hot)
ROBERT MAY'S STEWED PRAWNS WITH BROWN ROLLS (hot)
A BROILED LEG OF PORK● (hot)
JOHN EVELYN'S ROASTED TURNIPS (hot)
ROBERT MAY'S GRAND SALAT
A SULLIBUB●
HANNAH WOOLLEY'S BACON AND ALMOND TART● (warm)
COFFEE AND ORANGE COMFITS

(Recipes all from *Pepys at Table* by Michelle Berriedale-Johnson and Christopher Driver.)

RECIPES

The recipes in this section have all come from Catercall's files, gathered over fifteen years of catering. Many of them have been culled from historic sources in the course of my researches, but many others have been torn out of newspapers, written down at parties, and copied out of books. Inevitably, the originals have been lost, so I can only apologize to any cook or cookery writer whose recipe I am unwittingly quoting and hope that readers of this book may trace it to source. It must at least have been a good recipe or it would not have had such hard use!

I have not given recipes for standard dishes, which are to be found in any one of half a dozen good cookbooks. What I have given is recipes for dishes that we have evolved or found particularly useful or unusual and that you will *not* find in most cookbooks. All cooks have their own favourite guide or mentor. In our kitchens there is an extremely battered copy of Constance Spry's classic *Cookery Book* (first published by Dent in 1956, but I believe it is now out of print) and the *Reader's Digest Cookery Year* (first published in 1973, but still available). There are also an assortment of specialist books on cake decorating, pickling and spicing, preserves, and so on. Ninety per cent of our recipes, however, live on battered, egg-splattered, almost illegible cards – soon to be transferred to a word processor. It is from these that I have chosen the following selection.

Recipes are given for 10 people for all starters, main courses and desserts, approximately 25 people for a cocktail or finger buffet party, and 20 for a children's party. For larger, or smaller, numbers, the quantities can merely be multiplied or divided. However, remember that strong flavours get disproportionately stronger in quantity, so spices, curries, strong herbs, etc. should be treated with circumspection and only added by taste. See the section on portion control, page 32.

SPINACH AND HERB OMELETTE

Serves 25 as a cocktail snack/6 as a luncheon dish

Like the ARNOLD BENNETT OMELETTE, this is very good cold in little bits for cocktail snacks; it can also be used warm or cold as a buffet dish. The tongue is optional – just leave it out for a vegetarian dish. The whole thing is based on a sixteenth-century recipe for a spinach 'froise'.

75 g/3 oz butter
75 g/3 oz cooked spinach (fresh or frozen), chopped
50 g/2 oz currants, washed
75 g/3 oz cooked tongue, chopped
½ teaspoon ground cinnamon
¼ teaspoon each ground mace, cloves, black pepper and ginger
8 eggs
salt

Melt half the butter in a pan and add the spinach, currants, tongue and spices. Stir well and warm through gently. Whisk the eggs in a bowl and season with salt. Add the filling to the eggs. Heat the rest of the butter in an omelette pan until sizzling and pour in the egg mixture. Cook quickly until browned on the bottom, then place the pan under a hot grill to cook the top. Allow to cool completely, then cut into bite-sized pieces for cocktails; they can be served alone or on oatcakes. For a buffet, serve either warm or cold.

DEVILLED WHITEBAIT

Serves 30 for cocktail snacks

This is an unusual dish to serve for a cocktail party. The whitebait can be deep-fried several hours in advance and reheated gently in an oven before serving. They also go a very long way.

225 g/8 oz fresh or frozen whitebait

½ teaspoon each cayenne pepper and salt

25 g/1 oz flour

oil for deep-frying

1 lemon

Wash the whitebait (or defrost) and dry them thoroughly. Mix the cayenne pepper and salt with the flour and lightly coat the fish with the mixture. Heat the oil in a deep pan until it sizzles when you drop in a piece of bread. Put half the fish in a basket and lower them into the oil. Fry them until they are golden and crisp but not burnt, then turn them onto kitchen paper to drain. Repeat with the rest of the fish. If you want the whitebait to be very fiery, sprinkle over another ½ teaspoon of cayenne.

Reheat the whitebait in a moderate oven (180°C/350°F/Gas Mark 4) when you are ready to serve and squeeze lemon juice over them at the very last minute.

ARNOLD BENNETT OMELETTE

Serves 6–8 for breakfast/20–35 on oatcakes for a cocktail party or finger buffet

This is excellent hot if you are able to serve it that way, but retains its charms if cooked 4–6 hours before it is needed.

6 eggs

4 tablespoons cold water

salt and freshly ground black pepper

350 g/12 oz cooked smoked haddock

100 g/4 oz well-flavoured Cheddar cheese, grated

175 ml/6 fl oz double cream

15 g/½ oz butter

Whisk the eggs in a bowl with a balloon whisk. Add the water and some seasoning (do not oversalt as the haddock can be salty) and beat again. Mix in the fish, cheese and half the cream.

Melt the butter in a large omelette pan until it sizzles, pour in the egg mixture and cook over a high heat as for an ordinary omelette. When it is half cooked (a couple of minutes), pour the rest of the cream over the omelette and put it under a hot grill for 3–4 minutes to finish cooking the eggs and slightly brown the top of the omelette. Sprinkle with freshly ground black pepper.

Allow to cool completely, then cut into pieces of the size you need and remove with a spatula onto toast or oatcakes, or whatever you are using.

CHICKEN OR BEEF SATAY

Serves 25 as a cocktail snack

450 g/1 lb chicken meat or stewing beef, cut in small bite-size pieces

25 g/1 oz ground almonds

1 tablespoon shredded root ginger

1 teaspoon each ground coriander, turmeric and dark brown sugar

300 ml/½ pint coconut milk (see below)

2 tablespoons good vegetable oil

about ½ teaspoon chilli powder

2 medium onions, very finely chopped

225 g/8 oz good quality peanut butter

about 1 teaspoon pale brown sugar

about 1 tablespoon soy sauce

juice of ½ lime or lemon

salt and freshly ground black pepper

Mix the almonds, ginger, spices and dark brown sugar in a bowl. Add the coconut milk and use this mixture to marinate the meat pieces for at least 2 hours. Transfer the meat, in its marinade, to an ovenproof dish, cover it and bake in a moderate oven (180°C/350°F/Gas Mark 4) for about 40 minutes or until it is tender and cooked.

Meanwhile, heat the oil in a pan with the chilli powder and sweat the onions until they are quite soft. Take the pan off the heat and add the peanut butter with the pale brown sugar, soy sauce and lime or lemon juice to taste. Mix in the cooked marinade and adjust the seasoning to taste — although it is unlikely to need any more salt or pepper.

Spear the pieces of meat on cocktail sticks and arrange them in a dish with a bowl of the sauce in the middle for dipping. The satay freezes well both cooked or in the marinade, as does the sauce.

NOTE: Make the coconut milk by simmering 75 g/3 oz desiccated coconut in 300 ml/½ pint of milk or water for 20 minutes. Allow to cool and strain.

STUFFED TOMATOES

Serves 25 for a finger buffet

There are innumerable recipes for stuffing tomatoes, but we have found this one tasty and easy for the guests to manage. They can be made the day ahead but cannot be frozen.

13 medium tomatoes

12 anchovy fillets, chopped

2 medium onions, finely chopped

25 g/1 oz butter

75 g/3 oz breadcrumbs

1 teaspoon dried thyme

freshly ground black pepper

Halve the tomatoes and remove the pulp. Fry the anchovy fillets and onions in 15 g/½ oz of the butter until the onions are soft but not coloured. Add the breadcrumbs, thyme, pepper and a couple of tablespoons of the tomato insides, chopped very small. Mix well and pile into the tomato shells. Dot the tops with the remaining butter and put them under a medium grill for around 7 minutes to cook the shells lightly and brown the tops. Serve warm or cold.

STUFFED SQUID

**Serves 25 as a cocktail snack/6 as a cold or hot
main course**

The squid can be cooked in advance and freeze well.

12–18 small squid

---

350 g/12 oz smoked ham, thinly sliced

---

2 large handfuls parsley, finely chopped

---

200 ml/7 fl oz olive, sunflower or corn oil

---

2 medium onions, peeled and finely chopped

---

salt and pepper

---

3 eggs

---

3 tablespoons tomato purée

---

150 ml/¼ pint dry white wine

---

350 ml/12 fl oz water

---

a little Tabasco

Remove the tentacles and wings from the squid
and chop them finely. Mix them with the ham and
the chopped parsley. Heat 3 tablespoons of oil in a
pan, add the onions and soften them gently. Add
the chopped squid, ham and parsley and cook
them all together for a couple of minutes. Remove
the mixture from the heat, season it well and,
when it has cooled slightly, mix in the eggs. Clean
the bodies of the squid and stuff them with the
mixture and secure with a cocktail stick. Heat the
remaining oil with the tomato purée, wine and
water in a pan, lower in the squid and poach them
gently for 25–30 minutes. Season the juices to
taste with salt, pepper and a few drops of Tabasco.
Remove the squid and allow them to cool.

Slice the squid to use as a cocktail snack or for a
cold buffet and use the juice for soup. Serve them
whole in the sauce if they are to be served hot.

OATCAKES

Makes about 50 cocktail oatcakes

These are invaluable as a base for cocktail canapés
as they do not go soggy. They also freeze very well.

---

*225 g/8 oz mixed oatmeal (fine, medium and
pinhead)*

---

100 g/4 oz plain wholemeal or white flour

½ teaspoon salt

---

1 teaspoon baking powder

---

*40 g/1½ oz each butter and lard, or 75 g/3 oz low
fat margarine*

Put the oatmeal in a basin and sift in the flour, salt
and baking powder. Rub in the fats as for pastry
and mix to a stiff dough with hot water. Turn the
mixture onto a board sprinkled with oatmeal.
Knead the dough lightly, roll it out fairly thinly
and cut it into rounds with a glass or pastry cutter.

Place the oatcakes on a tray and bake in a
moderate oven (180°C/350°F/Gas Mark 4) for
20–25 minutes, but keep an eye on them to make
sure they do not burn. Cool on a rack and store in
an airtight container or the freezer.

MUSHROOMS STUFFED WITH GORGONZOLA AND SPINACH

Serves about 25

This is also excellent served as a starter using large, flat, field mushrooms and placed on brown toast. The mushrooms can be prepared in advance and just put under the grill before they are served.

---

40 medium button mushrooms

---

about 25 g/1 oz butter

---

225 g/8 oz fresh spinach

---

350 g/12 oz ripe Gorgonzola or Dolcelatte (not Danish Blue)

---

freshly ground black pepper

Remove any stalks from the mushrooms (keep for a sauce or casserole), dot each with a little butter and put them under a grill until the butter is melted and the mushrooms slightly cooked. Meanwhile, chop the spinach fairly finely and mix it thoroughly with the cheese. Fill the mushrooms with the mixture and put them back under the grill for 2–3 minutes or until the cheese is melted and lightly browned. Grind black pepper over the top and serve at once.

CURRIED PARSNIP AND APPLE SOUP

Serves 10

As both the parsnip and the apple are sweet, the curry contrasts particularly well with them. This can be prepared in advance and freezes well.

---

50 g/2 oz butter

---

2 tablespoons vegetable oil

---

2 tablespoons curry powder

---

450 g/1 lb leeks

---

675 g/1½ lb parsnips, scrubbed and thinly sliced

---

675 g/1½ lb cooking apples, peeled and chopped

1.7 litres/3 pints chicken stock

---

300 ml/½ pint milk

---

300 ml/½ pint dry white wine

---

salt and pepper

---

4 tart eating apples, peeled and finely chopped

Melt the butter and oil in a heavy-based pan, stir in the curry powder, followed by the leeks and parsnips and cooking apples. Cook together gently without burning for 10–15 minutes or until the leeks are quite soft and the parsnips beginning to soften. Add the stock, milk and wine, bring to the boil and simmer for 30–35 minutes or until the parsnips are quite cooked. Purée in a processor or liquidizer. Reheat and adjust the seasoning to taste. Just before serving, add the eating apples. NOTE: If the soup is to be frozen, do not add the eating apples until you are ready to serve it.

DEVILLED NUTS

Serves 25

These are delicious and 'moreish' – they are particularly good if you are also supplying the drinks. They keep for several weeks stored in an airtight container.

---

375 g/13 oz (about 15 g/½ oz per head) assorted mixed nuts (see below)

---

vegetable oil for frying

---

sea salt and cayenne pepper

Lightly coat the bottom of a frying pan with oil and heat. Fry the nuts gently until they are well browned but not burnt – you will need to put the larger nuts (for example, brazils) in first. Tip them out onto greaseproof paper and sprinkle to taste with salt and cayenne pepper – take care not to overdo the pepper. Allow to cool completely before storing.

NOTE: If you cook the nuts too quickly, they will be chewy and not crisp. You can use any nuts you fancy, provided they are not already salted or flavoured – almonds, cashews, peanuts, hazelnuts, walnuts, pecans, brazil nuts, etc.

SEEDY PASTRY SQUARES

Makes about 35 squares or triangles

I first saw these amazingly cheap, simple and easy cocktail bits in Demel's famous pastry shop in Vienna. They can be prepared in advance and frozen, although the cooking should be done on defrosting.

---

about 225 g/8 oz good shortcrust or puff pastry made with butter

---

1 egg, beaten

3–4 tablespoons poppy seeds, aniseeds, chopped sunflower, pumpkin or coriander seeds, sesame seeds, etc.

---

a little fine sea salt

Roll out the pastry reasonably thinly and brush it lightly with the beaten egg. Sprinkle your seeds, mixed with a little salt, liberally over the pastry, then cut into small squares, triangles or rounds. Bake in a moderately hot oven (190°C/375°F/Gas Mark 5) for 10–15 minutes, taking great care they do not burn. Serve warm or cold, but make sure they are crisp.

FENNEL AND GINGER SOUP

Serves 10

Equally good hot or cold, this can be made in advance and freezes well.

75 g/3 oz butter or low fat margarine

3 large onions, roughly chopped

900 g/2 lb fennel root, roughly chopped

50 g/2 oz root ginger, grated, or 2 teaspoons dried ginger

1.7 litres/3 pints chicken stock

300 ml/½ pint dry white wine

300 ml/½ pint milk

salt and pepper

100 g/4 oz ground almonds

200 ml/7 fl oz double cream

Melt the fat in a pan and add the onions, fennel and ginger. Sweat together gently until the onions and fennel are soft. Add the stock, wine, milk and a little salt and pepper. Bring to the boil and simmer for about 30 minutes. Purée in a processor or liquidizer – I prefer the soup with little bits of fennel floating in it rather than a totally smooth purée; if you would rather have a purée, process it for longer and then strain the bits from the soup. Add the ground almonds and cream and adjust the seasoning to taste. Serve either hot or well chilled.

PINK RHUBARB SOUP

Serves 10

This has a very pretty colour and delicate flavour. It can be made ahead of time and freezes well.

100 g/4 oz butter or low fat margarine

900 g/2 lb young rhubarb, trimmed and roughly chopped

100 g/4 oz young leeks, cleaned and finely sliced

50 g/2 oz cooked lean ham, finely chopped

100 g/4 oz fresh brown breadcrumbs

1.7 litres/3 pints chicken or light veal stock

300 ml/½ pint dry white wine

salt and a couple of drops of Tabasco

juice of 1 large lemon

4–6 teaspoons sugar

200 ml/7 fl oz double cream, lightly whisked

Melt the fat in a saucepan, add the rhubarb, leeks and ham and stew them gently for 10 minutes or until the rhubarb is soft. Add the breadcrumbs, stock and wine, bring to the boil and simmer for 15 minutes. Liquidize or purée the soup and return it to the pan. Add the salt, Tabasco, lemon juice and sugar to taste; how much of the last two you add will depend on how sweet the rhubarb and your own tooth are. Serve with a dollop of whipped cream in the middle of each bowl.

MRS BLENCOWE'S GREEN PEA SOUP

Serves 10

This soup must have been served at more 'Old English' dinners than any other dish we make. It is based on the recipe of a Mrs Anne Blencowe, wife of a seventeenth-century MP for Northampton. It can be made in advance and freezes well.

675 g/1½ lb fresh or frozen green peas

2 leeks, finely sliced

2 cloves garlic, crushed

50 g/2 oz bacon, very finely diced

100 g/4 oz butter or margarine

1.7 litres/3 pints ham or chicken stock

50 g/2 oz fresh spinach (or 25 g/1 oz frozen leaf if fresh is not available)

50 g/2 oz white cabbage, very finely sliced

½ lettuce, very finely chopped

a large handful of parsley, finely chopped

2 stalks celery, strings removed and finely chopped

1 carton mustard and cress

4 teaspoons fresh chopped mint, or 2 teaspoons dried

salt and pepper

a pinch of mace

Put the peas, leeks, garlic and bacon in a pan with half the fat. Fry gently until the vegetables are softened but not coloured. Add the stock, bring to the boil and simmer for 20 minutes. Liquidize or purée in a food processor.

Meanwhile, melt the rest of the butter in another pan and sweat the spinach, cabbage, lettuce, parsley, celery, mustard and cress and the mint until soft. Add the puréed peas to the sweated mixture and season to taste with salt, pepper and mace before serving.

ALMOND SOUP

Serves 10

This is rich and expensive and very much a luxury soup; it can be made ahead of time and freezes well. It is based on a medieval recipe.

2 cloves

1 blade mace

1 bay leaf

1 sprig basil

75 g/3 oz ham, diced

75 g/3 oz celery, diced

2 litres/3½ pints chicken stock

300 g/10 oz ground almonds

90 ml/3 fl oz medium sherry

150 ml/¼ pint double cream

salt and white pepper

Put the herbs and spices in a small muslin bag or infuser and place in a pan with the ham, celery and stock. Bring to the boil and simmer for 30 minutes. Add the almonds and simmer for a further 15 minutes. Remove the herbs and purée the soup in a processor or liquidizer; you may also want to strain it through a coarse sieve to remove any bits of celery or ham. Add the sherry, cream and seasoning to taste, and serve hot or cold.

CHEAP VEGETABLE TERRINE

Serves 10

This is a very flexible and effective way of serving vegetables for a buffet table. It can be made the day before but cannot be frozen.

900 g/2 lb assorted vegetables of differing colours (see below)

10 g/generous ¼ oz gelatine

450 ml/¾ pint thin, well-flavoured white sauce or mayonnaise

1 tablespoon white wine (optional)

Cut the large vegetables into matchsticks and blanch them all for 3–5 minutes according to type and size – you want them to be soft enough to cut through without being totally soggy.

Melt the gelatine in the white sauce over hot water. If you are using mayonnaise, melt it in a tablespoon of white wine over hot water, then mix gradually into the mayonnaise. Pack the vegetables loosely but decoratively in a soufflé or terrine dish and gently pour over the white sauce or mayonnaise. Chill until thoroughly set, then turn out to serve.

NOTE: You can use a variety of vegetables for this terrine – carrots, turnips, French or green beans, corn-on-the-cob, peppers, spinach leaves, courgettes, etc.

SMOKED MACKEREL AND COCKLE FLAN

Serves 10

This is a real old Catercall favourite. It has an excellent flavour, is just as good if cooked the day before and reheated, and will tolerate being frozen, defrosted and reheated with endless good humour. It can be used in fingers as a substantial cocktail snack; in small wedges as a starting course; and in large wedges as a cheap buffet dish.

350 g/12 oz wholemeal shortcrust pastry

25 g/1 oz butter

25 g/1 oz flour

300 ml/½ pint milk

350 g/12 oz smoked mackerel fillet

225 g/8 oz cockles (frozen will be fine)

1 large egg

salt and freshly ground black pepper

Line a 25-cm/10-inch flan case with the pastry and bake it blind. Meanwhile, melt the butter in a pan, add the flour, cook for a minute or two, then gradually add the milk, stirring continuously until you have a smooth sauce. Cook for another couple of minutes.

Skin and mash the smoked mackerel in a bowl and add the cockles, sauce and egg. Season to taste with salt and freshly ground black pepper and spoon into the pastry case. If you had pastry left over, you can use it to make a latticework on the top.

Cook the flan in a moderate oven (180°C/350°F/Gas Mark 4) for 20–25 minutes and serve it warm or cold.

AJWAR (RED PEPPER PÂTÉ)

Serves 10

Ajwar is a Yugoslavian pâté made with the red peppers so beloved in south-eastern Europe. Purists will skin the peppers by submerging them in hot oil until they blister, and look askance at the addition of aubergine, let alone brown bread. However, skinning the peppers is a slow and fiddly business which I feel is scarcely justified by the marginal improvement in the flavour, and the pâté is so rich in its native form that a little 'dilution' does not go amiss. It is delicious served either with fresh brown bread or toast or as a dip with crudités. It improves if made a couple of days in advance and freezes well.

10 fairly thick slices aubergine

about 5 tablespoons olive or sunflower oil

3½ large red peppers, deseeded and roughly chopped

5 large cloves garlic

3 thick slices wholemeal brown bread

salt and pepper

Fry the aubergine slices in the oil until they are just brown on each side. Put all the ingredients – fried aubergine, peppers, garlic and bread – in a food processor or liquidizer and purée them. The pâté should not be totally smooth when puréed; it should have the texture of a country terrine. Season to taste with salt and pepper, but do not be too heavy with the salt if it is to be frozen. The flavour of both the garlic and the salt will be exaggerated by freezing. Turn out onto a serving dish.

BEEF, MUSHROOM AND ASPIC MOULD

Serves 8

This is a very cheap and pretty dish for a buffet or a light lunch. It obviously needs to be made in advance but will not freeze.

25 g/1 oz gelatine

1 litre/1¾ pints good quality beef consommé

150 ml/¼ pint dry or medium sherry

12 very thin slices rare roast beef

50–75 g/2–3 oz button mushrooms, finely sliced

Melt the gelatine in the consommé with the sherry and use to line a 1.2-litre/2-pint ring mould. Allow to set completely. Cut the slices of beef into fingers and lay them crossways in the mould, alternating with slices of mushroom. Fix these in place with a little more of the consommé. When it is thoroughly set, chop the rest of the beef and the mushrooms and scatter them around the mould. Fill it up with the remaining consommé mixture and allow the whole thing to set firm. Turn out on a platter to serve.

LAURENT'S LAMB COUSCOUS

Serves 10

This excellent recipe was given to me by the proprietor of one of London's few couscous restaurants. It will give 10 generous portions.

Heat the oil in a large saucepan (a couscousier or double saucepan is ideal but not essential), put in the onions and garlic and cook until golden. Add the meat, sauté briskly, then add the tomatoes with their juice, seasonings and 1.7 litres/3 pints of water. Bring to the boil and simmer gently for 45 minutes until the meat is cooked and tender. Remove the meat with a slotted spoon and keep warm. Add the carrots, turnips, leeks and celery and continue to simmer for 10 minutes. Meanwhile, put the couscous in a bowl with 12 large tablespoons of lukewarm water and leave it to swell for 10 minutes, breaking up any lumps with your fingers. Add the remaining vegetables and the chick peas to the pan and pile the couscous into the steamer top of the saucepan, or into a large sieve or strainer that can sit over the vegetables. Cover the pan tightly with a lid or with foil and leave to simmer for 10–15 minutes.

To serve, turn the couscous into a long dish, adjust the seasoning of the vegetables to taste and serve these and the meat in separate warmed dishes for the guests to help themselves.

6 tablespoons olive or vegetable oil

3 medium onions, coarsely chopped

4 cloves garlic, crushed

1.8 kg/4 lb lamb (boned shoulder will do excellently), trimmed and cubed

2 × 400 g/14 oz cans peeled tomatoes

salt and pepper

2 teaspoons ground cumin

8 carrots, peeled or scrubbed and cut into large dice

8 turnips, peeled or scrubbed and cut into large dice

4 leeks, coarsely chopped

4 sticks celery, coarsely chopped

900 g/2 lb couscous

4 courgettes, coarsely chopped

2 large red peppers, coarsely chopped

2 large green peppers, coarsely chopped

675 g/1½ lb cabbage, coarsely chopped

2 × 400 g/14 oz cans chick peas

HERB TART OR PIE

Serves 10

This is an unusual variation on the quiche theme. You can bake it as an open flan or as a closed pie. Feel free to vary the herbs and, if you cannot get fresh, use dried, but only use half the quantity.

450 g/1 lb wholemeal or plain shortcrust pastry

550 g/1¼ lb lean rashers bacon, thinly sliced

300 g/10 oz leeks, finely chopped

300 g/10 oz fresh spinach, finely chopped

1 carton mustard and cress

1 bunch fresh watercress

a large handful of parsley, roughly chopped

3 sprigs each fresh thyme and savoury, chopped

4 sage leaves, chopped

4 large eggs

about 250 ml/8 fl oz chicken stock

salt and pepper

Roll out two-thirds of the pastry and line a 25-cm/10-inch flan case; bake it blind. Remove the rinds from the bacon, chop the rashers roughly and fry them in their own fat until crisp. Sprinkle the pastry case with half the bacon. Mix the leeks, spinach, cresses and herbs and pile them on top of the bacon. Beat 3 eggs, add the stock, season with salt and pepper and pour over the vegetables. Sprinkle the remaining bacon over the top. Roll out the rest of the pastry and cover the pie, using the trimmings to decorate the top. Beat the remaining egg and glaze the lid generously.

Bake the pie in a moderate oven (180°C/350°F/Gas Mark 4) for 40 minutes. Serve warm.

BEEF CASSEROLE WITH PRUNES

Serves 10

A tried and trusted favourite, this improves by being made in advance, and freezes excellently.

1.5 kg/3 lb trimmed stewing beef, cubed

4 onions, peeled and finely sliced

1 heaped teaspoon each thyme and parsley

3 bay leaves

3 tablespoons olive or vegetable oil

450 ml/¾ pint red wine

a little seasoned flour

2 large green peppers, seeded and finely sliced

about 450 ml/¾ pint beef stock

300 g/10 oz softened prunes

salt and pepper

Mix the trimmed beef with the onions and herbs in a large bowl and pour over 2 tablespoons of oil and the red wine. Leave to marinate for at least 6 hours. Remove the meat with a slotted spoon, dry it and coat it in the seasoned flour. Remove the onions from the marinade and fry them lightly with the green peppers in the remaining oil. Remove them to a casserole and briskly fry the meat, then add to the casserole.

Tip the marinade into the frying pan, cook for a few minutes to remove any bits off the bottom, then add to the casserole along with the beef stock. Cover and cook over a low heat or in a moderate oven (180°C/350°F/Gas Mark 4) for 1–1½ hours or until you are sure the meat is really tender. About 10 minutes before it is done, add the stoned prunes to the pot, leave for 10 minutes and then adjust the seasoning to taste.

TURKISH PRAWN PILAFF

Serves 10

This excellent prawn pilaff can easily be adapted for chicken, turkey or sausages. It can be served hot or cold, is fine if cooked in advance, and freezes well.

8 tablespoons olive or sunflower oil

1 large onion, peeled and finely chopped

3 large red peppers, finely chopped

2 cloves garlic, finely chopped or crushed

450 g/1 lb long grain Patna rice

1 teaspoon each ground allspice and cumin seeds

2 heaped teaspoons dried mint or basil

225 g/8 oz prawns, fresh or frozen

3 heaped tablespoons washed currants

salt and pepper

juice of 2 large lemons

2 handfuls parsley, finely chopped

Heat the oil in a large, flat pan and gently cook the onion, peppers and garlic until they are soft but not browned. Add the rice, spices and herbs, stir for a few minutes, then add enough water to cover the rice. Bring the mixture to the boil and simmer with the pan uncovered for 10–15 minutes or until the rice is just cooked but *not* mushy. (You may have to add a little more water if it dries up too fast.) Add the prawns, currants and a generous sprinkling of salt. Cook for a couple more minutes, then add the lemon juice and parsley and adjust the seasoning to taste. Serve warm, or cold.

SEAFOOD PLATTERS

These are immensely useful for almost any kind of meal. We serve the fish pulled or cut into small pieces for cocktail and finger buffet parties with a small tub of cocktail sticks in the middle of each platter so guests can spear whatever they fancy. For a buffet meal, obviously this is not necessary, nor for a starter or main course at a 'sit-down' meal. We normally serve a plain mayonnaise dip, but you can, of course, offer whatever variation on that you wish. You will need approximately the following quantities:

Cocktail party – 25 g/1 oz per head

Finger buffet – 50 g/2 oz per head

Starter – 75 g/3 oz per head

Main course – buffet or 'sit down' – 150–175 g/ 5–6 oz per head

Fish suggestions

Shell Cockles, mussels, clams, oysters, prawns of all sizes, crab claws, scallops, lobster, whole crab.

Smoked Salmon, trout, mackerel, eel, tuna (usually served in little rolls as they are easier to cope with and more economical).

Pickled Rollmops or pickled anchovies (in *small* quantities).

Fresh Any fresh fish that will hold together, lightly poached in a little white wine with lemon (salmon, sole, cod and monkfish are particularly good).

COLD BEEF STROGANOV

Serves 10

This was the invention of Catercall's founder, Pat Harbottle, and I think it takes a lot of beating for a cold beef dish. It really needs to be made the day it is served.

1.6 kg/3½ lb fillet steak, trimmed and cut into matchsticks

4 tablespoons vegetable oil

1 medium onion, finely chopped

300 ml/½ pint good mayonnaise

5 tablespoons double cream, lightly whipped

2 tablespoons mango chutney, finely chopped

2 teaspoons Worcestershire sauce

1 tablespoon tomato purée

5 medium tomatoes, peeled, deseeeded and finely chopped

1–2 tablespoons lemon juice

salt and pepper

Heat the oil in a pan and fry the matchsticks of steak lightly and quickly – they need to be only just cooked. Remove the meat and allow to cool. Add the onion to the pan and sweat for 5–10 minutes or until it is quite soft; then remove with a slotted spoon.

Mix the mayonnaise with the cream, chutney, Worcestershire sauce, tomato purée, tomatoes and 1 tablespoon of lemon juice. Add the cooled steak and onions and thin the sauce if necessary with the cooled cooking juices. Adjust the seasoning to taste with salt, pepper and more lemon juice.

A VICTORIAN 'BEEF CAKE'

Serves 10

This makes a cheap but tasty meat loaf based on one of Eliza Acton's recipes. It improves by being made a day or two in advance and freezes well.

900 g/2 lb minced beef, either cooked or raw

300 g/10 oz beef suet, fresh or 'packet'

225 g/8 oz onions, finely chopped

100 g/4 oz mushrooms (flat ones if possible), finely chopped

100 g/4 oz dark brown breadcrumbs (black rye crumbs are ideal)

1 teaspoon each sea salt, ground mace and ground cloves

½ teaspoon cayenne pepper

2 tablespoons each Worcestershire sauce and mushroom ketchup

120–180 ml/4–6 fl oz beef stock or red wine

Mix the minced beef, suet, onions, mushrooms and breadcrumbs in a bowl. Mix the spices with the sauces in a cup, then add 120 ml/4 fl oz of the stock or wine. Mix this thoroughly into the beef mixture. If it seems too dry (you want it moist but not runny), add a little more stock or wine. Spoon the whole mixture into a loaf tin or casserole dish and smooth the top. You can line the dish with foil to make it easier to get out when cooked.

Cover and cook it in a moderate oven (180°C/350°F/Gas Mark 4) for 1¼–1¾ hours – depending on whether you are using cooked or raw meat. If possible, cook the cake in a *bain-marie* as this helps to retain its moistness. Take the cake out of the oven and weight it lightly to cool. When it is completely cold, loosen the edges and turn it out onto a serving dish.

VEAL WITH MUSHROOMS IN SOURED CREAM

Serves 10

This Catercall recipe has truly stood the test of time. It freezes well, but it is better to add the cream on defrosting.

1.8 kg/4 lb lean stewing or pie veal, well trimmed

salt and pepper

75 g/3 oz butter or low fat margarine

3 tablespoons olive or sunflower oil

1 large onion, finely chopped

450 g/1 lb button mushrooms, wiped and halved or quartered

1 teaspoon paprika

2 tablespoons flour

300 ml/½ pint white wine

450 ml/¾ pint soured cream

Rub the veal well with the seasoning. Meanwhile, heat the fat and oil in a large pan and gently cook the onion until just soft, then add the mushrooms and cook for a further minute or two. Mix the paprika and flour, stir it into the pan, cook for a minute, then add the wine and the veal.

Cover the pan, bring it to the boil and simmer gently for 1–1½ hours or until the veal is tender. It can also be cooked in a moderate oven (180°C/350°F/Gas Mark 4) for the same time or a microwave for about 30 minutes. When the meat is cooked, add the cream and adjust the seasoning to taste. The veal is particularly good with green or white noodles.

BACON AND APPLE FLAN

Serves 10

Here is an immensely useful flan that is filling and tasty. It can be cooked ahead of time, freezes excellently, and will put up with being reheated several times.

300 g/10 oz shortcrust pastry, plain or wholemeal

350 g/12 oz rashers bacon, coarsely chopped

1 large onion, coarsely chopped, plus 1 medium onion, sliced into rings

225 g/8 oz sausagemeat

1 large cooking apple

50 g/2 oz rolled oats or porridge oats

salt and pepper

a large pinch of fresh or dried thyme

25 g/1 oz melted butter

Line a 25-cm/10-inch flan case with the pastry – it is not necessary to bake it blind. Fry the bacon in its own fat with the chopped onion for 5 minutes. Work in the sausagemeat and continue to cook for a further 5 minutes. Add half the apple, chopped fairly finely, the oats, seasoning and thyme. Pile the mixture into the flan case and flatten out. Slice the rest of the apple and lay it, with the onion rings, over the flan. Brush them well with the melted butter.

Bake the flan in a moderately hot oven (190°C/375°F/Gas Mark 5) for 40–45 minutes. If the apple and onion look like burning, paint them with a little more butter and cover them with foil or greaseproof paper. Serve warm or cold.

AUBERGINE AND SAUSAGE CASEROLE

Serves 10

This tasty and filling casserole can be made one or two days before it is needed and freezes very well.

15 tablespoons olive or sunflower oil
3 large aubergines, thickly sliced lengthways
25 g/1 oz butter or margarine
900 g/2 lb good-quality sausagemeat
1 bunch spring onions, wiped and chopped
450 g/1 lb mushrooms, coarsely chopped
300 ml/½ pint red wine
2 tablespoons wholegrain or French mustard
2 tablespoons Worcestershire sauce
salt and pepper
450 g/1 lb tomatoes, sliced
100 g/4 oz well-flavoured Cheddar cheese, grated
100 g/4 oz brown breadcrumbs

Heat the oil in a heavy-based pan and fry the aubergines until they are lightly browned on each side – you will have to do this in several batches. Melt the butter in a separate pan and briskly fry the sausagemeat until it begins to colour. Add the chopped spring onions and mushrooms and cook everything together for a couple of minutes. Add the wine, mustard and Worcestershire sauce and *a little* salt and pepper.

Lay half the aubergines in the bottom of an ovenproof dish, cover them with the sausage mixture, followed by a second layer of the aubergines. Cover the aubergines with the tomato slices. Mix together the cheese and breadcrumbs and sprinkle them over the top of the tomatoes.

Bake the casserole in a moderate oven (180°C/350°F/Gas Mark 4) for 30 minutes or until the top is well browned.

CHICKEN, APPLE AND PARSLEY SALAD

Serves 10

This is a very simple, but very refreshing salad – it can be made the evening before for a lunch, although I would not recommend leaving it much more than that.

1.25 kg/2½ lb cooked chicken meat, finely chopped
grated rind and juice of 4 large lemons
2 tart eating apples, cored and diced but not peeled
1 medium onion, very finely chopped
4 large handfuls parsley, coarsely chopped
sea salt and freshly ground black pepper
5 tablespoons olive oil

Mix the chicken, lemon rind, apples, onion and parsley in a large bowl. Sprinkle with sea salt and freshly ground black pepper, then add the lemon juice and olive oil. Mix well together and arrange on a serving platter.

A 'BATTERED' MEAT LOAF

Serves 10

This cheap, cheerful and tasty meat loaf can be eaten hot or cold – although it goes further cold! The 'battered' element is the cheesy batter with which it is coated. It can be made a day ahead and freezes well, although it would need to be reheated to crisp up the batter.

Beat the egg yolk, flour and beer in a food processor or mixer to make a batter and set aside.

Meanwhile, chop the meat reasonably finely in a processor or mincer and mix it with two-thirds of the cheese. Fry the onions in the butter until lightly browned and add to the mixture along with the apples, breadcrumbs, mustard and allspice. Mix the eggs with the yoghurt and mix well into the meat; season fairly liberally.

Form the mixture into a loaf shape on a baking tray or an ovenproof serving dish. Beat half the remaining cheese into the batter and spoon half of this over the loaf. Bake it in a moderately hot oven (190°C/375°F/Gas Mark 5) for 15 minutes. Remove from the oven, spoon over the rest of the batter, sprinkle the remaining cheese on top and return to the oven for another 15 minutes or until the top is nicely browned. Meanwhile, the extra batter will have dripped down the side and made a crunchy layer around the loaf. Serve either hot or cold.

1 egg yolk

50 g/2 oz flour

100 ml/3½ fl oz beer (real ale if possible, but any beer will do)

550 g/1¼ lb cold meat (beef, lamb, ham, pork, etc.)

350 g/12 oz well-flavoured cheese (Cheddar is ideal)

2 onions, roughly chopped

25 g/1 oz butter

2 tart eating apples or 1 cooking apple, peeled and coarsely chopped

100 g/4 oz brown breadcrumbs

2 tablespoons wholegrain mustard

2 teaspoons allspice

3 large eggs

4 tablespoons plain yoghurt

salt and pepper

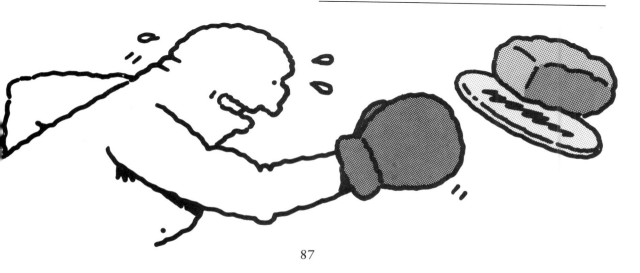

'PUPTON OF PIGEONS'

Serves 10

This deliciously rich and unusual cold terrine dates from the early eighteenth century. It can be made a couple of days in advance but goes watery if frozen.

4 pigeons
50 g/2 oz butter
450 ml/3/4 pint brown stock
450 ml/3/4 pint red wine
2 sweetbreads, cleaned and quartered
4 pickling onions, peeled
50 g/2 oz mushrooms
10 whole cooked chestnuts
salt, pepper and nutmeg
15 g/1/2 oz flour
1 large onion, finely chopped
450 g/1 lb sausagemeat
a small handful of parsley, chopped
1 teaspoon dried thyme
juice of 1/2 lemon
7–10 rashers bacon
juice of 1 orange
a large bunch of watercress

Clean the pigeons and fry them in 40 g/1½ oz of the butter to brown. Transfer the pigeons to a saucepan and add the stock and wine. Cover and simmer for 45 minutes or until the pigeons are almost cooked. Meanwhile, fry the sweetbreads and pickling onions in the remaining butter. Add them to the pigeons with the mushrooms, 6 chestnuts and the seasoning and simmer for a further 15 minutes. Remove the pigeons from the pan and bone them, keeping the flesh in as large pieces as possible. Remove the vegetables, sweetbreads and chestnuts and mix them with the pigeon meat. Add a little of the stock to the flour to make a paste in a small bowl and gradually return it to the stock. Boil briskly to thicken and reduce. Fry the chopped onion in the butter left in the pan and add it to the sausagemeat with the herbs and remaining chestnuts, roughly chopped. Add the lemon juice and season with salt and pepper.

Line a 15-cm/6-inch loose-bottomed tin or soufflé dish with the bacon rashers. Pack the bottom and sides of the tin with two-thirds of the forcemeat. Pile the pigeon mixture in the middle, flatten it and pour in 150 ml/¼ pint of the thickened stock. Cover the pigeon with the remaining forcemeat and smooth over the top with a knife.

Cover and bake for 45 minutes in a moderate oven (180°C/350°F/Gas Mark 4), then allow to cool completely. When quite cold, loosen the edges and turn the pupton out onto the serving dish. Just before serving, squeeze over the orange juice and surround with watercress.

CAPON OR TURKEY ROAST IN HONEY

Serves 8–10

This is a dramatic way to cook any bird as the honey keeps the skin dark and shiny and the flesh is blindingly white.

1 capon or small turkey (with giblets)

75 g/3 oz butter or margarine

1 medium onion, finely chopped

a large handful of parsley, finely chopped

1 tart eating apple or ½ cooking apple, peeled and finely chopped

75 g/3 oz plump raisins

grated rind and juice of 1½ lemons

75 g/3 oz ground almonds

75 g/3 oz brown breadcrumbs

1 teaspoon each ground ginger and salt

½ teaspoon black pepper

1 egg

2 tablespoons honey

Remove the giblets from the bird, keep the liver and chop it; use the rest for stock. Melt 25 g/1 oz of fat in a saucepan and gently cook the liver, onion and parsley until the liver is firm and the onion soft. Take off the heat and add the apple, raisins, lemon rind and juice, almonds, breadcrumbs, seasoning and egg. Mix the whole lot well together and stuff the bird at both ends. Secure with skewers and put it in a roasting pan. Melt the honey and remaining butter together and spoon them over the bird; as this mixture cools it will cling to the skin. Leave the bird to marinate in the honey, uncovered, in a refrigerator or larder for 24 hours, spooning over any excess mixture whenever you are passing.

Roast the bird in a moderate oven (180°C/350°F/Gas Mark 4), basting frequently with the honey and butter mixture, for 20 minutes to 450 g/1 lb; the skin will gradually turn black and shiny in contrast to the white meat below. Serve hot or cold.

SHERRIED POTATOES

Serves 10

This is an absolutely delicious way to serve 'mashed spud' – it can be cooked the day before and heated up.

2 kg/4½ lb potatoes

150 g/5 oz butter

50 g/2 oz soft brown sugar

1 teaspoon each nutmeg, black pepper and salt

3 eggs

150 ml/¼ pint medium sherry

juice and grated rind of 2 medium oranges

50 g/2 oz nibbed almonds

Peel and boil the potatoes. When they are cooked, mash them with the butter, sugar and seasoning. Beat the eggs, mix them with the sherry, orange juice and rind and beat them into the potatoes. Finally, mix in two-thirds of the almonds and pile the mixture into an ovenproof serving dish. Sprinkle the remaining almonds on top and bake for 20 minutes in a moderately hot oven (190°C/375°F/Gas Mark 5) until the potato is hot and lightly browned on top.

BONED, STUFFED CHICKEN

Serves 10–15

Any boned, stuffed bird will look effective and be easy to deal with for a buffet. Use the recipe below merely as a guideline to stuffing anything, just changing the quantities as appropriate. The bird can be successfully frozen either cooked or uncooked; if you intend to freeze it stuffed but uncooked, make sure that you use a fresh, not frozen, bird.

2–2.5 kg/4–5 lb chicken or capon

about 1.5 kg/3 lb good sausagemeat or minced veal

about 225 g/8 oz dark meat from a game bird

175 g/6 oz piece black pudding, cut in half lengthways

175 g/6 oz well-flavoured and coloured garlic or chorizo sausage, salami, etc., cut into large matchsticks

about 20 pistachio nuts

4–6 hard-boiled egg yolks

a little softened butter

Lay the bird out on a board and completely bone it, pushing the meat from the legs and wings back into the body. Sew up the apertures and any gashes in the skin (leaving just one big cut down the backbone). Line the inside of the bird with a layer (about 2.5 cm/1 inch thick) of the sausagemeat or minced veal – it is better to have too much than too little. Arrange all the other ingredients inside the bird, holding them all in place with layers of the sausagemeat or minced veal. Remember that when the bird is served, it will be cut across and look like a pâté, so lay the dark meat, black pudding, sticks of sausage or salami, etc. lengthways and sprinkle the pistachio nuts and egg yolks throughout. Remember also that the skin will have to meet to be sewn up, so do not get too enthusiastic as it will split in cooking if overfilled. Try to keep the shape of the bird in mind as you stuff it. When it is full, pull the edges together and sew up firmly.

Place the bird in a buttered baking tray, sewn side down, and rub it well with softened butter. Cover lightly with foil and bake it in a moderate oven (180°C/350°F/Gas Mark 4) for 20 minutes to 450 g/1 lb. About half an hour before it is done, remove the foil and baste the bird well so that it has a good brown top. Cool and chill well before slicing to serve.

PARSNIPS MOLLY PARKIN

Serves 10 as a vegetarian main course/20 as a vegetable

I have had this recipe for as long as I can remember, although I absolutely cannot recall where it came from. It can be used as a vegetable or a vegetarian dish, can be cooked several days before and heated up, and it freezes well.

1.8 kg/4 lb parsnips, scrubbed, topped and tailed and thinly sliced

---

about 10 tablespoons vegetable oil

---

150 g/5 oz butter or margarine

1.5 kg/3 lb tomatoes, peeled and thickly sliced

---

salt and pepper

5–6 level tablespoons soft brown sugar

---

350 g/12 oz grated Cheddar or other strong-flavoured hard cheese

---

900 ml/1½ pints double cream

---

6 rounded tablespoons fresh brown or white breadcrumbs

Heat the oil in a heavy pan and briskly fry the parsnips on both sides until they are golden brown. Meanwhile, grease a casserole dish with half the butter or margarine. Layer the parsnips and tomatoes alternately, sprinkling each layer with salt and pepper, sugar, cheese and cream and ending with a layer of parsnips topped with cream and cheese. Sprinkle the breadcrumbs over the top and bake in a moderately hot oven (190°C/375°F/Gas Mark 5) for 40–50 minutes or until the parsnips are cooked and the top well browned.

BONED, STUFFED GROUSE

Serves 2–3

This sounds more fiddly than it is and it does help expensive grouse go further; you can also freeze the birds once stuffed to serve later, or when out of season. The grouse can be served hot or cold; you should get two helpings from a hot grouse, three from a cold one. If they are to be served hot, a little thin gravy would be suitable. The quantities below are for each grouse.

---

1 grouse

---

15 g/½ oz onion, finely chopped

---

10 g/scant ½ oz butter

---

25 g/1 oz cooked spinach, chopped

---

15 g/½ oz cranberries, roughly chopped

---

25 g/1 oz medium oatmeal

---

salt, pepper and nutmeg

Bone the grouse by cutting through the skin down the backbone and carefully extracting the carcase. Do not try to bone legs or wings, just cut them off neatly. Gently fry the onion in the butter until it softens, then add the spinach and cook for a minute or two. Add the cranberries and oatmeal, mix well and season to taste with salt, pepper and nutmeg. Lay the stuffing down the middle of the boned bird and close the flesh over it. If you are going to sew it up, you will need to repair any gashes you made in boning, then sew up the main cut along the backbone. Alternatively, you can tie it very neatly or you can wrap it in a caul or a tight foil parcel that has been rubbed with butter. If the grouse is not in foil, it should be protected by draping over some rashers of bacon. Roast in a moderate oven (180°C/350°F/Gas Mark 4) for 30–45 minutes, depending on the size of the grouse.

TOMATO RING MOULD

Serves 10

You can make this cheap and simple dish a day ahead and fill it according to the budget available – watercress, interesting green salad, prawns or smoked fish in dressing, artichokes or avocado in mayonnaise are all delicious.

1 large can (800 g/28 oz) tomatoes

1 medium onion, sliced

2 bouquet garnis

a generous dash of Tabasco

½ teaspoon salt

1 dessertspoon sugar

1 heaped teaspoon dried basil or tarragon

350 ml/12 fl oz water

20 g/¾ oz gelatine

6 tablespoons red wine

Put all the ingredients except the gelatine and red wine in a pan, bring to the boil and simmer for 15 minutes. Remove the bouquet garnis and purée the mixture in a processor or liquidizer, then strain it if you want a totally smooth jelly. Soften the gelatine in the red wine, then add enough of the hot liquid to ensure it melts. Add this to the rest of the tomatoes and pour everything into a 1.2-litre/2-pint ring mould and leave to set firm. Turn out and fill the centre with whatever you have chosen.

CURRIED LENTIL SALAD

Serves 10

This looks pretty on a buffet table. It is filling and improves with keeping.

175 ml/6 fl oz vegetable oil

120 ml/4 fl oz wine vinegar

1 tablespoon sugar

3 teaspoons salt

2 teaspoons black pepper

1 heaped teaspoon each ground cumin and dry mustard

1 level teaspoon each turmeric, mace, ground coriander and ground cardamon

½ teaspoon each cayenne, ground cloves, nutmeg and cinnamon

500 g/18 oz red lentils

150 g/5 oz soaked currants

100 g/4 oz capers, chopped

2 medium onions, very finely chopped

Make the dressing by whisking together the oil, vinegar and all the seasonings and spices. Meanwhile, cook the lentils in plenty of boiling water for 3–6 minutes or until they are cooked but not disintegrated. Rinse them, drain well and combine with the dressing. Leave overnight.

Several hours before serving, add the currants, capers and onions and mix well.

Picnic hampers can be filled with a selection of cold
meats, cheeses and home-made pies. Pack
containers with interesting salads or rice, pasta and
vegetables, and provide plenty of crusty bread. A
choice of fresh fruit makes the perfect dessert.

For a winter buffet, offer a range of hot international dishes to cater for all tastes. Here there is a choice of Paella, Crispy-topped Mince, Chicken Véronique, Veal Cordon Bleu with Courgettes and Sweet and Sour Pork Balls with Noodles, served with pitta bread or French bread.

For a business lunch, it is better to serve lighter, more delicate foods and to offer just chilled white wine as the guests will have to work afterwards. Fish Quenelles and pâté with Melba toast are ideal for such occasions, and Caramelized Oranges are wonderful to finish off the meal.

For a summer buffet, make the most of the seasonal
fruits and vegetables. Serve light fish mousses with
cucumber and watercress, and fill melon shells with
summer fruits or make into delicious tarts. Chilled
rosé wine is a refreshing alternative to white.

IN SUMMER *there will be a demand for outside catering. Keep the table setting and food very simple. Serve plenty of fresh vegetables and fruit with dips, and cold pies and pâtés with crusty French bread. Arrange colourful pot plants around the table as decoration.*

A CHRISTMAS SALAD

Serves 10

Here is one of our more successful ways of dealing with the winter salad problem.

300 g/10 oz white cabbage, finely sliced

150 g/5 oz fennel, finely sliced

300 g/10 oz raw Brussels sprouts, finely sliced

300 g/10 oz raw parsnip or celeriac, grated

2–3 tablespoons chopped capers

about 10 tablespoons mayonnaise (not salad cream)

2 bunches watercress

150 g/5 oz broken walnuts

Mix all the vegetables except the watercress in a bowl. Add the chopped capers to the mayonnaise which should be of a light coating consistency; if it is too thick, thin it with a little boiling water. Toss the salad in the caper mayonnaise and turn it into a serving bowl. Just before serving, cover the salad with the watercress and sprinkle the chopped nuts over the top.

CABBAGE AND CAPER SALAD

Serves 10

Another good winter salad, this can be made the day before and finished off just before serving.

2 small, young green cabbages, washed and shredded

2 large onions, finely chopped

a small bunch of chopped fresh tarragon (if available), or 1 heaped teaspoon dried

8 tablespoons French dressing

4 tablespoons double cream

3 tablespoons capers

2 hard-boiled eggs, sliced

Mix the shredded cabbage with the onions and tarragon. Mix the cream with the French dressing in a large bowl, then toss the cabbage in the mixture. Turn into a salad bowl, sprinkle with the capers and decorate with slices of hard-boiled egg.

CHOCOLATE AND ORANGE MOUSSE

Serves 10

This expensive but luscious dessert can be made a day in advance or frozen.

300 g/10 oz good-quality dark chocolate

grated rind and juice of 3 oranges

2 tablespoons water

2 tablespoons Grand Marnier or Cointreau

25 g/1 oz cocoa

10 g/scant ½ oz gelatine

3 large whole eggs

3 egg yolks

75 g/3 oz sugar

150 ml/¼ pint double cream

Break up the chocolate in a bowl over hot water. Add the orange rind and water and stir until the chocolate is melted and creamy. Add the liqueur and remove from the heat. Meanwhile, mix the cocoa and gelatine in a bowl with the orange juice. Melt the gelatine by heating the bowl over hot water. Mix the eggs and egg yolks with the sugar in yet another bowl or double saucepan and whisk them over hot water until they are light, fluffy and thick. Carefully add the chocolate and gelatine mixtures to the egg, folding all well together until thoroughly amalgamated. Set aside in the refrigerator until it is just beginning to set.

Meanwhile, whisk the cream until it just holds its shape. Once the chocolate mixture is ready, fold in the cream and pour into a serving dish or individual glasses. Chill thoroughly and decorate with grated orange rind, flaked almonds or extra cream.

SYLLABUBS

Serves 10

The original syllabub was a frothy drink of wine, sherry, Madeira or brandy that was sweetened, spiced with nutmeg or cinnamon, and mixed with milk or cream; over the years syllabubs have become more solid and are now normally served in a glass with a spoon. They are a useful and simple dessert as they can be made a day in advance. You can also change the flavour with the liquor, the fruit juice (orange or lime) and the spices (cinnamon or cloves) and make it more or less rich by varying the proportion of cream to liquid. Use the proportions below as a guide.

rind and juice of 3 lemons

300 ml/½ pint medium sweet white wine or cider, or any combination of white wine, medium sherry, cider and brandy

about 2 tablespoons sugar

600 ml/1 pint double or whipping cream

about 1 teaspoon grated nutmeg

Put the lemon rind in the wine and allow it to infuse for several hours, then remove it. Pour all the ingredients into the bowl with the wine and whisk well until the mixture holds its shape without being too stiff – it will stiffen up further in the refrigerator. Taste the syllabub and add more sugar if it needs it. Pour it into glasses (preferably stemmed) and chill. Decorate with a further sprinkling of spice.

98

'FROG' SACHERTORTE

Serves 10

This recipe is based on the chocolate dessert cake served in the Frog Commissary restaurant in Philadelphia – it is very rich and very delicious.

Melt 225 g/8 oz of the chocolate in a double saucepan or microwave, then allow to cool until it is lukewarm. Cream the butter with the sugar and vanilla essence until light. Toss together the flour and ground walnuts. Separate the eggs and add the egg yolks, one at a time, to the butter and sugar mixture, then stir in the chocolate and the nuts and flour. Beat the egg whites until they hold their shape in soft peaks, then stir in about a quarter of them to lighten the mixture and fold in the rest. Pour the batter into a buttered and floured 23-cm/ 9-inch loose-bottomed cake tin and bake it for 1 hour in a preheated moderate oven (180°C/350°F/ Gas Mark 4). When it is cooked, let the cake cool in the pan for 20 minutes, then push down the puffed-up sides so they are flush with the middle. Invert the cake onto a rack so that the bottom becomes the top.

Cool the cake completely, then glaze with apricot jam. You may need to heat the jam and, if it has large pieces of apricot in it, you should sieve it so that you do not get lumps in your icing. Let the glaze set for about an hour.

To ice the cake, scald the cream in a metal pan, then whisk in the coffee and add the rest of the chocolate. Cook over the heat for a minute, remove from the heat and continue to stir until the chocolate has melted. Allow to cool until just warm and pour over the cake, turning it while spreading the icing as smoothly as possible with a spatula. Chill the cake on its rack until the icing is completely set and then transfer to a plate. Serve with whipped cream.

375 g/13 oz good-quality dark chocolate

225 g/8 oz softened butter

175 g/6 oz sugar

½ teaspoon vanilla essence

50 g/2 oz plain flour

225 g/8 oz broken walnuts, finely ground in a food processor or liquidizer

7 eggs

apricot jam

120 ml/4 fl oz double cream

2 teaspoons instant coffee

CHOCOLATE ROULADE

Serves 10 on a buffet table with other desserts/8 on its own

This is cheap and quick to make and a sure-fire winner.

225 g/8 oz plain chocolate
6 eggs
225 g/8 oz caster sugar
4 tablespoons hot water
about 25 g/1 oz icing sugar
300 ml/½ pint double cream

Line a swiss roll tin with greaseproof paper and brush it well with oil. Break the chocolate into a double saucepan or basin over hot water and melt it slowly. Meanwhile, separate the eggs and whisk the yolks with the caster sugar until lemon coloured. Remove the chocolate from the heat, stir in the hot water and mix the chocolate into the egg yolks and sugar. Whisk the whites until they hold their shape, then fold them into the chocolate mixture. Pour this into the swiss roll tin, making sure it is evenly spread, and bake in a preheated moderate oven (180°C/350°F/Gas Mark 4) for 15 minutes or until it holds its shape when lightly pressed with the finger. Make sure the oven shelf is level or you will get a lopsided roll. Once the roulade is cooked, take it out of the oven, cover it with a clean sheet of greaseproof paper and then with a wet tea towel. Leave it for a couple of hours or overnight.

To finish the roulade, turn it onto a third piece of greaseproof paper that has been well dusted with icing sugar. Carefully peel off the lower sheet of paper – as long as you greased it well it should come off quite easily. Whisk the cream until it holds its shape, spread it over the roulade, then carefully roll it up with the lower sheet of paper and turn it onto a serving dish. Shake a little more icing sugar over the top. You can eat it immediately, but it will be very 'squishy', or chill it for a couple of hours to 'firm it up.

LEMON BOODLES FOOL

Serves 10

Our version of the traditional Orange Boodles Fool is a little sharper and so better after a rich meal. It can be made in a bowl or in individual glasses, but if you use glasses, you may need to pour a little of the juice mixture over the sponge in case sufficient does not soak through the cream. It can be made a day in advance, but cannot be successfully frozen.

1 medium sponge cake
6 lemons
2 oranges
900 ml/1½ pints double cream
about 50 g/2 oz caster sugar
lemon twists to decorate

Break up the sponge and scatter it over the bottom of a soufflé dish or glass bowl – you want a layer about 5 cm/2 inches thick, depending on the size and shape of the bowl; if you are making this in individual glasses, the layer needs to be no more than one-third of the way up the glass.

Grate the rind from the fruit and squeeze out the juice. Lightly whip the cream and fold in the rind and juice. Sweeten to taste with sugar and add more lemon juice if the mixture is not sufficiently tart. Spoon the mixture over the sponge cake – if you pour it, the sponge will float to the top. Cover and chill for at least 6 hours. The juice will gradually soak through the cream into the sponge below, leaving only the frothy cream on the top. Decorate with lemon twists.

PINEAPPLE WITH FRESH GINGER

Serves 10

This unusual and refreshing dessert is adapted from an eighteenth-century recipe. It can be cooked in advance and heated up gently.

75 g/3 oz sugar

450 ml/¾ pint water

juice of 2 small lemons

15–25 g/½–1 oz fresh root ginger, peeled and very finely sliced

1 large, very ripe pineapple

Melt the sugar with the water and lemon juice in a large pan. Add the sliced root ginger (according to how strong you want it), bring the mixture to the boil and simmer for 5 minutes. Cut off the top of the pineapple and reserve, then slice the fruit into rounds and remove the core and skin. Add the slices of pineapple to the liquid and simmer for a further 10 minutes.

The dessert can be served warm or cold (I prefer it warm as it is more unusual). However you serve it, the top of the fruit should be placed in the middle of a large flat dish with the slices arranged around it. The syrup is then poured over the top.

RUM (OR BRANDY) AND WALNUT GÂTEAU

Serves 10

This rich, simple and luscious dessert can be made the day before but cannot be frozen.

30 sponge fingers

about 150 ml/¼ pint rum or brandy

600 ml/1 pint double cream

sugar to taste

about 175 g/6 oz walnuts (some broken, some whole)

Lay 10 sponge fingers out on a dish and sprinkle them with a little rum or brandy. Whisk the cream until it holds its shape but is not too stiff and sweeten to taste. Spread a thin layer of cream over the sponge fingers and sprinkle with broken walnuts. Repeat the process with another 10 sponge fingers, then lay the last layer of sponge fingers on top. Mix the remaining rum or brandy into the cream and use to generously cover the gâteau. Decorate with the whole walnuts.

LYCHEE AND BLACK GRAPE SALAD

Serves 10

This is a good winter fruit dessert when it is so hard to get anything reasonably priced. It can be made the day before but cannot be frozen. You can use fresh lychees, but they are very expensive and it seems rather a waste when the canned lychees taste fine in this context.

675 g/1½ lb canned lychees

1 level tablespoon arrowroot

150 ml/¼ pint strong China tea

about 2 tablespoons sugar

juice of 1–2 lemons

450 g/1 lb black grapes, peeled if the skins are very coarse, halved and pipped

Drain the juice from the lychees and make up to 900 ml/1½ pints with water. Mix the arrowroot with a little of the lychee juice and water to make a paste, transfer it to a saucepan and add the rest of the liquid and the tea. Heat it slowly and simmer for a few minutes, stirring continuously until the sauce thickens. Add sugar and lemon juice to taste, remembering that it will be served cold which will dull the flavour slightly. Mix the fruits in a bowl or individual glasses and pour over the syrup. This should be made at least a couple of hours before serving to allow the flavours to amalgamate. You can serve the salad with cream, but I think it is better without.

DRIED FRUIT COMPOTE

Serves 10

If you are fond of dried fruit, this is addictive. It can be served warm as a winter fruit salad or cold for breakfast. It keeps excellently; its flavour improving the longer it is kept.

1.25 kg/2½ lb mixed dried fruits (apricots, apples, prunes, figs, large raisins, etc.)

750 ml/1¼ pints water

450 ml/¾ pint dry red wine

about 225–350 g/8–12 oz sugar (depending on the fruit used and how sweet you like your desserts)

1 stick cinnamon

finely pared rind of 2 lemons, cut in strips

Unless the fruit is very plump, soak it overnight, then drain and discard the water. Put the fresh water, wine, sugar, cinnamon and lemon rind in a saucepan and heat gently. Add the fruit and simmer for 10–15 minutes until it is cooked. Remove the fruit with a slotted spoon and continue to cook the juice for a further 30 minutes or until it is slightly reduced and thickened. Remove the cinnamon, pour the juice over the fruit and leave to cool.

HOME-MADE LEMONADE

Serves 20 (about 5.5 litres/10 pints)

You may find that you want to dilute this even more for small children – in which case it will go further. If you wish to convert it into an adult drink, substitute 1.5 litres/2½ pints dry white wine for the equivalent amount of water.

30 lemons

5.5 litres/10 pints water

about 550 g/1¼ lb sugar

juice of 5 large oranges, strained

Peel the lemons and put the rinds with 2.75 litres/5 pints of the water in a pan. Bring them to the boil and simmer for 5 minutes. Remove the pan from the heat, add the sugar and stir until it has melted. Add the juice of the lemons and another 1.5 litres/2½ pints of water and allow the mixture to cool. When cold, add the remaining water (or wine) and the orange juice. Chill thoroughly and strain before serving.

JELLY WHIPS

Serves 20

These may sound revolting to adults, but they always seem to go down well with kids, especially if you make them in fun shapes in individual moulds.

3 packets jelly (any flavour)

900 ml/1½ pints hot water

about 600 ml/1 pint evaporated milk (1 large can and 1 small)

Dissolve the jelly in the water and leave until it is just starting to set – about 45 minutes. Whisk in the evaporated milk with an electric beater until it is thick and stiff; it should expand considerably in volume. Pour into different shaped moulds to set and unmould to serve.

ORGANIZING FUNCTIONS

Dealing with Clients

It may seem self-evident to say that keeping the client happy is the most important part of organizing a function, but it is all too easy to forget in the mild hysteria that accompanies the setting up of any large affair. Clients need to be kept happy not only so that they end up pleased with what you have done and pay your bill, but so that they recommend you warmly to all their friends, relatives and business contacts – worth more in promotional terms than thousands of pounds spent on advertising. A happy and relaxed client will also make your life as function organizer a lot easier – nothing can fray your nerves more than having to constantly reassure nail-biting hosts when your attention is desperately needed to organize their seating arrangements.

Not that you can blame a client for feeling a little nervous. A vast number of outside catered functions are 'one-offs', but, whether business or private, they are usually important parties for the hosts concerned. In a business context, 'heads may roll' if the function does not come up to expectations; in a club situation, the organizer carries the heavy responsibility for all members enjoying themselves; a private party is normally a celebration of some kind that will be quite ruined if the caterers fail to come up to scratch. Moreover, clients often have little experience of organizing such functions so are entirely dependent on the caterer giving them the right advice and service. If caterer and host are used to working together, they will presumably have developed a reasonably successful working relationship, but if it is the first time round, it will take a very laid-back client indeed not to be just a little nervous. It is, therefore, up to you as caterer not only to justify your clients' trust in the long run, but to convince them from the start that they are in good and capable hands.

To do this, you must above all else give the impression that you are efficient; it will, of course, help if you manage to live up to your image! No matter what the function or how inspired your menus may be, if there are no forks to eat the 'nouvelle' delight you are serving, the party is unlikely to be a success. It is also wise to be pleasant, imaginative and a good cook, but the smooth running of the event is the priority uppermost in everyone's mind.

To appear, and be, efficient, you must know your subject and be in a position to advise on every aspect of the function. I shall expand at length on the subject of checklists later, but this is where the first one comes in. A master checklist of every aspect of organizing a function that can be discreetly consulted will prevent you forgetting anything vital, and impress your client with your thoroughness (see overleaf).

Your first contact will probably be on the phone, so a good confidence-inspiring telephone manner is essential (see telephone manner, page 156). In the majority of cases, the initial contact will be followed by one or several meetings either on site or in your office or your client's. On site is obviously the most sensible, but if there are to be subsequent meetings, it might be wise to try and have them in the client's office or home rather than your own kitchens. This way you will get some idea of the 'class of operation' you will be expected to produce. It will also prevent the client seeing you at work. Since most catering kitchens are in back streets and designed for working in and not to be seen, many of them could give a quite false impression of what their owners can do! Wherever they happen, any subsequent meetings must reinforce the client's conviction that the caterer knows exactly what he or she is at and is quite capable of handling the matter in hand. It pays to follow up the first serious meeting about any function with a really detailed letter covering all the points raised at the meeting plus anything else that may have occurred to you later. If the client is not used to entertaining, there may be innumerable details (coat racks for the guests' coats, table plans, gifts for relevant VIPs, etc.) that never occur to him or her at all.

The letter should be laid out as clearly as possible so as not to cause unnecessary confusion. It should also be made to look as professional as possible – it should be neatly typed on headed paper, etc. This will come naturally when you are established, but is important when you are trying to get off the ground and 'look professional'.

It should, obviously, deal with possible menus, drinks, locations, staff, etc., but it should also talk about money. Pricing is dealt with in more detail on pages 142–5, but I do find that clients appreciate a breakdown of costs (especially if they are going to be substantial) so they know exactly what they are spending their money on. I also find that it pays to be a prophet of doom – tell them the *most* it could cost them as well as the least, and do not leave out any nasty little extras (VAT, service charges, etc.) that will dramatically distort the final figure. A client is always delighted if the final bill comes out close to or even below the original estimate, although this is not always possible to achieve. (See the sample letter overleaf.)

Keeping the client happy for the rest of the run-up to the function will merely be a matter of re-inforcing the initial impression of efficiency. Always return any phone calls promptly – with the file in front of you when you do so! Copy your client in on any relevant correspondence with other contractors involved, etc.

This doesn't mean that all clients are shrinking violets who need to be led by the hand. You may also have to deal with ones who have extremely fixed ideas of what they want, whether or not their schemes are feasible – for example, freshly roasted sides of beef and Yorkshire pudding when you only have two electric hot cupboards to deal with food for two hundred. In this case, you will need to know your stuff even better and be firm about what is or is not possible, even if it means losing the job. A disaster with soggy Yorkshire pudding and raw beef will do you more harm in the long run than the blow to your overdraft through losing the job. A certain amount of firmness may also be necessary in the matter of costs as, despite wishful thinking, it is not possible to make a silk purse from a sow's ear, or a smoked salmon sandwich out of a sardine.

Master Checklist for Setting up Functions

Client's name, address and phone number This should not be demanded at the beginning of the conversation as it makes you sound as though you are selling insurance, but for goodness sake do not forget to get it before the end.

Type of function Cocktail/buffet/dinner party, press or product launch, club or society dinner, wedding, private celebration, etc.

Date

Time of day and expected duration

Estimated numbers

Location If they don't have one, you might suggest finding one.

Budget This is tricky since many people do not know or are not prepared to reveal how much they want to spend, but if you can get some kind of indication, it will help you enormously – a slightly jocular approach ('It would help if we knew whether you were thinking of spending 50 p or £50 per head. . . .') will usually produce some kind of lead.

Billing details This should probably not be discussed at the first meeting unless you are going to ask for a deposit, in which case you will need to say so. However, do make sure that you get the details right in good time and that you make your terms quite clear to the client.

Kind of food wanted Hot or cold, substantial or light, rich and luscious or health conscious, traditional or 'nouvelle', etc.

Special food requirements This is applicable to hosts and guests – vegetarians, any allergies, non-pork, beef, lamb or fish eaters, etc. Guests' peculiarities are something you will need to check at a later meeting, but even if the host decides not to worry about them, you should cover yourself by raising the point.

Leftovers What they want done with any food not used – for example, should it be left in the refrigerator, taken away, fed to the staff, etc.

Equipment available or needed This will probably have to wait until you have an on-site meeting, but at least you can give the client some idea of what he or she may be in for if all the equipment has to be imported. For detailed lists of what might be needed, see page 115–16. At some point, you will also want to discuss the quality of the equipment to be used – antique silver or disposable plates.

Flowers, lighting and other decorations Ask what needs to be provided for the venue. Depending on the function, bouquets or buttonholes may also be needed.

Staffing requirements Since this is one of the most expensive elements in a catered function, you need to be quite sure that you know what kind of service your clients want – some, for example, like a very 'professional' approach with well-trained staff in uniforms; others prefer a more relaxed atmosphere with girls and guys in jeans. You will also need to find out whether they want toastmasters, commissionaires, cloakroom attendants, etc. where appropriate. You should ask whether they have any special requirements about how they want the food or drink served, or if there are any unusual things that they want the staff to do – announce guests, man the record player, feed the cat, etc.

Drinks What kind of beverages are to be provided and how much do they want to spend on them?

Cigars and cigarettes Are these to be supplied and by whom?

Table plans, place cards, menus and invitations Who is to be seated where and whether they wish you to arrange for place cards, menus and invitations to be printed?

Entertainment Music, speaker, 'entertainers', dancing, etc. – a *sound system* may be necessary for some speakers and musicians.

Gifts Do these need to be provided for guests?

Transport Is this to be laid on for guests or hosts (where appropriate)?

Photographer Do they wish photographs to be taken?

Letter of Confirmation

This sample letter is confirming early arrangements for an 'Old English' dinner at a small stately home near Windsor. In this case, a meeting has already been held on site. The client also has some idea of the budget available and has chosen the type of evening that she wishes to hold. Although the booking is not yet definite, assuming that it may become so may help it along the way, as will making it quite clear that you will attend to every need of both host and guests. The letter should be written as soon as possible after the meeting, but not so soon that its recipient might think that you had not had to do any actual work on her behalf! Enclosing menus, place cards, etc. from previous functions also gives some concrete proof of what you can do.

Crystal A . . . . .
X Ltd.,
Slough,
Berks SL1 1QQ

Copy:
Peregrine Palmer,
Dorney Court

Dear Crystal,
Re: **Dorney Court Dinner – 18th July – 35–40 guests**
(*all relevant details should be included in the heading*)
Further to our meeting yesterday, I have been putting together some ideas for your evening at Dorney Court with the relevant prices and the various options we discussed.

Arrival

Guests will arrive at the house *around 7pm*, in cars rather than coaches so that they can use the main drive which gives the most spectacular view of the house.

Cocktails

Assuming that the weather is good (which it should be in July), we will serve *drinks and 'heavy' cocktails* on the lawns; if not, in the Elizabethan parlour. (Coats, if any, will be stored upstairs in the Great Chamber.) For drinks, we would suggest *an Elizabethan punch* backed up by a standard mixed bar. I have suggested *cocktail eats* below, all of which are from the period and which should be substantial enough to give your guests energy for a tour of the house before dinner!

Depending both on the weather and the kind of entertainment we go for, the guests could be *briefly entertained before dinner* while they are having their cocktails.

Tour of the house

At whatever time you felt right (between 7.30 and 7.45 pm I would think), the guests would be taken on a *conducted tour of the house* – in two groups. I am sure that they would all like to have a *brochure* (cost 90 p) on the house, but I do not know whether you would rather give it to them before they arrive so that they have some idea of where they are going, or whether you would prefer to wait until the tour, thus keeping the venue a surprise. The tour takes around 20 minutes and ends up in the Great Hall which would be laid up for dinner.

Dining Hall (Great Hall)

Depending on the final number, we would *seat the guests* at the old oak tables either in a horseshoe in the lower part of the hall or on three tables using the dais as well.

The *tables* would not be covered but would be *decorated* with iron candlesticks, candles and small arrangements of old English flowers and herbs. We would arrange for calligraphed *menus and place cards* (samples from the period enclosed), but we would need to liaise with you about the table plan. *Gifts* (possibilities listed below) could also be waiting for the guests in the Great Hall.

The *tables would be laid* with conventional porcelain, silver and glassware and white damask table napkins, unless you decided to opt for wooden platters and pewter goblets. This would, however, increase the costs substantially. *Staff* would be in Elizabethan costume – I would suggest four 'damsels' and two 'serving men'.

Dinner

I have suggested two possible *menus* (both eschewing the use of ginger in deference to your MD). One is specifically Pepysian, one more generally 'Old English'. I am also enclosing a list of our more conventional set menus. We would rather wait to suggest *wines* to go with the dinner until you have chosen a menu; however, we do think that you should include an English white wine with one course. We will serve port, brandy and mead with the coffee and will arrange for cigars (but not cigarettes) to be available for anyone who wants them.

Entertainment

As regards entertainers, we can go for a harpist/singer; a singer with a lutanist; a small group of early musicians; a medieval troupe to include a juggler; or we could combine a musician with a magician! Their costs vary from around £200–600 + VAT, depending on how many of them there are and how much they do.

I would also be happy to give a short talk on the food at the beginning or at some point during the meal – just so that everyone knows what they are eating! My fee would be £100 + VAT.

Photographer

I have checked and our photographer would be free on July 18th. His basic fee would be £150 + VAT; prints at cost thereafter.

Costings

I am listing some estimated costings for the evening, although at this stage they are very tentative. However, they will give you some idea of the overall sums involved.

I hope I have covered everything, but please give me a call if you have any queries or would like to discuss any aspect of the evening further. Otherwise, we will look forward to hearing from you when you are ready to take the arrangements on to the next stage. However, I would point out that the musicians do get quite busy during the summer, so it might be wise to book them as soon as possible.

With very best wishes,

Yours sincerely,

Sample menus (*with explanations where necessary and a total per head cost excluding VAT*)

Possible Gifts

Pot of Dorney Court honey:	£2.00 each
Dorney Court paperweight or etched whisky glass:	£2.50 each
Bag of old English herbs:	£1.50 each
Hand-painted silk scarves:	£9.50 each
Old English cookery books – signed:	£6.95 each
Gift wrapping:	75 p per gift

Tentative costings – assuming 40 guests
(*These costs are only intended as a guideline.*)

Facility fee:	500.00
Tour of house @ £1 per head:	40.00
40 brochures @ 90 p:	36.00
Pedestals of *flowers* in the hall and parlour:	225.00
Flower decorations for tables:	185.00
Hire of crockery, cutlery, glass, etc. @ £3.50 per head:	140.00
(Supplement for wooden platters and silver goblets – £3 per head)	
Delivery of equipment, food, etc.:	40.00
Waiting *staff* to serve drinks, dinner, etc.:	250.00
Elizabethan costumes for staff:	180.00
Handwritten *menus and place cards* in Elizabethan script @ approximately £3.50 per head:	140.00
Photographer:	150.00
Entertainment – musicians, etc.:	400.00
Talk on historical food:	100.00
Food:	
Cocktail snacks @ £3.75 per head:	150.00
Dinner – 5 courses @ approximately £15.00 per head:	600.00
Drinks:	
Punch and mixed bar on arrival; two or three good-quality wines with dinner (including an English white); soft drinks, sparkling water, etc.; brandy, port and mead with coffee @ approximately £12.50 per head:	500.00
(*Cigars* @ £5.25 sale or return)	
	3,636.00
VAT	545.40
Total:	£4,181.40

(£90.90 per head exclusive of VAT; £104.53 per head inclusive of VAT)

Locations

Unless you operate premises of your own (which some of the bigger caterers do very successfully), you will be working 'away from home'. This may be in your client's home or office or in some outside location hired for the event. Whichever it is, it will pay you to examine it and its facilities very carefully. I have drawn up a list of what you should check below, but you will also need to know how many people have to be accommodated and what they will be doing.

Area Needed for Various Functions
Table Space
Straight-sided tables Each person needs a *minimum* of 45 cm/18 in of table space.

Round tables 1.5 m/5 ft diameter = 10 people; 1.35 m/4 ft 6 in = 8 people; 1.05 m/3 ft 6 in– 1.2 m/4 ft = 6 people; 90 cm/3 ft = 4 people.

Floor Space You will need the following *absolute minimum* of clear floor space:

Banquet/formal dinner: 1 sq m/10 sq ft per person
Dinner dance: 1.2 sq m/13 sq ft per person
Buffet reception/ theatre-style lecture: 0.8 sq m/7 sq ft per person

If the space is obstructed with pillars, etc., you will have to adjust your calculations accordingly. Drawing a scale plan of the room and the table layout will be of great help to both you and your client – use graph paper and cut out little templates of the tables which you can move around on the plan. However, do take care to leave enough room for your staff to get between the tables. You will need a minimum of 2 m/6 ft between tables to allow the staff through, so if you are dealing with 1.5 m/5 ft tables you should cut your templates 3.5 m/11 ft in diameter. The same applies to rectangular tables, sprig arrangements, and so forth.

Marquees and tent functions require basically the same sort of area, but if you find yourself organizing a marquee, you can depend on the supplier to know exactly what you will need and to advise you accordingly.

Checklist of Points to Note in Any New Location

Accessibility If you are using an outside location, it may be difficult to find; a small map of how to get there – and how to get into the building – will be invaluable to your staff and delivery people. It might also be worth your clients enclosing a copy in the invitations if the guests are to show up even remotely on time. In addition, you will need to consider the following questions.

How are you going to deliver whatever you need to deliver? If you are going to have a big truck, will it get through the gate? Will tables and chairs get through the door or in the lift, etc.?

What time are you going to be able to get into the building before the function and what time will you have to be out after it?

Where can you park after you have delivered?

Are there extra rooms where you will be able to store your back-up equipment, dirty dishes, etc?

Can you get to the 'dining hall' from your working area (wherever and whatever it may be) reasonably easily?

If it is to be a big function, is there somewhere to 'feed and water' your staff before or during the affair?

Where are the fire exits?

Facilities for the caterer Are there cookers, hot cupboards, plate warmers, hot-water boilers, refrigerators, freezers, plenty of hot water, and working space for laying out dishes, doing final decoration, etc.? If any of these are lacking, you may have to import them at quite considerable extra cost, so you need to know before you do your estimate.

Are tables and chairs available and if so will you want to use them? If not, do they have anywhere to store them while you bring in your own?

What is the power supply like? We are by no means the only caterers to have fused all the lights in the middle of the party by trying to squeeze on just one more electric hot ring.

What are the rubbish dumping facilities like or will you have to take all your garbage with you?

Facilities for the client/guests If it is winter, what is the heating like? If it is summer, what is the ventilation like?

What are the toilet facilities like – will they need tarting up with flowers, towels, etc.?

Where can coats, etc. be stored and will you need coat racks?

Are there telephones available should they be needed?

What is the parking like for guests?

Lighting Is the 'in-house' lighting going to 'do' anything for your function or should you suggest using something better – fluorescent bulbs do not add to the romance of an engagement party!

Can you use candles? A lot of 'stately homes' and antique buildings will not allow them because of the fire risk.

Restrictions Does the location have any particular restrictions – the time the function must finish; noise level; in-house 'retainers' who have to be fed or paid; subcontractors – florists, musicians, etc. – who have to be used; restrictions on hanging things on walls; electricity supply, etc.

Finding Locations

You may find that a client comes to you with a party but nowhere to hold it. It will pay you therefore to file away details of any buildings or locations that might be available for hire locally. Obviously, church halls and town halls are widely used for entertaining of all kinds, but you will be surprised how many museums, art galleries, health clubs, trendy shops and 'stately' and private homes are happy to swell their incomes by letting themselves out when they are not busy selling pictures or organizing exercise classes!

An afternoon spent combing the Yellow Pages and local directories, followed by a day 'viewing' locations (and noting all relevant details about them) could provide you with a really interesting selection of potential venues to offer your clients. Exactly how you charge for this service will depend on how you choose to treat your ancillary services (see page 131), but even if you were not to charge for it at all, you may find that the contacts you make with locations bring more business to you than you take to them!

Equipment

Never be fooled into thinking that running a catering business has only to do with food; a vast amount of your time will be spent organizing, transporting, laying out, clearing up, washing up and taking back equipment – most of it heavy, awkward and, after a function, revoltingly dirty. Try sorting out a couple of hundred knives and forks covered in mayonnaise, cream and gravy the morning after a dinner and you will wonder how you ever got involved in such a disgusting job! However, fortunately, that bit does not take too long – and if the function is big enough, you will be able to hire the whole lot in, which means that someone else will have to wash it up!

Crockery, Cutlery and Glass

No matter how small the function, you are going to need plates, cutlery and glasses. Some locations where catering is a regular part of their day will already be stocked with most of what you need – although you should check with your clients to make sure that it is suitable for their particular party. If there is none on site, it will be your responsibility to supply it. Equipment can always be hired from 'dedicated' hire companies, but if you are hiring in very small quantities, they will charge you a heavy premium – if they are prepared to do it at all.

Your client may, of course, prefer to use disposable equipment – by no means the cheap and tacky option that it used to be. There are very high-class and attractive plastic plates, glasses and cutlery to be had – although not necessarily cheaply. The advantage from your point of view is that there is no clearing up to be done – but the host of a five-course banquet may not see it that way! The disadvantage is that to buy disposables at a reasonable price you have to buy them in very large quantities – we still have about 3,000 plastic forks left over from a monster picnic we did about ten years ago. This means a large investment in both money and space; the alternative, if you want a relatively small amount, is to cut your profit on them and just buy enough small domestic-sized packets to cover your needs.

Buying Your Own Depending on the type of catering you are going for, it may pay you fairly early on to equip yourself with a certain number of 'covers' that you can hire out to your clients. The initial investment is relatively high, but once you have made it, there is virtually no upkeep apart from replacement of breakages and losses, which should, obviously, be kept to a minimum.

Hiring Lists To keep your breakages and losses to a minimum, you must provide yourself with a 'hiring list' of some kind on which all items sent to a function are noted and against which the returns can be checked off. A hiring list is also essential to make sure that you have got everything you need, but we will come to that later. The only way you can really keep track of your belongings is to be conscientious about checking off returns; it is all too easy for staff to be careless – or, I am afraid, dishonest – and pocket a few knives or drop plates unnecessarily, both of which will eat holes in your profits.

You can charge clients for any losses or breakages that happen during their 'job', although some clients might, with some justification, feel that if your staff break or lose your equipment you should absorb the cost. The exception to this can be if you are hiring very expensive equipment on their behalf that has to be specially insured; in this case, the client will normally bear the cost of the insurance and be responsible for settling any claims. If you are going to charge clients for your losses, you must tell them so when you give them your initial estimate.

Whether you choose to include the cost of supplying the equipment in your food charge or whether you charge separately for it is merely a matter of book-keeping, but whichever way you do it, hiring out equipment can provide you with a very nice bit of extra income.

Crockery If you are going to buy your own equipment, do not be tempted by some pretty domestic china; it is going to have to withstand very rough treatment, so you *must* get a make that won't break as soon as someone sneezes. There are now dozens of hotel wares in attractive and totally

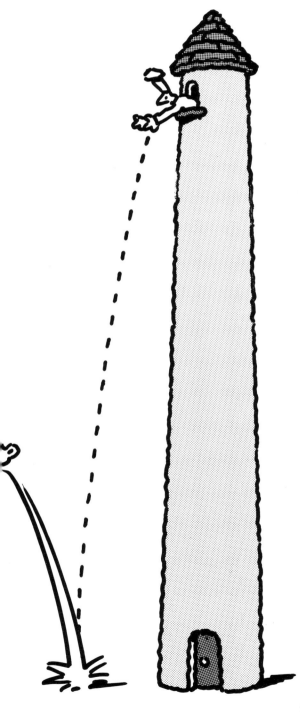

'non-standard' patterns that put up with the most appalling treatment. When you choose your pattern, remember that it is going to have to look 'right' in many different situations, so avoid anything too unusual. Often plain white crockery with a simple gold rim is the safest and most attractive. Also make sure that the supplier is *not* about to discontinue that pattern.

Cutlery Buying silver-plated cutlery is now really beyond the pockets of small caterers – once you have made your fortune, you can consider it! However, there is some good-quality stainless steel around which can look quite smart; if you do need silver for a particular event, you can always hire it in from a hire company for that occasion.

Glassware Glass is the one area where you will have heavy breakages. As yet no one has produced glassware that is both attractive and tough, but since the standard 'Paris goblets', tulips, tumblers, etc. are perfectly acceptable (well polished) and relatively cheap, you will just have to resign yourself to buying a lot. Incidentally, you should always allow two glasses for each guest as all guests have a terrible habit of dumping their glass in a corner and picking up a new one when they want a refill. Again, if you need 'posher' glasses for a specific function, you can always hire them in.

Hiring In Equipment The disadvantage, of course, of owning your own equipment is that you also have to clean it. Hiring everything does not entirely cancel out this problem, because some hire companies require their plates and cutlery to be washed, or at least rinsed, before they are returned to them. You should check this out when you arrange the hire so that you can provide buckets if there are no sinks or running water available. You may be able to persuade the hirers to take the gear back unwashed or rinsed (if your facilities are going to be so negligible as to make it impossible even to rinse), but they will normally charge you a supplement for the extra cleaning that will therefore be needed.

Cleaning Your Own Equipment A small caterer falls between two stools as far as dishwashers go as small commercial dishwashers are only moderately effective, if pretty speedy, whereas domestic dishwashers are efficient but terribly slow. Fully-fledged commercial dishwashers are effective but very bulky, very expensive, and need someone to man them all the time. The other alternative (which is often the best when you have awkward or bulky dishes or foods that spot or stick in a dishwasher) is to wash by hand. Most of the non-bulk caterers end up with a combination of all three methods – domestic dishwashers for glassware and cutlery where it pays you to have them really well washed and dried; small commercial dishwashers for plates; and a good 'washer-up' for soup bowls and serving dishes.

But, whether the equipment is your own or hired in, you must make sure that it is *sparkling clean and well polished* – nothing will put a client or a guest off a caterer faster than seeing some of yesterday's Bœuf Bourgignon stuck to the plate.

Serving Equipment
(See page 128.)

Linen
Damask cloths and napkins, like silver cutlery, have now become so expensive to buy that few small caterers can, or should, afford them. Most big laundries have contract hire departments (which are more or less efficient) if you think you will need a regular supply; alternatively, you can hire cloths and napkins for a specific function from any hire company. Do, however, check out your hire company before you use them as all too many supply stained or torn cloths that are very difficult to disguise on site.

Damask is available in white and normally in pink and gold as well; I personally prefer to use white for all functions as I feel it makes a better backdrop for your flowers and other decorations, but your client may prefer a colour.

Paper napkins (and cloths if you need them) are now available in a very wide range of patterns, colours and qualities and are really a much better idea for any informal party as they look jolly, are easy to use, and are also a lot cheaper!

Furniture
Furniture (mainly tables and chairs) is large and bulky to store and transport and relatively expensive to buy. Some caterers feel it is useful to own a few buffet tables for emergencies (we did for a few years but used them less and less); most people merely hire in what they need when they need it. There are plenty of hire companies ready to supply tables (round, rectangular or almost any other shape you want), chairs (folding wooden, 'folding padded', 'gilt banqueting', etc.), dance floors, bars, etc., and they will deliver the furniture for you. However, as with the linen, you do need to check your company to make sure that neither the chairs nor the tables are going to collapse at the crucial moment (it has been known!) and that seats are respectably clean. As with most things, you will get what you pay for, so be wary of any hire company offering particularly cheap rates.

Cooking Equipment
Depending on what is available on site, you may need to bring in heating and cooking equipment – hot cupboards or trays, water boilers, plate warmers, coffee makers, etc. To decide what you want, you will need to liaise carefully with your cooking department. Most large hire companies do have a certain amount of equipment, but you need to check out exactly what it is and what it can do. Hot cupboards, for example, are just that and, although they can get very hot (if you turn them on far enough in advance), they will not cook things – they will only reheat food that has been previously cooked. Many of these items are also extremely bulky, so they may be a real pain to transport and to squeeze into your venue. Do make a great fuss with the hiring company to ensure that the equipment works – on more than one occasion I have hired hot water boilers only to find that they either flatly refused to heat a cup of tea or leaked like a sieve.

The only bit of heating equipment that I think it pays most caterers to own is a few electric hot rings. They are cheap, small, easily transportable and, combined with a couple of large pans, will rescue you in all kinds of tight corners!

Marquees or Tents

If you need these, use a marquee specialist. You will find a list in the Yellow Pages, or may be recommended one by your hiring company. Most are efficient and reliable and will be of great help in matters of size, etc.

'Fancy Goods'

Apart from the standard crockery and cutlery, you could find yourself needing fancy silver candelabra or serving dishes, pewter mugs, oak carver chairs, eighteenth-century waitress costumes, flags to represent the nations at a dinner, umbrellas to keep the rain off the guests, and so on. Your standard hiring company may be able to supply some of them or suggest others who could; if not, you will have to head for the Yellow Pages again. Firms hiring theatrical props are the best bet, although since they all specialize, you may have to plough through several before you hit the right one. They may also be able to recommend costume hire firms. Toy shops sometimes have small flags; otherwise, you will have to go to a flag maker. For your more bizarre needs, you will have to use your own imagination!

If you work in the country or a relatively small town, your imagination is going to be doing overtime since the majority of suppliers I am suggesting live in large cities. You will, of course, be able to hire from them, but it is going to be a great deal more difficult to organize (firms supplying theatrical props will only hire to you if you go and visit them) and a good deal more expensive.

Quantities

It is always wise to supply or hire slightly more of everything than you expect to need; you never know whether extra guests will appear and, whereas you can usually stretch one portion of smoked salmon to cover two people, you cannot stretch one plate.

Hiring List and Miscellaneous Equipment

There is a vast range of miscellaneous bits and pieces that you will need 'on the job', although exactly what they will be will depend on your particular operation. As a guideline I am giving overleaf the basic hiring list which we have used very successfully for many years. You could add your own particular requirements to this. If you are hiring from an outside hire company, you should also enlist their help in suggesting anything you may have forgotten; they make their profit from hiring to you, so it will be in their interest to suggest anything that you might have missed and that they may be able to supply.

Nevertheless, hiring lists and checklists will only work *provided you check through them carefully*. All lists are vital for organizing functions, but none is more vital than the hiring list – you will be sunk without any bit of your equipment. So a *very* comprehensive list, *very* carefully checked and rechecked is absolutely essential for big and small functions.

You can, of course, do this easily if you are supplying the equipment yourself; it is not so easy when you are hiring it in. Experience will soon teach you who is reliable and who is not, but you do not want to have to learn the hard way. Personal recommendation as always is best. If you cannot get a personal recommendation, have a long talk to the company on the telephone (maybe even go and visit them) before you put in your order. That way you should be able to assess whether or not they sound efficient. Obviously, no one is perfect and even the best company will make the occasional boob – but if they do, the good company will be the one who gets your two hundred missing forks to you somehow, no matter what time of day or night.

Apart from the equipment needed for each function, it is wise to have an emergency or function box that gets carted along to every 'do'. This should include:

A first aid box, with plasters, aspirins, etc.

Scissors, sellotape, pens and some white cards.

Small sewing kit, including plenty of safety pins of various sizes.

Clothes brush and some spray-on dry cleaner.

Hiring List

Name: .... No: .... Date: ....

Crockery
Soup bowls and saucers....................
25-cm/10-inch plates....................
23-cm/9-inch plates....................
16-cm/6½-inch plates....................
Cruet sets....................

Cutlery
Soup spoons....................
Table knives and forks....................
Small knives....................
Small forks....................
Dessert spoons....................
Teaspoons....................
Serving spoons....................
Salad servers....................
Pie slices....................
Soup/sauce ladles....................
Cheese knives....................
Butter knives....................
Wedding cake knives....................

Coffee and Tea Equipment
Cups and saucers – large....................
Cups and saucers – small....................
Spoons – large....................
Spoons – small....................
Jugs – large (milk)....................
Jugs – small (cream)....................
Sugar bowls....................
Coffee machines....................
Extra jugs – coffee....................
Coffee and filters....................
Decaffeinated coffee....................
Tea pots....................
Kettles....................
Tea....................

Linen
Cloths – 70 × 144 cm/28 × 58 in....................
      90 × 90 cm/36 × 36 in....................
      70 × 70 cm/28 × 28 in....................
Linen napkins....................
Paper napkins – white/coloured....................
Pins/drawing pins....................
Aprons....................
Serving cloths....................

Glass and Bar Equipment
Tumblers....................
Red wine....................
White wine....................
Sherry/port....................
Brandy....................
Liqueur....................
Jugs....................
Measuring jug....................
Rubbish bags....................
Trays....................
Ashtrays....................
Lemon plate and knife....................
Ice bucket and spoon....................
Can opener....................
Bottle opener....................
Corkscrews....................
Cocktail sticks....................
Teacloths....................
Absorbent cloths....................

Miscellaneous
Bread/biscuit baskets....................
Butter dishes....................
Cheeseboards....................
Oil and vinegar sets....................
Vegetable saucepans....................
Vegetable dishes....................
Colander....................
Rubbish bags....................
Absorbent cloths....................
Teacloths....................
Oven gloves/cloths....................
Rubber gloves....................
Mop and bucket....................
Trays....................
Hot rings/plates....................
Oven....................
Urn....................
Extension flex....................
Adaptors....................
Matches....................
Candles....................
Menu holders....................
Coat rail and hangers....................
Cloakroom tickets and pins....................
Trestle tables....................

Delivery and Transport

No matter how small the function, you are going to have to get yourself, the food and whatever equipment you need 'on site'. Your normal car or van may not be big enough if you are dealing with a fairly large function. If you are hiring in most of the equipment, the hiring company will normally deliver to, and collect from, the venue direct. None the less, you will have a lot of extra equipment yourself and it is better to have too much room than too little. Incidentally, hiring special equipment from theatrical props agents, etc. can create a problem as very few of them provide delivery or collection services.

Hiring Transport

Although it will cost more, it will pay you to hire a decent-sized van for a night or two to cover your large function – nothing is worse than spending hours (when you are already running late) trying to cram what you need into the back of a Mini. In any case, you should be able to incorporate the cost of the hired van into your overall charge for the function.

It may seem obvious, but remember to *check tyres, spares and petrol* the day before – you do not want to have to stop for petrol (or, perish the thought, run out!) on your way. Also, make sure

that you know how to get to where you are going. Check out the route thoroughly on a map and, if you are really nervous, do a dummy run.

Packing

Leave *plenty* of time for packing your van – it always takes longer than you expect. And train yourself to do it neatly and methodically; you will get far more in if it is all properly stacked, and your precious mousses and jellies will stand less chance of being destroyed.

A final and comprehensive checking off of all your various checklists as you load the van is also vital. We work with two basic lists: the *hiring list*, which covers all the equipment, drinks and miscellaneous extras, and the *kitchen list*, which covers all the food (noting how many platters or pots of each dish) and which should include things like cream for the coffee, butter, cheese biscuits, salt and butter for the vegetables, etc. Nothing is loaded into a tray or container without being ticked off on one list or the other.

A trolley of some kind is a boon when you are carting loads of equipment and food around, but because sturdy ones are so bulky (and expensive), you usually have to just hope there will be one available at your destination. You can get sideless

trolleys with wheels that are easy to transport and that can be piled with containers. These do help, although your perilous pile has a horrible habit of sliding off the trolley when it is pushed too hard!

Labelling To ensure that you get the right things in the right trays, *everything* must be labelled for the relevant function. It is as well to get into the habit of labelling every dish even when you are not busy. Otherwise, once you start trying to pack dishes for two or three different orders at the same time, you will be in total chaos.

Getting There
Always leave extra time for the journey, especially if you don't know the route well. You never know where there will be a traffic jam or some unforeseen hold up. We once got caught in a bomb scare in the heart of London and finally were escorted to the venue (nearly an hour late) by a flotilla of police motorbikes! You will also have to allow time for unpacking at the other end and parking your transport somewhere.

Staff
Unless the venue is within easy reach of public transport, you will probably have to arrange transport for your staff. Many waiting and bar staff have their own cars and are happy to act as taxi to others provided you pay them generous petrol money; if not, you are going to have to arrange something else. Even if it is easily accessible, should the party go on late you will have to arrange taxis to get the staff home – don't forget to include this in your costings.

Insurance
Obviously, you will have notified your insurance company that you are using your own car or van for transporting food, but if you should borrow anyone else's car or van, you must make sure that those insurers know as well. If you hire a vehicle, it would be wise just to tell the hire company what you will be using it for.

However, these insurances will only cover you for damage to yourself and passengers, your vehicle and the third party; it will not cover the loss of your food and the crisis created by its failure to turn up! After much negotiation, we did arrange a policy that would at least partially cover us for sending the client and guests out to a restaurant, or getting other food in, or refunds and compensation. Our insurers were, however, extremely unwilling to do it, so if you feel that you want to attempt to cover this, you will have to go and negotiate with your insurers direct.

Food

Planning the food for a function has been covered in the menu planning section on pages 46–69, but the larger the function, the more important it is that a good liaison should exist between the person organizing the equipment and the person organizing the food – even if you are doing both! You would be surprised how easy it is to forget something like baskets for the cheese biscuits because 'equipment' thinks they are a serving dish so 'food' will be dealing with them, while 'food' thinks they are part of the hiring equipment and therefore 'equipment' will be dealing with them.

Liaison is also essential in the planning stages to decide what it will be possible to 'finish off' on site or whether everything needs to go complete, what the heating facilities will be able to manage, etc. It is also important to make sure that the menu planned is as easy as possible to transport and will reach its destination in pristine condition.

Feeding Staff

If the function is large with a lot of staff, you will have to supply a meal for the staff (don't forget to include it in the costings). This does not need to be what the guests are having – the hosts would probably refuse to pay for fillet steaks for their staff, but even if they didn't, most of the staff would not want it. Good cold meats, a choice of cheeses, lots of fresh bread and butter, some soup if the weather is cold, fresh fruit and maybe a gâteau of some kind is usually what goes down best, with possibly a taste of the guests' food if there is any left over at the end. Plenty of coffee and tea, lots of soft drinks and maybe a few cans of beer or the odd bottle of wine will keep away the thirst. Most waiting and bar staff (well, the ones you would want to employ anyhow) do not drink 'on the job', although they might have a glass of wine or a can of beer once the function is finally over.

Quantities

Since you are not operating in a hotel or restaurant situation with a back-up of extra food and

equipment, you must have a deadline for the final number for any function; we normally make this 48 hours in advance. After this, clients cannot reduce their numbers (because by then you will have ordered all the food so you would be losing out), although, obviously, you will do your best to help if they get some last-minute, unexpected acceptances. In fact, we encourage clients to keep us posted on how the acceptances are going right from the start so that we can work ahead. The only thing more annoying than finding that you have just cooked forty portions of Chicken Véronique too many (you can at least try to sell them to someone else) is to have cooked a hundred and fifty portions of Chicken Véronique, only to find that you need another five.

Although you will be supplying food for a set number of guests decided on with the client one or two days ahead, if the meal is a 'sit-down' one, it is wise to allow a few extra portions just in case some last-minute guests show up – I have divided one portion of potted crab between four, but it is not a good idea! You should allow a little extra in your costings to cover these portions. If it is a buffet, there is usually little difficulty in 'stretching' the supplies to cover the extra guests – but do warn your serving staff, if you have them, so that they 'ration' greedier guests until they are sure everyone has been fed, and so the late-comers are not faced by an embarrassingly empty table.

Leftovers

In most cases, fewer people actually turn up to a party than you expect – someone always has flu, a late meeting or a flat battery – so there nearly always are leftovers. In business entertaining situations, especially if the event is being held in an outside location, the hosts are seldom able to do anything with the leftover food, even if they want to, and are only too pleased for the caterer to feed it to the staff (or cats) or just get rid of it. However, at a private party the host may well be hoping to live off the remains for the next week. So, whatever you think the answer will be, it is wise to check.

Drinks

Supplying drinks is one of the caterer's most cherished sidelines because it is a high-profit area that involves very little work. On the other hand, it does require a relatively large investment. Nor can you guarantee that you will get the chance. Many private hosts reckon, quite correctly, that they will be able to buy their drinks from one of the chain wine stores or supermarkets as cheap, if not cheaper, than you will be prepared to sell it to them. You can refuse to provide them with food without also getting the drinks order, but I would not recommend it. Business hosts are usually a better bet. They are not quite so concerned about the costs (it is not their money) and they do not have the time to go trailing around the countryside picking up odd cases of wine and tonic water.

Licences

In the UK today, anyone is entitled to buy wines or spirits by the case and sell them on to a third person for consumption at a private party. If the drinks are to be consumed in a public place or you want to run a cash bar, you will have to apply to your local town hall for a licence – and, needless to say, the regulations vary depending on where you live! Alternatively, you may be able to persuade a local publican to give you an extension to his or her licence – for a certain fee.

Mark-up

The mark-up (or profit) that caterers put on wines and spirits varies from around 30–150 per cent. The latter is nice, if you can get it, but you might do better to decide on a more realistic figure for your particular market; 60–70 per cent seems to be about the norm.

Remember, however, that your mark-up has to cover your time in buying and transporting the drink and your investment, which can be high if you are supplying a mixed spirits bar. Some people also include the cost of supplying bar equipment (glasses, corkscrews, measures, lemons, ice, etc.) and the bar staff in their drink prices; others charge separately for staff and equipment.

Quantities and Sale or Return

It is always difficult to know how much people will drink and the last thing you will want to do is to run out. But almost as bad from your point of view is to be left with large quantities of drink that you have paid for but cannot sell to your client.

One way to get over the quantity problem is to buy and sell your drinks on *sale or return*; this means that whatever is not used you take back from your client and send back to your supplier. Clients will usually be very happy with this arrangement, but you may have more trouble finding a supplier who will agree to it. If you are going to work on sale or return, it is wise to stick only to whole bottles of spirits and soft drinks and whole cases of wine; the only exception to this is 'house' wines, where you can be sure that you will be able to get rid of odd bottles quite quickly.

If you are not able to work on sale or return, you will need to estimate your quantities pretty carefully. It pays to discuss the guests' drinking habits with your clients who presumably will have some idea of what, and how much, their friends or colleagues are likely to drink. However, if you can get no lead from the client, below are a few rough guidelines that might help you.

Spirits and Mixed Bars Consumption varies enormously according to the type of guest. Men normally drink more than women; Americans drink larger measures of spirits than Europeans; young and middle-aged people drink more than the elderly. Weather will affect appetites – more heavy spirit will be drunk in the winter – as will what the guests have been or are doing – if they have been playing tennis or are dancing, they will be thirsty and want lots of soft drinks and beers; if sitting around a conference table, they will want gin and tonic and whisky and soda. However, on average, allow two generous (30 ml/1 fl oz) measures of spirits, with the appropriate mixers, per head and you should be fairly safe.

More difficult to gauge is the type of spirit. There can be a wide variation in the kinds of spirits that different groups like. In very rough terms, the younger groups go mainly for white spirits – vodka, bacardi, gin – whereas older

120

groups, especially if they are at a business party, will stick more with the traditional whiskies and sodas and gins and tonics. If you are using a barman or barlady whom you know, ask them about the current trends in spirits and, particularly, in mixers.

Beers If guests want to drink beer, they usually want to drink it in pretty large quantities. Again, check with the host, but I would allow at least a pint per head on average. If beer or lager is being used merely as a back-up to a spirits bar, an average of a quarter of a pint per head should be ample, unless the weather is very hot, when that should be increased to half a pint.

Punches, Fruit Cups, Cocktails, Mulled Wines, etc. These can be delicious and give a festive air to a party. How much is drunk will depend on how strong they are (or how strong they taste), how sweet they are, and the surrounding temperature. On a cold winter's night, or a blazing June day, you should allow at least two wine glasses of hot mulled wine cocktail or chilled punch per head.

Soft Drinks You should allow plenty of these; more and more people no longer wish to drink during the day, or have to drive home after a party and don't want to be 'over the limit'. It pays to use good-quality soft drinks – fresh orange juice, *not* orange squash – although you do not need a very wide range. We always supply orange juice and mineral water with extras of tomato juice and lemonade on occasions. On average, allow one wine glass per head of soft drinks unless you expect the guests to be very thirsty (lots of dancing or a very hot night), in which case you could increase that to two or three. They are not expensive so you will not have a large outlay.

Wine For most *dinners*, an average of half a bottle of wine per head will be ample; allow one glass of white with the first course plus two of red with the main course. If you are serving two or three wines, you may end up by supplying rather more than this, but it is unlikely that it will get drunk. At *lunch*, people tend to drink less and an average of two glasses per head should be more than enough. This is especially true of business lunches with a high proportion of women where you will find that the most common drink will be mineral water. At receptions and buffets you will normally serve two bottles of white wine to every one of red.

Ports, Brandies, etc. Since these are served at the end of what you hope will have been a good meal, they will be indulged in somewhat more freely than the wines, especially if it is a mainly male group. An average of two 90 ml/3 fl oz glasses of port per head should be more than safe. Brandies (and in far smaller quantities, malt whiskies and liqueurs) tend not to be drunk as freely as port, but the measures will be large, so allow an average of one normal size brandy per head.

121

Corkage

If you do not manage to persuade your clients to buy your drinks but they still want you to serve them, you are quite entitled to charge corkage, or a charge for serving the drink. Some caterers set this purposely high (£5 per bottle of wine) so as to discourage clients from buying elsewhere; this is not a good idea in my opinion. It will depend on how much drink is to be consumed, but for a large party a charge of, say, 50 p per bottle of wine and £1 per bottle of spirits or champagne would probably make you a reasonable profit without overcharging the client. If it is only a small group who will drink relatively little, you should make a separate charge for hiring out the equipment and the staff needed to serve it.

Buying Your Drink

Spirits, soft drinks and beers can be bought wherever you can get the best price – 'cash and carry's do sell them, but they are very little, if any, cheaper than some of the chain stores and large supermarkets. If you have a large party in the offing, it is worth doing a little research on the 'special offers' available. For 'classier' parties, you may want to buy well-known brand names; for informal parties or where the spirits are to be used in mixed drinks, you will do very well with the cheaper but less-known brands.

Wines are a rather different matter as the selection is so enormous and the quality so variable. Again, you can get very good bargains in chain stores or supermarkets, but you may not get much in the way of advice. Own-label brands in supermarket chains are usually excellent, but clients, although happy to drink them at home, may feel it rather 'infra-dig' to serve them at a party. What's more, they may resent you putting your mark-up on a wine they buy every week with their Saturday shopping!

The best idea is to set up a relationship with a wine merchant, preferably one who will supply you at wholesale rates. You will, of course, be restricted to the wines the merchant imports, but you will, hopefully, be able to rely on him or her for good advice as to what you should serve with what, at which price, and how you should treat it.

Once you are established as a caterer, you will no doubt have wine suppliers hammering on your door, but to start with you may have to go out and find them. The competition is keen in the wine trade, so if you ring up a few suppliers (out of the Yellow Pages), I am sure you will find them keen to talk and do business with you in the hope that you are going to be successful and turn into an excellent client.

Transporting Drinks

Spirits and soft drinks, although bulky, are no trouble to transport, but wines are a different matter. If you are going to serve really good wines, you have to arrange to have them delivered weeks or even months before they are needed, or risk spoiling the wine and ruining the function. This is feasible if the party is to be in a private house or office, but more often than not it is being held in a location where you would not want to leave a cheese sandwich overnight, let alone valuable wines for several months. Consultation with the client is obviously necessary, but the simplest answer is to find wines that, although good, are not of such quality or age as to require a long period to settle. Similarly, we try to serve late-bottled ports that are not heavily sedimented.

Serving Drinks

Fast and efficient bar service does a lot to make a party run smoothly, especially if the drinks are complicated. Filling trays with drinks ready to be offered to the guests as they arrive avoids endless queues at bars. If you are serving wine or champagne and soft drinks, this is easy; if you are serving mixed drinks, you will need to put a selection on a tray.

You do not need fully trained butlers to serve your wine, but you do need staff who will treat it with reasonable respect; no wine, no matter what its price, improves with shaking. Corks should always be pulled with care and the tops of the bottles wiped. White wine, especially if it is cheap, should be served really well chilled; red wine is best 'chambré' or just above a reasonably warm room temperature. Most red wines benefit by being opened well in advance and allowed to 'breathe', but a few are better opened just before they are needed. If you don't know from experience how to handle the wine you are serving, ask your wine merchant or supplier who will normally be able to advise you.

Chilling large quantities of white wine or champagne, or even of beer or soft drinks, is often a problem. The best solution is a large refrigerator or wine cooler at your home base where the wine can be stored in the boxes 24 hours in advance. It is then so thoroughly chilled that, provided it is kept in the boxes, it will remain really cool for four to five hours even on a relatively hot day. The trouble with using your refrigerator is that, if you are organizing a large party, your refrigerator space will no doubt already be bulging with food! If so, you will have no option but baths and quantities of ice on site. Baths can be hired from most hire companies (do ensure you get ones that don't leak!) and ice can be bought in bulk from specialist ice merchants if you cannot cope with making enough yourself.

If you are serving a really 'up-market' dinner, it would be wise to employ fully-trained butlers or bar staff (if you can) just to serve the drinks. At more informal 'sit-down' parties, guests are normally very happy to have the first glass poured for them and then for the bottles to be left on the table for them to help themselves. Slightly more informal still is just to leave bottles on each table and allow the guests to help themselves.

At receptions, the most practical solution is to give each guest a full glass as they arrive and then for waiting or bar staff to circulate with bottles refilling glasses. Inevitably, guests 'lose' glasses, so you will need plenty in reserve.

Bar Equipment

Even if you are only serving wine, you will need a good selection of corkscrews; more complicated drinks will require more complicated equipment. Opposite is a checklist that should help. I am giving the most basic names for glasses; hire companies have their own jargon, but since companies differ, so does their jargon.

Glasses

Large tumblers or water glasses

Small tumblers or spirits glasses

½ pint or pint glasses or tankards (for beer)

Red wine glasses (usually 250 ml/8 fl oz)

White wine glasses (usually 175 ml/6 fl oz)

Champagne flutes (most people use tulip-shaped white wine glasses)

Sherry or port glasses

Brandy balloons

Liqueur glasses

Other Equipment

Corkscrews – plenty that are easy to use

Can and bottle openers

Champagne cork 'easers'

Jugs for water and soft drinks

Ice buckets and spoons

Plenty of ice, especially if it is hot

Lemons (with plates and knives for slicing)

Cocktail sticks for spearing cherries etc.

Optics or spirit measures – these are only really necessary if you are running a cash bar or if you are trying to restrict the amount of drink used

'Druggett' or protective carpeting for laying down behind a bar or bar table to protect the floor

Napkins, paper and linen, for bar staff

Tablecloths and pins or drawing pins for fastening them

Tea towels – allow plenty for polishing glasses

Wiping-up cloths and lots of rubbish bags

Trays

Ashtrays

Measuring jug for punches and cocktail shakers for cocktails

Staff

No matter how wonderful your food or your organization may be, the success of your function will, to a large extent, depend on your staff. Good waiting staff and butlers will make the most complicated event run smoothly; bad ones will turn the simplest one into chaos. Moreover, it is the staff who are at the sharp end once the party starts – they are the ones who make contact with the guests, not you. So your reputation for friendliness and efficiency depends entirely upon them. All of which makes it vital that you find, and keep, really good ones.

You may also need 'kitchen staff' at a big function to help organize matters backstage. They need to be efficient, but since they are not on 'public view', that is really all they do need to be – although a sunny temperament is a boon in the overheated frenzy that precedes a large function.

Formal banquets and dinners may also call for toastmasters and commissionaires. Toastmasters are usually to be found through agencies; commissionaires can be tracked down through the Corps of Commissionaires or recommended by a toastmaster. Fees will need to be negotiated with them direct.

Finding Staff

In the early days, many caterers call on friends and relatives to don the black and white gear, and there is nothing wrong with this at all. For many more informal functions, out of work actors, students and a whole range of secretaries and computer programmers looking to make a little extra money are perfect. The work is not usually very skilled or complicated, so as long as they are friendly, helpful and not totally thick, they will get along fine.

However, once you move into more formal entertaining and larger functions, it will pay you to find some 'proper' trained waiting staff. Bar staff are not so important, as good waiters or waitresses can usually also serve behind the bar and deal with drinks. An efficient and experienced 'pack' of waiters or waitresses will, if they have to, lay up the tables for a five-course banquet for two hundred in half an hour, will work like slaves to get the meal out on time and as it should be served, and will deal with all the little crises and requests that pepper any large function without batting an eyelid – or bothering you. The problem is how to find them.

Fortunately, they really do work in 'packs', so if you can get yourself plumbed into a group, you will find that they will have enough friends and relations to fulfil almost all your needs. Personal recommendation is, as always, the best way. If you have any friends in the catering business, try them; try local pubs – their part-time help might quite likely be interested in waiting work; or follow up any other leads that look hopeful. Good 'packs' do not register with agencies – they do not need to – so it will just be a question of following leads until you find one. Agencies will provide you with staff if you are desperate, but it is an expensive way of doing it and you are always a little nervous as to what you will get sent.

Just as a good waiter or waitress or butler can make your evening, so a bad one can ruin it. Staff who drink, are dirty, careless or rude are a copper-bottomed disaster area and must be got rid of as soon as possible. If you are using people you do not know personally, keep an eagle eye on them to make sure that they are okay; it would be better to send them home and be short-staffed rather than risk them being rude to or offending guests or the host either by word or deed.

Booking

Once you have established your lines of communication, give your staff as much notice as possible both of bookings and cancellations. You (or your client) will also have to be responsible for paying them if they are cancelled at such short notice that they cannot get another job.

Uniforms

When you book your staff, make sure that both they and you know what they are going to wear. Unless it is a very run-of-the-mill function, it is worth checking with your client whether they want the staff to be formally dressed (few will go so far as to insist on caps these days) or not. Most professional staff prefer to work in 'uniform' – usually a white jacket and black trousers for the men; a white blouse, black skirt and white pinny for the women – and from your point of view you do at least have some control over what they look like. We have employed 'informal' waitresses in the past who have appeared wearing black leather mini skirts and scarlet tights and with their hair all frizzed! If it is to be an 'informal' party, it would still be wise to discuss the degree of 'informality' with the staff.

Timing

Make sure that you give the staff plenty of time to get organized, especially if it is to be a big job. Discuss the job with them when you book them; it is always better to be safe than sorry, so even if

you have to pay them a bit extra, it would be wise to have them there an hour earlier. A small party should only take 30–45 minutes to set up, but a big function could take 2–3 hours.

Numbers

You should also discuss the number of staff needed for any function, no matter how small, with the staff you are booking to do it – both because they probably have a great deal more experience than you, and because they are the ones who are actually going to have to do the work. What is more, if you take their advice and they suggest too few, they are the ones who will have to live with the extra workload – and they will not be able to blame you for overworking them. If they advise too many, then you will know for the next time and temper their suggestions accordingly. However, if you find yourself having to make the decision, here are a few pointers.

For a '*sit-down meal*', one waitress or waiter should be able to deal with ten place settings or covers, provided she or he does not have to dispense wine as well. One butler or bar person serving wines should be able to deal with around thirty covers.

Buffet parties are less rigid as the number of staff you will need will depend on the complexity of the food, whether you want the guests to help themselves or be helped, and how much clearing up there will be. On average, one waiter or waitress should be able to deal with around twenty guests.

For *cocktail parties and stand-up receptions*, you will need one person for food and one person for drinks for approximately every thirty guests, although as the numbers increase, the staff will reduce proportionally. Again the staffing level will depend on the complexity of the drinks.

One problem that can occur when clients are trying to restrict the cost is that they will suggest that their daughters, sons, secretaries, wives, boyfriends, girlfriends, etc. 'help' the waiting staff so you do not need to employ so many. This can work, but more often than not the daughters or whatever will be inexperienced and only too easily distracted into chatting to the other guests, thus leaving the poor waiters or waitresses to battle with far too heavy a workload. This is not only most unfair to the professional staff, but it reflects badly on you as, no matter how hard your waiters and waitresses work, the service will probably be slow and patchy. Unless you know the daughters, secretaries, etc. really well and can be sure that they genuinely will help efficiently, you should be firm with your clients and insist on the right number of professional staff.

Fees/Wages

Staff charges vary enormously depending on where you are working, so you will have to agree a fee with them for each job when you book them. There is normally a standard fee for a lunch, cocktail party or evening function up until a certain time. After that, they would expect to be paid overtime at an agreed rate until the end of the function. Weekend and bank holiday work should, of course, also be paid at overtime rates.

As waiting work is not very well paid, most of your waiting and bar staff will want to be paid in cash. Provided that their total earnings from all sources are below the current minimum earning limit, that they sign the relevant form (P46) to that effect, and that what you pay them does not exceed the minimum earning limit, there is no reason for you not to pay them in cash without filing any other returns. However, if their earnings exceed these limits, then you have the legal responsibility of ensuring that they pay income tax on any earnings they receive from you. You will have to discuss with the individuals how they want their money dealt with, but you may find that if they are going to have to pay tax on it, waiting staff will ask for higher wages in order to leave them with the same net amount. You would also be wise to discuss the situation with your local Inland Revenue office to make sure you are quite clear on what your duties and responsibilities are. It is you, as the employer, who will be liable for any of your staff's unpaid tax, so you need to be very careful how you deal with the matter and not be tempted to forget about this.

Tips

The fee you agree will be what your staff will expect to get paid for the night. If you feel that they have worked particularly hard or the client offers to pay a tip, then, obviously, no one is going to refuse it. However, that is a bonus and should be treated as such – it should not be considered as part of the fee for the job.

Transport

Most staff will make their own way to a job on public transport and do not expect to be reimbursed unless the job is particularly far away and expensive to get to. If it is, they may also ask to be paid for at least some of their travelling time. However, they will expect, quite rightly, to be got home by car or minicab after a late party. They will also expect you to arrange transport if the job is a long way away. As mentioned on page 118, you can often arrange for one waiter or waitress with a car to take three or four others if you pay petrol money.

Feeding and Watering

Like anyone else, waiting staff work better if you treat them right. If it is going to be a long job, you must plan in time for them to have a rest and some refreshment.

A pot of tea or coffee fairly soon on arrival is always welcome, especially if everyone has come a long way. The function should then be set up – tables laid, wine opened, etc. Once the dining hall is ready, everyone (including you) should be able to sit down and have something to eat before getting changed. Some waiting staff will already have eaten or prefer not to eat before a job, but even if they are not going to eat, you should still give them the time to sit down for a rest. Apart from anything else, it gives you a chance to plan how the meal is to be served and answer any queries they may have. After the meal they will probably all be anxious to get home as soon as possible, but it is nice to at least offer a drink and a taste of what the guests had – assuming there is any left! If there is any transportable food (cheese, etc.) over, which is not wanted by the host or needed for anything else, the staff might like to take some home. If you are thinking of making the offer, remember to put a roll of cling film in with your hiring equipment in which to wrap everyone's titbits.

Organizing and Instructing Staff

For a small or relatively simple meal, there will not be a lot of instruction – merely to say whether it is to be silver service (served from the platter onto the guest's plate by the waiter or waitress), butler service (served by the guests onto their own plate from a platter held by the waiter or waitress) or a buffet. The waiting staff should, however, know what the menu is and roughly what went into it in case they get asked any questions about food allergies. They should also know about any special preferences, likes or dislikes of hosts or guests that you know about. Most experienced staff will ask the relevant questions themselves, but it does no harm to double check.

For your own sake, you should tell them (if it is not already perfectly obvious) how you would like the dishes served and how you would like the clearing up done. For a small function, the waiting staff would normally expect to have to wash up, whereas with a large one that is not usually feasible and you will need extra staff for this.

Large Functions At a large affair the whole thing becomes more complicated.

1 You will need to allocate particular duties to each member of staff – cloakroom attendant, service of drinks, food service, etc.

2 You will need to allocate 'stations' to the serving staff. This means deciding which waiters or waitresses are going to serve which tables. Although one person will deal with ten covers, a lot like to work in pairs, thus covering twenty people or (usually) two tables between them.

3 If the function is big enough, you will need to decide from which area of the 'servery' each waiter or waitress (or pair of them) are to collect their food and where they are to dispose of their 'dirties'.

4 Wine-waiting staff should also be allocated tables and know where to get their supplies and dispose of their empties – they will usually want to set this up and organize it between themselves, but you must make sure that it is done.

5 All the staff must know what the menu is, in what order and how each dish should be served, and, roughly, what has gone into it. They also need to know at what point condiments, butter, bread and finished glasses should be cleared.

6 All the staff must know what the schedule and programme is for the evening, so that some sort of timetable is kept to.

7 Everyone must know where to find you or whoever is in charge of running the function in case of queries.

For a large and complicated function, it would pay you to make big posters with all this information on them and stick them up in the servery area so that everyone can refer to them.

Serving Banquets If you are working with experienced staff, they will guide you on the finer points of serving a banquet, but in case they cannot, here are a few rules that you should remember.

1 The 'top' table with the host and chief guests on it should always be served first; the lady on the right of the host being the first person on that table to be served. As soon as she has been served, a start can be made on the other tables.

2 Plates should be laid in front of everyone before the service of food starts. It speeds the operation

up if all the plates have been counted into the hot cupboard in piles of the relevant number for each table.

3 Food should always be served from the left; dirty plates must be removed from the right.

4 The wines appropriate to each course should be served *immediately* after the food.

5 No table should be cleared until everyone has finished. However, sticking rigidly to this rule can slow down service somewhat, so it is acceptable only to wait until everyone on a particular table has finished before that table is cleared. However, no table should be cleared before the 'top table'.

6 Cruets, bread and butter can be removed after the main course, although they can also be cleared earlier or left to the end if they are to be needed later in the meal – salt to use with celery and cheese, for example.

7 Ashtrays need only be put on the table with the coffee, unless specifically asked for earlier.

Equipment

Many waiting staff always carry their own serving spoons and forks and their own serving cloths – to protect their hands from what you hope will be your very hot dishes! However, you should always provide at least two sets of servers (a large spoon and fork) for each staff, and at least one napkin or suitably respectable cloth for carrying the dishes so you are sure they will be well equipped.

Setting up 'Back Stage'

If you want a function to run smoothly, you must be organized behind the scenes; there is no way that the serving staff can get the food out quickly and hot unless you can supply it to them that way. The facilities you will be working with will vary enormously from location to location. In some, you may have a complete catering kitchen; in others, there may be nothing. The worst I have ever had to contend with was a seven-course dinner for one hundred and fifty guests where the dining hall was along a two-hundred-yard corridor and up a spiral staircase from the only room we had to work in. This was equipped only with the buffet tables and hot cupboards that we had brought in. The only running water was from one cold tap several yards down another corridor from the 'servery'.

You will need to plan your 'back-stage' area carefully to allow you to do any finishing off and decoration needed, to lay out the dishes for the waiting staff to collect, and to give you space to stack and clear the dirties. This takes longer and is more work than you think, so remember to allow time in your planning and do allow in your costings for a couple of helpers to aid and assist you so the food is ready on time.

Running the Function

No matter how small the function, someone has to be in charge of it. When it is merely a dinner for six served by one waiter or waitress, then he or she effectively runs it in conjunction with the host. When you are dealing with a large party, it is vital that you, as caterer, are there throughout to refer to as a troubleshooter and representative of your own organization. Incidentally, always carry a good stock of visiting cards or small promotional cards; if the event is successful, you are bound to get at least one person ask you for a card with a mind to future parties, so this is the ideal opportunity to get more business

You should plan so that you have no specific jobs to do yourself. Your role is as a co-ordinator, and if you are busy laying out plates of smoked salmon, you will not be available to answer queries about the table set up, what has happened to the cloakroom tickets and pins, where can the red wine best be put to chambré, and did the host order a corsage for the chief lady, and if so where is it. You also need to be free to lend a hand in any area that is running behind schedule, and you must be available to cast an eye over every finished product, be it the laid-up table or plate of smoked salmon, to make sure it is exactly as you want it as your reputation will suffer if something is not up to scratch.

Once the function has started, you need to be unobtrusively available for anyone who may want you. You should let the host (or his minion if more appropriate) know that you are there in charge and that any queries can be referred to you. All staff, similarly, should know where to find you in case of problems. When anyone doesn't want you, just 'wander', keeping an eye on what is happening and an eye out for anything that may have been overlooked – brimming ashtrays, empty glasses, empty butter dishes, and so on. Whatever you do, however, you must discreetly fade into the background, so that no guest is aware of your presence.

Incidentally, you need to dress fairly carefully. Choose something quiet but smart that will make it quite clear that you are not one of the serving staff, but not one of the guests either. Whatever it is, it must not show stains as you will inevitably get part of the dinner thrown over you at some point during the event, and it should be *comfortable* – especially in the shoe department!

Finally, you should be available at the end in case people want to tell you what a wonderful time they have had. If the party has been a success, both guests and host may want to congratulate the caterer and will be upset if they do not get the chance to do this.

Importance of Organization

It must by now be clear that the one thing that can make a function stand or fall is organization. Functions need to be planned as military campaigns, and as long as they are treated with military thoroughness, they will run smoothly.

Lists are vital – you cannot have too many of them or check them often enough. When I sit down to organize a major event, be it a lunch, dinner or a buffet, I effectively open a separate file for each aspect of the function into which go lists of everything that needs to be done in that particular area. *Everything* gets written down and filed into that file; *every* arrangement with subcontractors gets discussed with them,

confirmed in writing and reconfirmed by telephone a couple of days before the event. Hiring lists are cross-checked with the kitchens; food lists with the hiring department. Instructions are written out for staff, delivery people and anyone else working on site, as the very business of telling someone else what has to be done may remind you of a detail you had forgotten.

All this may seem very laborious, but it is the *only* way to ensure that everything will go 'right on the night'. Just one badly checked list that leaves you with lemon for the smoked salmon but no smoked salmon, or candelabras but no candles, will teach you the value of being pernickety.

Disasters

No matter how well prepared and organized you are, disasters will happen – you just hope they don't happen too often! I could fill half this book with crises that have faced caterers – ourselves included – but somehow we all survive. Every disaster is different so there are no ground rules as to how to cope – except to stay calm and employ a bit of lateral thinking. There is nearly always a way round the problem if you can but find it. If you are employing experienced staff, ask their advice – they have probably faced more catering crises than you can ever fear to. If necessary (especially if it is a disaster that is not really of your making), take the host into your confidence – after all, if the guests do not know what was meant to be happening, they will not know that things have changed!

To encourage – or depress – you, I will briefly quote a very few of the crises that we and others have faced over the years.

Arriving at the location (80 miles from home base) with only half the right quantity of fish – but not discovering until a third of the guests had been served. The waitresses were sent out to bring the plates back with the excuse that we had just discovered that the fish was not hot enough. When they got their plates back, their fish was hot, but it had shrunk.

Going to serve a champagne sorbet at an extremely smart lunch only to find that the freezer had packed in at some point and that the sorbet was liquid. It was served – very successfully – in champagne glasses as a post-prandial 'cocktail'.

Running out of Pimms two-thirds of the way through a very boozy city party on a Sunday afternoon when there were no pubs or shops open. We made a cocktail of red wine and tonic water (both back-up drinks) with masses of fruit in the jugs and a napkin wrapped well round – most guests never even noticed.

Blowing up the ring main when a quarter of the way through cooking the vegetables for a dinner for a hundred and fifty people – we ditched the potatoes and served the beans, 'blanched', on a separate plate as a salad.

Dropping one complete container of coffee cups down the lift shaft at a livery hall lunch. Fortunately, the guests were at separate tables; one half just had to wait for their coffee until the other half had finished!

Running out of ready-mulled wine on a particularly cold December evening. We put some of the dinner wine with some spices and some of the dinner orange juice in the microwave – it tasted surprisingly good!

Arranging a photographer for an international conference dinner the night before the guests dispersed all over the world and the photographer's flash synchronization unit failing to work – only we did not discover that it hadn't worked until two days later. We had a special picture of the house (fortunately, a stately home!) taken and framed for the delegates.

Arriving at a wedding *very* late. In a panic to get the drinks out to the bride and guests, tripping over a rug and throwing twenty glasses of champagne at her feet. Finally, staggering as far as the cake-cutting ceremony only to have all four tiers topple over in a heap just as the bride and groom were about to cut it!

Ancillary Services

As main organizer of a large event, you may get the chance to supply a wide range of services to your clients other than just feeding them. Hire of location, equipment and drink have already been mentioned, but if you are already providing these, there is no reason why you should not also provide some of the following or anything else that might add to the success of the party.

Flowers or other decorations

Lighting – internal or external

Marquees

Portable loos

Entertainment, musical or otherwise

Costumes for staff or hosts – or guests!

Gifts

Menus, invitations, place cards and table plans

Transport

Photographers

Fancy or wedding cakes

Many hosts will prefer to organize these things themselves, but some, business hosts in particular, are only too pleased to have someone else take the whole responsibility of organizing their party off their shoulders. If you are going to provide ancillary services of this kind, you should keep a well-stocked file of contacts and be constantly on the look out for new services you could offer. You do, however, need to be careful; paper does not refuse ink and not every service that looks wonderful in a brochure will be so wonderful in the flesh. If possible, try to check out any service that you are thinking of using – ask for references if you cannot see it in action. Once you have found a good service or supplier, stick with them – you will soon build up a relationship with them that will make the whole business of working together so much easier.

Charging

How you charge for arranging these extra services is up to you. Some caterers take a commission from the subcontractor for giving them the work; some charge the client a flat rate for arranging extra services no matter what the latter may cost; others charge a percentage to the client on top of the subcontractor's fee.

If a commission is taken from the subcontractor, the latter can bill the client direct; you merely claim your commission from the subcontractor after the job. My personal objections to this system are that most clients would rather get one bill for the whole job from the caterer than lots of small ones from everyone involved. But, more important, the commission system may put you under a certain amount of pressure to use that subcontractor because you know he or she will pay you a fee, whereas another, who might be more suitable for the job in hand, would not.

If you charge a flat rate to clients for arranging things for them, you will be under no pressure to use any but the musician or florist best suited to that particular function. If you want to escape the financial burden of paying the musician or florist, you can also get them to bill the client direct for their work and you will then bill him or her for your fee.

The third alternative is for you to engage the musician or florist at a fee agreed between you and them, for you to pay them, and for you then to recover the money from your client plus whatever percentage you care to add for having arranged the service. This way you are under no pressure to use any but the best person for the job, you have total control of what they do as you are paying their bill, and you will be able to add whatever handling fee you think is reasonable – somewhere between 10 and 25 per cent, depending on the work involved, seems to be about normal. The disadvantage, of course, is that you may have to pay your musicians or florists before you get paid by your client – and in the, hopefully, remote possibility of your client not paying at all, you would still be liable for all your subcontractors' charges.

Weddings

Weddings are like every other function in all respects but two: they often happen on sunny Saturday afternoons in June; and because of the importance of the occasion to the hosts (usually the bride's parents) and their inexperience in organizing such affairs, the caterer bears an even heavier responsibility than usual for ensuring that all goes well. Some people find this too much like hard work and prefer to stick with less traumatic business functions; others find it very rewarding, fun – and lucrative! However, to do weddings well, you do have to be prepared to act father confessor to the harassed mother, deal with obstreperous younger brothers, and, if necessary, take affairs into your own hands. At one wedding we did some years ago, I found myself racing around the suburbs of north London half an hour before the guests arrived trying to find an open wine merchant because the wine that the bridegroom had sworn he was having delivered hadn't turned up. It finally emerged that he had told the wine merchant to deliver it on the wrong Saturday!

None the less, you can make a very good business of doing nothing but weddings and christenings – with the occasional funeral thrown in. Just develop the knack of putting the hassled parents at their ease and giving them confidence in your ability to make the event enjoyable (even if they cannot stand their prospective son-in-law) without bankrupting them in the process. They will be singing your praises if the event goes off well and may recommend you to their friends.

Ancillary Services
Good contacts with all the ancillary services that seem to be required to get people married will also help. You will make your clients' lives much easier if you can recommend – or even organize – good florists, cake makers, printers, marquee hirers, limousine services, photographers, string quartets – even dressmakers and travel agents – as well as providing a location, food and drink. Good contacts with other wedding suppliers could bring you more business than you take to them!

Food

Weddings often happen at the most awkward of times – 2 o'clock in the afternoon – so you need to be imaginative about your menus. Soggy egg canapés, greasy sausage rolls and warm champagne will do little for your reputation. Light but interesting food is what you need for mid-afternoon, with a good balance between sweet and savoury. Lunches (wedding breakfasts) and evening receptions are much easier to cater for and, for food purposes, can be treated like ordinary functions.

Drinks

Because cost is usually a prime consideration at a wedding, many people prefer to buy their own drink as they believe it will be cheaper. There is not a lot you can do about this – unless you can find some really good, cheap suppliers, but do not forget to charge corkage for serving it. If you do have chilling facilities at your home base, it would pay you to offer to chill their wine (for a small fee) rather than have to battle with leaking bath tubs and dripping ice.

Equipment

You will, of course, need the usual range of hiring equipment, but below are extras that should not be forgotten:

An extra round of glasses for the toasts (by that time everyone will have lost the ones they started without)

A smart wedding cake knife for the bride and groom to cut the first slice and plenty of long, sharp knives for the waiting staff to cut up the rest of the cake for the guests to sample

Serving dishes for the cake to be circulated on

Lots of extra white napkins (paper) for eating the cake or wrapping up to take with them

A few chairs strategically placed for elderly aunts and anyone who may be overcome by the whole affair and need to sit down

A well-filled function box – especially aspirins, safety pins and sewing kit

Particularly friendly and helpful staff.

RUNNING A BUSINESS

Cooking at Home or in Outside Premises

As you will have realised by now, there is much more to running a catering business than just cooking, so here is a run down of some of the preparations and decisions you will have to make before you start and the various factors involved in keeping it going.

Where you cook your food is going to dramatically affect the investment that you will need to get you off the ground. Provided you have the space (and agreement from other members of the household), it is cheaper and safer to start from home – this way you will have invested relatively little in the venture should it turn out to be a total flop. There are also very real economic advantages to working from home.

You will not be paying rent or mortgage charges.

The extra electricity, gas and telephone charges that your business will use will be marginal and you will save extra standing charges.

You will be able to use all your home cooking equipment rather than having to buy new.

You will be able to charge a proportion of your rates and services accounts against the profits of your business – although care should be taken here as any part of your house that is used for business purposes becomes liable for capital gains tax should you decide to sell it.

In other words, your overheads will be negligible. The obvious virtues of this state of affairs can lead to a rather false assessment of how profitable a catering business can be. After all, any business that has no overheads cannot really fail to make money. The real proof of the pudding is whether the business would still be making money if it were paying rent, rates, service charges and all the other hidden costs of keeping up a property. To work these out, make out a chart using the sample analysis sheet on page 148 as a guide.

If you are investing your own money in buying your new premises, do not forget to include a return on your invested capital in your calculations. When you have added in every possible cost you can think of, allow a reasonable 'contingency sum' as no matter how hard you try you are guaranteed to overlook something. *Then* compare the cost of running your operation with what you think you could bring in.

On the other hand, running your catering business from your own kitchen, especially if it is not very large, is going to cause considerable disruption. How much disruption will depend on how much and what sort of catering you do. Suppliers of pâtés to pubs, for example, can probably do their cooking during the day when the other members of the household are at school or at work and have got the whole lot out of the way by the time the kitchen is needed for supper. A successful supplier of cocktail or dinner parties may be hard pushed to be so organized. I suppose that the ideal would be to have a house large enough to accommodate two kitchens – but those are few and far between! Even if you do start in your own kitchen, if you are successful, the time will probably come when you have to move out into something larger and better designed to allow you to expand.

If your home really cannot be persuaded to accommodate you, then you will have to go elsewhere. You may be able to find a kitchen, either private or commercial, that you can rent part of, or rent time in. These are not easy to come by, but it is certainly worth looking around. It would also be worth approaching the owners of food shops who may have large, unused basement areas. I know several caterers who have started in the basement of a delicatessen, supplying the shop with many of its needs but cooking for outsiders at the same time. You may have to invest in a certain amount of equipment, but the rent should be relatively low (see pages 21–6 for suggestions on equipment).

If none of these possibilities appeals, you may decide to go ahead and rent or buy a full-time catering kitchen, but be warned, it will not be cheap. Depending on where you are, however, buying premises could be a perfectly respectable property investment. Such a venture should really only be embarked on if you have a sizeable amount of capital to invest in doing up the building and equipping it (even second-hand equipment will be costly), and sufficient backing to see you through a couple of years of losing money while you build the business to the point where it can support its overheads. If you decide to rent rather than buy, you need even more backing to see you through the first few years as a substantial rental charge will be added to those overheads.

Wherever you decide to cater, your first consideration must be whether the premises will comply with the relevant rules and regulations.

Working Conditions

You cannot sell cooked food to the public without the risk of being closed down unless you have been passed by the Department of Environmental Health. This can be located through your local council offices and an officer will need to inspect the kitchen in which you want to cook. Because the department is attempting to cover an enormous range of establishments, some of the regulations may seem rather irrelevant, but on the whole the officers are helpful and they are prepared to be reasonably flexible with small businesses. However, you would be wise to enlist their help and advice over a cup of coffee and a home-made biscuit rather than objecting to the recommendations! If you are lucky, they may require you only to make very minor changes (repainting chipped surfaces, etc.), but you should be aware that they could insist on quite major and expensive alterations. You can start your business without being inspected, but you risk being closed down out of hand (with all the accompanying loss of business and damage to your reputation) if the authorities discover what you are doing and do not pass your kitchen as fit to work in. As soon as you start to get custom, you can be sure that noise of it will reach those authorities.

Planning Permission

If you are going to cook at home and propose to do so in a large way or for any length of time, you could hit problems with the planning authorities. Regulations in each area are different, but commercial use of residential property is normally frowned upon. As long as you are discreet about your activities, you will probably be fine, but if you put the neighbours' backs up by parking your delivery vans in their drive or stinking them out with the smell of frying sausages, they could complain to the council who would then come to investigate. If the council thought your business was serious, they could refuse you permission to use your home for it. Check before you start what their attitude would be – just in case.

If you find yourself working in outside premises, you will need to check with the local council that that particular building has planning permission for commercial catering. As long as it is already being used as a shop or something similar, and the neighbours do not object, the permission is not hard to get.

There should be no other objections that you have to deal with, but it would be wise to check with your solicitor that what you are planning to do in no way infringes any law or by-law.

Insurance

The next thing to deal with is insurance. You will need to make sure if you are cooking at home that your household insurers are aware of what you are going to be doing. Otherwise, if you burn your kitchen down, they may refuse to pay on the grounds that they have not been notified that you are using it commercially. If you are working in outside premises, then obviously they will have to be insured. You will also need to insure your equipment and your stock – the loss of a freezer full of food could make a nasty hole in a month's profits. Incidentally, your stock should include your recipe books, diaries, etc., the disappearance of any of which could cause you substantial losses.

In addition, you must have a public liability insurance in case you damage a member of the public – especially by poisoning! Your broker or an insurance company will advise you on exact

figures, but make sure that you have generous cover – eighty people suing you for several thousand pounds each because you had given them all a severe bout of food poisoning adds up to a vast sum of money. Don't forget that as long as you are not a limited company, you would remain personally liable for such a claim. In other words, you might be forced to sell house and home to pay for it.

If you are going to employ anyone, you will need employer's liability insurance and it would be wise, while you are at it, to insure yourself against accidents at work; and to insure yourself against losing your driving licence if you intend to deliver your food.

Insurance is important, so make sure you are covered – to help you here is an insurance checklist.

1 The premises in which you work, be they home or independent.
2 The equipment you use, including your diaries, recipe books, etc.
3 Your stocks – food, wine, etc.
4 Employer's liability if you employ anyone.
5 Public liability (and this must be high) in case you injure any member of the public – normally by food poisoning. If you employ anyone, you must also have third party coverage for them.
6 Insurance for yourself and anyone you employ against injury or accident.
7 Motor insurance for your delivery vehicle or vehicles.
8 Insurance of the contents of your delivery vehicles (see page 118).
9 Insurance against losing your driving licence if you do your own deliveries.

Finance, Backing and Cash Flow

Starting any business obviously requires some capital – the amount needed depends on whether you are working from home or in separate premises. But even if you are using your own kitchen and already have enough equipment, you will still need some 'start up' capital for brochures, literature and marketing as well as a cushion of money or borrowing power to cover your cash flow needs.

Unless you only accept contract work (see page 145), you are bound to go through periods, often seasonal, when there is very little work as well as

periods when you are run off your feet. The trouble is that your overheads have to be paid whether or not you are doing any business. As long as you are cooking from home, this may not matter too much as your real overheads (regardless of how you may calculate them for the purpose of assessing whether or not you are making a profit) are very low; once you move into separate premises, it becomes a great deal more important.

What is more, you will have to pay for most of your raw materials (food, drink, etc.) very soon after you buy them. Few food shops give more than a week's credit – a month at the outside if you are a regular customer – and many none at all. You will also have to pay your staff, both casual and regular, as soon as they have done their work for you, but you may not get paid by your client for several weeks – and sometimes months – after the job. You need some back-up to bridge the gap.

Obviously, if you have the money yourself or you have a friend or relative who is prepared to 'invest' in you, you will not have a problem. If you don't, then you will have to arrange finance elsewhere. It is certainly worth finding out what business schemes may be available in your area – most town halls will point you in the right direction. Some can work well, although some take so long to arrange and are so tied up with restrictions that you may think them not worth the effort. Your alternative is to go to your High Street bank and arrange borrowing terms.

The advantage of borrowing money from a bank is that you can usually do it on an overdraft basis which means that you only pay interest on the money borrowed during the time you need it – you do not have to borrow a fixed amount for a fixed period at a fixed rate of interest. Banks on the whole (especially the smaller, local branches) are reasonably sympathetic to small businesses with cash-flow problems. They will, of course, ask you to guarantee the overdraft personally (so that if your business does go down the tubes, they are entitled to reclaim the money from you personally), but they will grant quite generous temporary overdrafts, provided they can see what they call 'movement' in the account. In other words, they don't mind you being £5,000 overdrawn this month as long as you are likely to be £5,000 in credit next month or the month after. This should be enough to tide you over a sticky patch. However, bank interest rates are usually fairly high so it is not a service you want to avail yourself of more often than you can help.

When you go to see the bank manager, especially for the first time, you should be as organized and business-like as you can. Take along any printed literature or designs you may have, details of costings, cash flow, possible future work, etc., and make them all as neat and tidy as possible, preferably typed. Attractive and vibrant people with wonderful ideas are all very well, but banks only lend when they are sure that their loans are safe, so you need to impress them with your efficiency as well as your charm.

Incidentally, the bank manager may ask you do a 'cash-flow forecast' – in other words, what money you expect to get in against what you will have to pay out. The latter is usually quite easy, but unless you do a lot of contract work, the former will be almost impossible. Most banks understand this but be warned. The best way to avoid overdrafts is, of course, to be permanently busy! Failing that, you need to lay hands on the money that you do earn as quickly as possible.

Getting Money In

Deposits There is much to be said for taking a deposit from your clients. It guarantees that they won't change their minds at the last minute and go elsewhere – or even if they do, that you will not be out of pocket. It gives you some money 'up front' with which to buy the food and drink for the party. It ensures that even if they fail to pay your bill afterwards you will not be totally out of pocket. Certainly, if you are in any way dubious about the financial probity of your client, a deposit would be a good idea. Similarly, if you are in business in quite a small way and the function you are organizing is going to involve a large investment on your part, you should ask for a substantial advance. Whether you do so in other circumstances will depend entirely on the type of business you intend to run, and your opinion of the financial standing of the people you are selling your food to. For what it is worth, in fifteen years of running a catering company we have only had two genuine 'bad debts', both for quite small amounts, but we have, on the whole, dealt with relatively large business operations or well-heeled private individuals. Someone working in a different area might be less fortunate and be glad that they at least got some money in advance.

Payment Terms Again, the terms on which you decide to do business will depend entirely on the sort of business you want to run and the clients you are dealing with. If you are selling pâtés to the local pub or sandwiches to an office complex, you should look for cash on delivery, although in both cases if you get a regular order you could decide to run a weekly or monthly account with them. Many caterers ask for cash on delivery for small, one-off functions; others will ask for their money by return; others again will give seven or thirty days' credit. Private clients usually pay very promptly – but are more difficult to pursue than a company if they do not pay. Large companies – with large accounts departments – are slow.

Most large companies work on a thirty-day accounting system which it is possible but difficult to circumvent. For an exceptional case (if you are doing an especially big job and you do need some money in advance or at least as soon as the job is done), they can usually rush a cheque through, but since it is a hassle for them, they are not anxious to do it more often than they have to. Your problems arise when they do not pay at the end of the thirty days. All you can really do is to make such a nuisance of yourself that it is easier to pay you than put up with you. This is a bore for you, but if you are paying 18 per cent interest on an overdraft, it is worth the effort. Send them reminders, ring them up, talk to the accounts department, talk to the person who organized the function or indeed anyone who can help. If the situation gets bad enough, try to talk to or write to the managing director – marking it 'personal' – explaining your plight. Often it is merely bureaucracy that causes the delay, but sometimes it is company policy; if you have any suspicion that the company you are about to do business with is of that kind, get a large deposit! Similarly, if you have doubt about the financial soundness of a private client, get a substantial deposit.

Paying Your Bills

This is a lot simpler than getting paid. The basic principle is never to pay anything or anybody before you have to. This may sound like sharp practice, but if you are struggling to keep your overdraft within manageable proportions, you will have no option. Since that is the way that all large companies work, they have already allowed for the fact that you will not pay them until the last possible moment, so you need not feel sorry for them.

On the other hand, you must pay within their specified limit. A regular supplier who knows you will put up with one or two very overdue bills, but if you stretch their patience, or credulity, too far, they may get suspicious and withdraw credit. This means that they will refuse to supply you at all unless you pay cash on delivery. Neither do you want to get onto any of the innumerable 'bad debt' lists that are circulated around larger firms; once your name gets onto one of these lists, it is very hard to get it off again.

Small, individual suppliers should be treated with more sympathy – often their cash-flow problems are even greater than yours and they can only operate if they get paid quickly. You will have to judge each one on its own merits, but even though it seems hard, do not be too generous; your duty is to your own overdraft before anyone else's.

Accounting for the Money

The mention of book-keeping or accountancy is enough to strike terror into the hearts of many competent cooks and organizers, but it is not as bad as it sounds. If you really don't think you can cope, you can employ a book-keeper, usually quite cheaply, but if you do so, it will not be as easy to keep your 'finger on the pulse' of your business as if you do the books yourself. The line between success and failure is often so thin and can be crossed so quickly that having to do your own books each month is a very good way of keeping an eye on what is happening and how your business is going.

Computerization Home and small business computers are very cheap these days, so it makes perfect sense for even a one-person business to invest in one. There are all kinds of simple accountancy packages that will cover most of your needs. If you buy one with a word-processing facility, it will also make writing estimates and replying to letters *infinitely* easier – especially if

you are not a great typist! If you decide to computerize yourself, examine carefully what packages are on offer. We have never found it worth computerizing more than our accounts. Our food, stocks and suppliers were too diverse for any of the 'off the shelf' packages to handle and too many people would have had to use the system for it to be totally reliable. But what is available is changing so fast that you might be able to find 'just the thing'.

Book-keeping Even in the smallest business, you will need three basic account books – whether they are in ledger or floppy disk form. A 'cash book' (for the money that you pay out by cheque), a 'petty cash book' (for the money that you pay out in cash), and a 'day book' in which you enter the goods or services that you sell. You will be able to detail in these exactly what you have spent your money on and what you have been paid for. At the end of the year your accountant (and/or the tax man) will need this information, but long before then, you will want it in order to 'analyse' how your business is going.

Bills, Receipts and Vouchers At the end of the year, the accountant/tax man will want 'supporting' bills or receipts to cover all your payments and receipts. Ideally, they also want receipts for all petty cash spent, but discuss this with your accountant or the tax man as you will go berserk if you have to get a receipt for every bottle of milk that you buy.

Cheque Books, Paying In Books and Bank Statements Apart from your account books, you will also need cheque books, paying in books and you will get, whether you want them or not, bank statements. As anyone who has attempted to keep control of their personal finances will know, entries in cheque books and paying in books need to be regularly checked against the bank statement to make sure that all is in order. Charges on your bank statement (standing orders for rent or services, interest, etc.) should all be entered in your cash book as 'payments out' otherwise your 'analysis' will be completely to pot.

Once you get established, it would be worth investigating some of the accounting 'systems' that are available. Many of these include cheque 'books' that double as 'cash books', and cut down the book-keeping work enormously. There are also systems for sending out invoices and statements and innumerable other refinements. The systems are quite expensive but often worth the investment.

Analysis of Your Accounts This sounds sophisticated, but is vitally important if you are going to discover how and why you are – or are not – making money. All it means is comparing what you spend with what you make. This allows you to identify areas where you seem to be overspending or the amount you are spending does not tally with what you receive – maybe too many casual staff for the amount of work they are turning out; too much spent on food in comparison with what you are receiving – or are your prices too low? It will also allow you to identify particularly profitable sectors which you should develop.

Some areas of your business will be quite clear cut – what you spend on your delivery cars or vans versus what you receive in delivery money; what you spend on your hiring equipment, including the dishwashers and their operators, versus what you receive for hiring it out; and so on. Others will be far more complicated. You could, for example, analyse exactly how much food (how many pounds of butter, slices of bacon, cocktail sticks) you used for each function and compare the cost with the money received for that function, but you will end up spending more time analysing your figures than cooking your food. However, a general comparison of what it costs you to run your kitchen and buy your food with what you receive for it will be educational. If you have subdivided your expenditure fairly carefully, you will be able to discover what percentage of your costs are going on food, electricity, staff, cleaning up, etc., and whether they are reasonable.

However, remember that you cannot judge your figures accurately on just one month's figures; overheads (electricity, gas, etc.) tend to spread over two or three months. Moreover, you may buy something in month one but not pay for it until month two or three. Even more likely, you will buy and pay for something in month one for a function in month two. This means that three months is really the shortest time over which you can do a vaguely accurate analysis of your business; six months or a year is even better.

That is not to say that you should only do it every six months or a year. Ideally, you should do your analysis every month when you complete your other book-keeping. You will always have the previous two, three or four months to look

back on and you will get a feel of how things are going – you will also quickly become aware if a discrepancy has developed in some area of the business. However, once every three or six months you should sit down in a corner with a wet towel and your analysis sheets and look very carefully at how your business has been developing. On page 148, I have provided an excerpt from a typical year's analysis for a small catering company to show how it works.

Accountants Whether you use an accountant or deal direct with the Inland Revenue will be up to you. There is no reason why you should not deal direct; just contact your local tax office and ask their advice as to what you need to do – they are usually very helpful. This is, of course, cheaper than using an accountant. However, many people feel, quite justifiably, that they would rather have an 'expert' handle the tax side of their affairs while they got on with running their catering business. If you do use an accountant, remember that they charge by time, so the less sorting out of your accounts they have to do, the less they will cost.

PAYE and National Insurance

If you employ staff who are earning over the statutory minimum wage, you will be responsible for paying their tax. You should contact the local tax office and tell them what you are doing. They will then deluge with you with an enormous amount of literature, a lot of which you will

probably find totally incomprehensible – most people do! However, the actual filling in of the deductions cards and calculation of the tax is quite simple, once you know how. I would suggest that you ask your accountant or someone who deals with it regularly to show you how it works.

Single Owner, Partnership or Limited Company

Running anything but a very small operation on your own is *very* hard work. The hours are long, the physical work hard, and the skills demanded of you are many. Although you can close down for annual holidays, that is guaranteed to be the moment when the one really big job of the year comes along. Of course, you can employ someone else to run the operation when you are not around,

but in the early days it may be hard to afford the kind of person who would really be capable of running the show in your absence. Once you are established, it is a rather different matter, although even then employees who are good enough to be confidently left in charge are usually good enough to want some share in the business, so you may still find yourself going without holidays.

A partnership is the simplest and easiest way for two or more people to operate together. You should check with your solicitor about special provisions, but a basic partnership means that you are equal in everything – responsibility, investment and earnings. Obviously, it does help if you get on with your partner or partners. For a partnership, accounting is relatively simple – and therefore cheap. You need only submit your books with their receipts to the Inland Revenue each year, they do not have to be 'audited'. Although tax laws and rates are constantly changing, paying tax personally (as you do with a partnership) rather than as a company is usually beneficial.

However, as a partnership you do all remain personally liable for the debts that your business incurs. This probably does not matter very much if you are small when you will remain in total control of everything yourselves. However, if the business grows and you start to employ a lot of people, there is always the danger you may no longer have such tight control and you could find yourself paying for other people's mistakes.

Turning yourself into a limited company means that if everything does go wrong, your business can go bankrupt without your personal possessions (house, furniture, car and everything else) being affected. Although if you have a bank overdraft, this will not be the case as banks will normally only grant overdrafts to small limited companies if they have personal guarantees for the money from the directors. On the other hand, a limited company is much more tightly watched

over than a partnership. As a limited company you will have to submit audited accounts each year (expensive) and pay company tax on your profits. This may well be worth doing, but be sure to discuss it thoroughly with all your advisers before you make the change.

If you do decide to go ahead, your accountants, bank manager or solicitor will all be able to advise you as to what you should do.

Pricing Your Food and Your Services

If you are going to sell your food and services, and make a profit, you have to get the price right. It is all too easy to underprice or underestimate and find that you have made a loss on a function that you had hoped would pay the rent for the next two months. On the other hand, you do not want to charge so much that you lose all your clients. A good rifle through your competitors' brochures will give you some idea of what they are charging, but you will need to work out your own prices.

Freelance Cooking
As I said in the introduction, most freelance cooks charge on an ingredients plus time basis – the cost of the ingredients for the meal plus an hourly charge for your time. Others charge for the ingredients and then a per head fee for the number of people at a party – this will work out about the same as the hourly rate for a small group, but you would do better on a large group where the time taken to prepare all the food will not be

proportionate to the extra number of people, and therefore the extra fee. To find out what a suitable hourly rate would be for your area and clientèle, you will have to do a little local research – agencies are usually quite useful for this kind of information.

'All-in' Pricing of Food

When you charge an 'all-in' price for your food, it has to cover not only the cost of the raw materials but all the costs of producing it – in other words, all your overheads. Some people price their food by the dish, others prefer to price it by the whole menu. If you price by the menu, you can also include the cost of hiring equipment (crockery, cutlery, etc.), service (staff) and delivery in the menu costs. However, unless you are quite sure that you will always be supplying these items, it may be wiser to cost them separately.

When you have been operational for a while and are able to calculate your overheads with some degree of accuracy (see pages 140–1), you will be able to work out exactly how much profit you make on any particular function, but because of the very fluctuating nature of most small catering businesses it is very difficult to forecast this. A general rule of thumb for pricing has therefore been adopted by most catering companies which, although not appropriate for every circumstance, is generally fairly reliable.

Working Out the Charge for Each Dish

1 When you start, quite likely working from home but anyhow with relatively low overheads in terms of staff, etc., take the cost of the ingredients for the dish concerned for six people; multiply this by three and then divide by six to get the amount that you should charge for each person. This *should* cover your overheads and give you a reasonable net profit of around 15 per cent.

2 Once you expand – maybe move into separate premises – and once you start employing staff, you will have to raise the multiple to four (the ingredients for each dish for six people multiplied by four and then divided by six to reach the price per head) in order to cover your greater costs.

3 Larger companies with several staff, fancy telephones, small computers, etc. will often increase the multiple to five to cover their yet further increased costs. They will justify their higher prices on the grounds that they are supplying a much more comprehensive service – which, of course, they are.

As always, there are exceptions to this rule. If you are serving very expensive food (smoked or dressed salmon, caviar, shellfish, fillet steak, etc.), multiplying the cost of the food by four or five will produce a ridiculously high figure – especially since the labour involved in high-cost foods is usually quite small. You will have to use your own judgement in these cases, but usually two or three times the raw material cost is enough. On the other hand, if you are serving foods (many cocktail snacks, for example) where the raw material cost is negligible but the labour cost very high, then you will have to increase the multiple. It usually pays to have a fixed minimum cost for a cocktail snack, even if it is appreciably above what your calculations say you should charge for it. Above that, work on a multiple of five or six for all cocktail bits until you reach the high-cost ingredients, such as smoked salmon, caviar or prawns, at which point you could revert to four times the cost.

Pricing Individual Dishes When pricing individual dishes, you will need to establish what size portions you are going to serve and stick with them. You will find advice on portion control on page 32. Remember also to allow for wastage. Some foods – some meats in particular – have an enormous amount of waste and, if you fail to allow for it, you will throw your costings totally out. It will often pay you to buy a better quality ingredient with less waste for a higher price; once prepared, the difference in cost may not be that great and you will save yourself a lot of labour.

Ingredient costs will, of course, change, some of them very frequently, and you cannot keep on changing your prices. On a week-to-week basis it is very much a case of what you gain on the swings you lose on the roundabouts – tomatoes go up in price while cucumbers come down. Some ingredients are totally seasonal and if they are to be got at all out of season cost a fortune. If you are going to quote these on a menu or list of dishes, it is better not to give a price at all – just put 'seasonal prices', which means that you can cost them according to the going market price when they are ordered.

However, it will pay you to keep an eye on all prices in case some ingredient goes up and stays up. About once every three months you should re-price half a dozen representative recipes just to check that your prices are still fairly accurate. It is very easy to let your pricing slip and suddenly find that you are driving yourself like a slave to no end as your prices are too low. On the other hand, it is not wise to change your prices too often, partly because it is expensive to continually have to reprint and mail price lists, and partly because if your clients are for ever receiving revised (upwards) prices, even if the increase is only slight, they will pigeon-hole you as a company who is always putting its prices up. Try not to change your prices more than once every six months, preferably every year. This means that when you do change them you will have to pitch them slightly high for current prices so as to cover you for the six months or year to come. When you do change your prices, make it an excuse to change your menus or dishes too – this will help to disguise the price rise, and be more interesting for the client.

Costing Your Other Services

How to charge for the ancillary services that you offer (finding locations, drinks, flowers, entertainment, etc.) has already been discussed on page 131, but you still have to deal with hiring out your own equipment (if you have any), delivery of your food, and staff. As I said before, some caterers prefer to include all of these in the overall cost of the meal; some prefer to quote for them separately. Especially when you are starting, you may find that many of your clients will not actually want all these services (or want to provide them themselves), so it is probably better to quote for them separately. Even if you do, there is nothing to stop you adding them up at the bottom of your estimate to give them an 'all-in' figure.

Hiring Equipment Pricing your equipment will really be a matter of finding out what everyone else charges for theirs. Depending on how nice yours is compared with theirs, you may be able to charge a little more – or a little less – but you will not be able to step far out of line or you will not get the business. You may also wish to charge people who only want to hire equipment but not buy your food a little more, although on the whole we always found that too complicated to be worth the effort. Remember that if you want to charge for the breakage or loss of equipment, you will have to warn clients before they hire it from you.

Staff To avoid complications over taxation and PAYE, some caterers insist that their staff are employed directly by the clients, in which case they may charge a small booking fee. Others will book the staff free of charge as part of their service. If the caterers pay the staff themselves, again they may, or may not, charge a small booking fee. However, when estimating the staff cost for any function, do always allow a little leeway for overtime or a small tip. And don't forget to allow for extra kitchen or delivery staff.

Delivery Unless you do a very high turnover indeed, your delivery charges, even if they are astronomically high, will not pay for the cost of buying, running and servicing a van or car. So you will have to resign yourself to subsidizing the running of your delivery van out of the profits you make on your food. However, there is no reason why you should not make a delivery charge, probably starting with a flat rate and moving on to a per head sum for larger parties. Again, try to find out what other people in the area are charging and pitch your prices in line with theirs.

Extras
Don't forget, when you are doing your costings and your estimates, all those little extras – emergency portions of food, food for the staff, drinks for the staff, extra delivery charges, staff overtime, etc. It is so easy to forget just one of them and they can make quite a dent in your profits if you do. You can charge them as 'extras', but it is much better to cost them in at the beginning.

Discounts for Quantity

Some clients ask for, and some caterers give, discounts for quantity. It is, in fact, perfectly reasonable for clients to assume that it will cost you proportionately less to provide food for one hundred than it will for ten (not in food terms, but in labour) – and that they should therefore be entitled to some of that saving. Obviously, if you can avoid sharing that bonus so much the better, but depending on the area of business that you are in, you may find it pays you to disgorge a little of your profit in the interests of securing the contract.

Contract Catering

This means signing a contract with a client to supply him or her with a certain amount of food for a certain period of time. It can be a contract to supply a pub with four tins of pâté each week, a contract to supply business lunches to a small office three times a month, or it can be a contract to supply factory canteens for 2,000 workers with four meals a day. In each case, its virtue from your point of view is security. Unless you make a total mess of the job, it guarantees you a certain amount of income each month or each year, thus saving you cash-flow problems, keeping your bank manager happy, and allowing you to do your financial planning far more accurately.

Much contract work involves actually taking over and running canteens, restaurants or other 'in-house' facilities. There is nothing wrong with doing this – indeed it can be very lucrative – but take care not to leap in without finding out exactly what it is all about. Running what amounts to a subsidized restaurant in someone else's premises is not at all the same thing as running a catering business in your own. If you are thinking of doing it, read up on industrial catering, talk to other people running similar enterprises, and do your sums *very* carefully before you go any further.

Without going to the lengths of running a canteen, it is sensible to secure a small amount of contract work to at least ensure that the rent is paid. The danger of taking on too much, especially if you are small, is that if a really luscious, big, 'one-off' job comes along you may not be able to handle it because you are too busy fulfilling your contracts.

Transport

Even if you are not proposing to deliver your food, you are going to have to shop, since the days of delivery to your door (except in much larger bulk than you are likely to need at first) are long gone. So you will have to deal with the problem of transporting your goods.

A bicycle or motor bike is feasible, but unless you are operating in a very small way, pretty impractical – and very hard work. Many a family car has been pressed into service for delivering meals for dinner parties, but again do watch your insurance. If you do not inform your insurers that you are using the car for business purposes, they could refuse to pay out on a claim if you were delivering someone's birthday cake at the time. Be warned, they will probably charge you extra.

The ideal is a small van or flat-bottomed hatchback that will not suffer too much if the Bœuf Bourgignon spills and that is reasonably spacious. A compromise between something fairly cheap that will survive the rough and tumble of a delivery van's life but will not 'ruin your image' by looking as though it belongs on the rubbish tip is what you should aim for.

You will also need something in which to carry your food. You can easily spend a fortune on packing containers, but if you keep an eye open, you will find that many of the big firms scatter their plastic trays far and wide and you may be able to build up quite a respectable collection without paying a penny. A flick through the classified pages of a local paper might also turn up a bankrupt business where you could pick up a few bargains. (See also pages 117–18.)

Internal Organization

I know that I have droned on endlessly already about the importance of organization in running any kind of catering business, but it really is vital. So I shall allow myself one further section on the subject and hope you will bear with me.

Although it may be a great effort, especially for someone who is not by nature very organized, it is worth 'planning' your time very thoroughly as soon as you can. Checklists are the caterer's life-support line. There are so many disparate elements to be tied together in running a cooking or catering business that it is very easy to forget something small. But so often that small something can be the lynch pin that holds the whole operation together – the electric hot rings to heat the soup and cook the vegetables, the dessert you had left to chill for as long as possible in the refrigerator, the wine to go in the glasses – or the glasses to hold the wine. The only way to ensure with reasonable certainty that you have got everything is to have everything written down and checked off on a checklist. So, to get you in the mood, here is a checklist of the things I think you should have.

Office Equipment

You cannot have enough pencils, pens, rough paper, rubbers, 'whiteout' paint, sellotape, staplers, etc., as there is a gremlin in all catering kitchens who eats them. There is nothing more infuriating – or inefficient – than having to leave your client hanging on for five minutes while you grovel for a pencil or a bit of paper, and you would be amazed how useful all the other bits are.

Diary

You need a general diary for recording tentative and confirmed bookings. It is very important that this is kept up to date so that you do not overstretch or double-book yourself. Some caterers also keep a large daily diary in which the individual orders can be listed in greater detail and any special requests can be noted.

Main Order Form

This is very important as it is your main source of reference for any order. The details on this will obviously vary according to the kind of business you run, but it should always include:

Client's name, address and telephone number

Location, date and time of function plus any relevant delivery instructions, etc.

Number of guests

Menu with prices quoted

Details of any special requirements – drinks, hire of equipment, flowers, etc., with prices where relevant

How the client got your name.

(See sample below.)

Client's name: ....

Client's address: ....tel. no. office:......

.... home:......

Any special billing instructions:......................

Delivery address: .... Delivery time:......

Any specific delivery instructions: ....

Date order for: .... Date order taken:......

Number of people or covers (where relevant): ....

Details of order – menus/specific dishes/

quantities, etc.: ....

Prices quoted: ....

Equipment needed: 1 to be hired to client: ....

2 to fulfil or serve the

order: ....

How the client got your name: ....

This order form can come in two versions – a preliminary one when you are dealing with a query rather than a definite order. In this case, it serves as an *aide-mémoire* for you – what you should remember to ask the client – and a record of the enquiry in case you need to follow it up. These can be quite cheaply printed or run off on cheap paper as they are only for reference. There should then be a final version which will be the one from which the order will be supplied. There need to be as many copies of this as you have departments, but no matter how small you are, you should have two – one for your records and from which to do the bill, and a working copy for the kitchen. We have always used three: one office copy, one kitchen copy and one copy for the hiring department. The most convenient way to get your copies is to use NCR or self-copying paper; this can be printed according to your requirements in pads so your copies get done automatically. However, NCR is quite expensive, so in the early days you could make do with carbon paper.

Kitchen Department

Your kitchen lists should include the following.
1 An order form or list for each order or function; this can be kept as a list or written into a daily diary, but wherever it is to be found, it must include everything in the food line that has to go to that function – cream for coffee, butter for bread, biscuits for cheese, salt for cooking vegetables, as well as the fillet steak and the trifle.
2 A daily cooking list.
3 A forward cooking list.
4 Shopping and ordering lists for your suppliers.
5 Basic item shopping and ordering checklist.
6 Blank shopping list for everyone to add to.
7 For large functions, lists of serving dishes.

Labelling Don't forget that *everything must be labelled*. If you are preparing more than one function, it is vital that each item is labelled for the relevant party so that the prawn cocktails do not end up at little Johnny's tea party and the packets of crisps at the managing director's posh dinner. Even if you are only preparing for one event, it is worth labelling to separate the mayonnaise that is

going to the party from the spare pot that is to be left in the refrigerator. Indeed, once you get into the habit, you will label everything (labels are very cheap when bought in bulk) as it will save you all the time spent sorting through pots in refrigerators or freezers if they all say what they are!

Hiring Department

1 Hiring lists of your own equipment – see page 116.
2 Comprehensive lists of whatever equipment you may be hiring in.
NB Again, it is worth labelling each tray or container load of equipment. It is fine when you are only dealing with one function, but when you graduate to more, you could run into trouble.

Office or Administration Department

1 Copy of main order form.
2 Subcontractors – checklists of who you are using for what and what they are supplying or doing.
3 Staff – who you have booked, what you are paying them, what times they are arriving and leaving, and how they are to be transported.

PR or Publicity

1 Lists of old clients who should be contacted with new menus, etc.
2 Lists of enquiries that came to nothing, but names that might be worth contacting again with new menus, etc.
3 Lists of 'media' contacts who should be informed of any new venture.

Accounts

1 Lists of any outstanding debts – in other words anyone who has not paid you within the specified time and therefore should be sent a reminder, rung up, or whatever.
2 Lists of outstanding bills – what you owe and how soon you will have to pay.

Sample of accounts analysis
for a small catering company
over a 2-month period
(see also pages 139–141)

TAKINGS FOR YEAR 1 EXCLUDING V.A.T.

MONTH		0% V.A.T. FOOD	15% V.A.T. FOOD	HIRE EQUIPMENT	HIRE LOCATION	STAFF	WINE	MIXED BAR	DELIVERY	MISC.	TOTAL
MAY	CHEQUE	4601·95	687·00			325·00	1283·07	91·90	245·00	404·00	7637·92
MAY	P.C.										
MAY	TOTAL	4601·95	687·00			325·00	1283·07	91·90	245·00	404·00	7637·92
JUNE	CHEQUE	5374·05	1498·70	2207·75		954·50	770·21	396·85	445·00	1941·10	13,588·16
JUNE	P.C.										
JUNE	TOTAL	5374·05	1498·70	2207·75		954·50	770·21	396·85	445·00	1941·10	13,588·16

RUNNING COSTS FOR YEAR 1 EXCLUDING V.A.T.

MONTH		FOOD	BUSINESS EXPENSES (INC. RENT, RATES, PHONE, CLEANING)	BANK CHARGES	REPLACEMENT OF HIRING EQUIPMENT LAUNDRY	HIRE OF LOCATIONS RE FUNCTIONS	SALARIES/ STAFF	VANS	WINES AND DRINKS	MISC.	TOTAL
MAY	CHEQUE	1278·83	894·77		285·48	228·00	2521·25	274·57	114·14	444·00	6041·04
MAY	P.C.	262·01	251·74			20·90	237·00	158·68	27·61	14·39	972·33
MAY	TOTAL	1540·84	1146·51		285·48	248·90	2758·25	433·25	141·75	458·39	7013·37
JUNE	CHEQUE	1333·21	363·73	227·21	75·03	691·34	2485·07	249·10	434·08	389·00	6247·77
JUNE	P.C.	187·33	248·63				709·00	105·37	14·23		1264·56
JUNE	TOTAL	1520·54	612·36	227·21	75·03	691·34	3194·07	354·47	448·31	389·00	7512·33

ANALYSIS FOR YEAR 1 EXCLUDING V.A.T.

MONTH		FOOD	BUSINESS EXPENSES (INC. RENT, RATES, PHONE, SALARIES, BANK CHARGES, EQUIPMENT, ETC.)	HIRE OF EQUIPMENT, LAUNDRY	HIRE OF LOCATIONS AND MISC. SERVICES	STAFF	WINE AND DRINKS	VANS/ DELIVERY	MISC.	TOTAL	PROFIT/ LOSS
MAY	INCOME	4601·95	687·00			325·00	1374·97	245·00	404·00	7637·92	
MAY	EXPENS.	5208·60	285·48	248·90		237·00	141·75	433·25	458·39	7013·37	
MAY	PR/LOSS	606·65	401·52	248·90		88·00	1233·22	188·25	54·39	624·55	624·55
JUNE	INCOME	5374·05	1498·70	2207·75		954·50	1167·06	445·00	1941·10	13,588·16	
JUNE	EXPENS.	4845·18	75·03	691·34		709·00	448·31	354·47	389·00	7512·33	
JUNE	PR/LOSS	528·87	1423·67	1516·41		245·50	718·75	90·53	1552·10	6075·83	6075·83

Marketing

Selecting your Market and Getting to Know It

This sounds rather grand, but it really means investigating the competition in whatever line of business you have chosen. Indeed, it is something you should do before making any absolutely final decisions about what line you are going for. It may be a wonderful idea to do a daily sandwich delivery, but if there are already ten people doing sandwich deliveries in a small town, you might be pushed for work. You should also be able to pick up some tips and ideas from people who are already operational.

First of all, find out who is doing what in your area. Yellow Pages, local directories and the regional Chamber of Commerce should be good sources of information. Ring up anyone who looks interesting and ask them to send you their brochure – you can give a false name and pretend that you are a potential client. You needn't feel bad about it, everyone does it! Once you have got all the literature, sit down and read it carefully. Take particular note of *how* they sell themselves; what points they emphasize, how they have laid out their brochure, and so on.

Next, take good note of their menus – how many they give, what areas they cover, what sort of numbers they are catering for. You will almost inevitably get ideas from what they suggest without necessarily copying them. Finally, look at their prices. What do they include in those prices? Do they give discounts for quantity? These are the people you will be competing against, so you need to make sure that what you offer is at least in the same league.

It would then be a good idea to talk to some of them. Most people who run a small business are very sympathetic to others who are setting out – they remember what hard work it was when they first started! If they are successful, they will not be that bothered about someone else wanting to come into their line of business – there is always room for more. If they are not successful, you don't want to talk to them – unless you want to learn how *not* to do it. However, it would probably be tactful to suggest that, although you want to start in *generally* the same line as them, you will be trying to specialize in something they

are not interested in – barbecued tropical fish? – thus you would present less of a potential threat.

You could ask whether they would let you work with them for a few days – obviously, you would offer your services free in return for what you would be learning. This is probably the ideal solution as it gives you a chance to see a business in operation. However, it can sometimes be more trouble than it is worth to have an extra body hanging around a busy kitchen not really knowing what to do, even if it is free, so do not be surprised if your contacts do not leap at the chance. Alternatively, you could ask whether they would mind just talking to you for half an hour. You should certainly offer to buy them a drink or lunch or whatever, but make it quite clear that you are more than happy to show up at their kitchens at 6.30 am for a chat before work starts if that is what suits them best.

If you manage to do all this, apart from picking up tips about how to run a business, you may also discover that your skills or expertise are a bit lacking in some area. You will obviously learn a lot as you go along in your own business, but since it might be wise not to treat all your clients as experimental guinea pigs, it could be a good idea to go to work on your skills before you start. How you do this will depend on how much time and money you have to spend. If you have plenty of both, you can take yourself off to a specialist cookery course; if not a lot of either, you should try to get yourself a temporary, even if not very well-paid, job with someone already working in that field. In that way, you will at least earn a bit of money and learn 'on the ground'. Of course, this may be easier said than done, but it is certainly worth a try.

Choosing a Name

This must be the most fraught part of starting any new business. There are various stylistic options and the one that you choose should reflect your own personality and your attitude to your business. Here are a few general ideas to help you decide.

1 The 'family name' type of business – this is what most of the old established catering companies have and denotes a certain reliability and respectability: Payne and Gunter, Ring and Brymer, Searcy Tansley, Gardner Merchant, Sutcliffe's, etc. On the other hand, some might say it was boring and made you sound like a solicitor!

2 The practical, explanatory-type name that indicates to the world exactly what you do: Party Food, Party Organizers, City Food Services, Danish Catering, Party Fare, etc. These have the virtue of being immediately comprehensible and can also be quite fun – Travelling Gourmet, Movable Feasts, Catering à la Carte, The Sandwich Plant, and so on. But do be careful not to be too clever. Our own company's name, for example, Catercall, theoretically was self-explanatory – unless people read it as Cat-ercall and thought we were a stray cat rescuing service!

A variation on this is the allusion-type name, which is fine – as long as your clients 'get' the allusion. 'Figaro', for example, is an excellent name for an organizational catering company *as long* as the clients are familiar with Mozart and realize that Figaro was the world's best 'in-house' organizer; if not, it is pointless.

3 The personal name. When specifically linked to food, these can all too often verge on the twee – 'Katy's Kitchen', 'Kevin's Katering', 'Susie's Sandwiches', 'Jack and Jill Catering'. This may be all right, or even positively beneficial, when you are doing kid's parties and filling freezers, but becomes rather out of place when you are doing grand dinners. On the other hand, a simple, but unusual, name can be amazingly successful. Who would have thought, for example, of calling a food company 'Justin de Blank', but look how well that has done. Once you are into this area it becomes a matter of luck as to whether or not your bizarre choice can catch on and become fashionable.

4 The 'witty' name. Again these can be fun, but there is a danger of type-casting yourself. 'Guzzles Catering' is a winner when you are doing cheap and cheerful buffet parties, but if you want to graduate to up-market gourmet dinners, it just might give the wrong impression.

Unless you have already had your brainwave and know what you want to call yourself, the best answer is to get a group of your most inspired friends together, give them a good dinner and get them all to throw ideas into the pot. You may not decide on one there and then, but at least you will have plenty of material to work with. One other thing to remember – whatever you choose, it needs to be easy to say in a hurry, and understand, on the telephone.

Printed Literature and Brochures

Before you try to sell your services to anyone, you need to have something to show them. We are so paper-orientated that no one will think you are 'serious' unless you can produce a piece of paper supporting what you do. You may think this is a waste of time if all you are going to sell is blocks of Terrine Maison to the local pub, but even then a smartly typed sheet of paper with your name, address and telephone number, a description of your pâtés, their sizes, prices, how often you can deliver and whether you charge for delivery will make a much better impression than scruffy bits of paper with prices scribbled on them.

However, fancy literature can be astronomically expensive, especially if you are only printing small quantities, so it would be worth spending time and effort on designing something that will look good without costing a fortune. You also want it to be fairly flexible, especially at the start when you are not quite sure how the business may develop. Today we are lucky as the mushrooming of High Street photocopying shops means that printing only fifty of something can be done for a sensible price; in the 'old days', you had to print thousands to cover the cost of the initial setting. Many of these shops also offer 'artwork' services, so if you are dubious about your own artistic abilities, you can get professional advice for a relatively small fee on how to 'lay out' your brochure to achieve maximum effect. What is more, the arrival of word processors means that you can make a quite simple typed sheet look as though it has been printed. If you cannot dragoon a friend with a word processor into letting you use it for your brochures (or even do them for you), there are agencies that will type out what you need for quite a reasonable fee.

Contents All brochures need to contain certain basic bits of information.

1 Who you are and where people can contact you – you must make absolutely sure that this is clearly stated in one or several obvious places. Nothing is more irritating than having to search three times through someone's brochure in order to find their telephone number.

2 A short introduction about you and what services you offer.

3 What specific foods you offer – usually in the guise of set, priced menus.

4 If you wish to include them, what drinks you offer with prices and what other special services you offer – with or without prices.

5 Your terms of business.

How you dress them up is a different matter.

Layout This needs to be clear and simple. I am personally in favour of giving a relatively small amount of well-chosen information; just enough to tempt clients to enquire further, rather than drowning them in a forty-page booklet. What you have to say needs to be easy to read and understand – potential clients will not be bothered with a company whose brochure they cannot make head or tail of.

Design Design is very dependent on fashion and the particular image you want to create. Once you start talking to printers and designers, you will get involved in all kinds of technicalities about the 'in' typefaces and print styles, but remember that getting a brochure set up is an expensive business, so you do not want something that is going to be the rage today but old hat tomorrow; on the other hand, you do want something distinctive. The danger in trying not to be too trendy or fashion-conscious is that you may become boring. On the whole, visually simple design is the most successful: a clear and easily readable type style and an uncluttered page.

What size brochure you produce is a matter of taste. Most people use A4 (standard UK letter size) or A5 (A4 folded horizontally). A4 is rather more expensive to send as it requires larger envelopes and possibly more postage, but I find it gives you more scope for getting the information you want in without it looking crowded.

A catering brochure presents particular problems in that, while part of it (the general introduction) will not need to be changed for some time, other parts (menus, prices, etc.) will – or at least should – change quite frequently. Reprinting the whole of an expensive glossy brochure every time you have a price change is really not practicable. The solution that most people opt for is to have a 'fixed' introductory section – often in the shape of the cover – with changeable contents. This can be done with a flap into which you slot the changeable menus or price sheets which can be cheaply reprinted whenever necessary, and you could also insert details about any new ventures you are setting up or copies of newspaper write-ups about your firm.

Another slightly more expensive option is to have the cover (always the most expensive bit) and maybe one inside page printed in a large quantity but not bound. You can then print smaller quantities of menus and prices whenever necessary and have the whole lot bound up as needed. Yet another alternative is to use plastic clutch or ring binders which allow you to change the contents of the brochure at will. These are cheap and extremely convenient but can look a little 'tacky', so make sure you choose carefully.

The *cover* of the brochure is all important as that is what creates that vital first impression. Many people spend a lot of money on expensively photographed covers, but my own feeling is that unless they are *exceptionally* well photographed, which the vast majority of them are not, they do not work. A tableful of food is almost impossible to photograph successfully at any time and when reduced to A5, or even A4 size, it always looks cluttered. Yet, a really good photograph of a single dish (easier to achieve) may not give the right impression of bounty for a catering company. A logo can, of course, be substituted for a photograph and is a lot cheaper to reproduce. Combined with attractive lettering, it can look very effective. This was the option for which we finally settled. The third alternative is just to use your name, attractively printed and laid out. This may sound, and can be, boring, but if you have an interesting typeface and layout and use an unusual colour, card or laminate, it can also be very effective and eye-catching.

Logos A logo of some kind is very popular these days and there is no doubt that an unusual and apposite logo does help to lodge your name in potential clients' minds. However, finding an unusual and appropriate logo is not easy – and the one thing you do not want to do is send out vibes through your logo that will be totally at variance with the service you are trying to sell.

Some years ago we went through a long soul-searching process trying to find a logo that would suit our particular style of business: dealing in the main with an expensive, up-market business clientèle and providing an efficient, comprehensive, personal, sophisticated and imaginative entertainment service. Much of our business had also to do with period entertaining in stately homes, but we were afraid of typecasting ourselves too much if we overemphasized this angle. To concentrate our minds, we asked our designer to sit down one evening and just jot down any ideas that occurred to him for logos for a catering company. The results were very helpful. Many of them were attractive and fun but none of them actually gave off quite the vibes we were looking for. In the end we opted for some adaptations of eighteenth-century political cartoons that I had done some time before. Although not great works of art, they had the advantage of being individual and slightly quirky,

and when combined with a very clear and well-laid out brochure, and an efficient back-up service, they (and therefore we) stuck in people's minds. The moral of which is, if you can find the right logo, use it; if you can't, don't bother but concentrate on a good typographical design.

Photographs These are an expensive luxury inside a brochure , so if you are going to use photographs, make sure they are good. All too many brochures are filled with unflattering 'mug shots' of the directors of the company and even less flattering shots of their product.

Style What you write in your brochure is as important as how you present it. This will depend even more than the design on the market you are aiming yourself at. If this is a traditional or rather conservative bunch of businessmen, you should play safe and straight – purely factual information, well-laid out and comprehensive. If you are aiming for the wedding and home celebration market, you can afford to be a little more 'homely'. If you want to attract the young and trendy, PR and advertising, computer whizz kids, and so on, then you will need plenty of hype. But whatever the case, your brochure must not be boring – a failing in all too many catering brochures. And do make sure that it is grammatical. You would be amazed how many expensive and much-slaved-over brochures are ruined by the most basic grammatical, or even spelling, mistakes.

The best way to set about brochure writing is to get as many of your competitors' (or potential competitors') brochures as you can lay hands on and study them – hopefully you will be able to learn from their mistakes, and successes! But don't think you will be able to sit down and do it overnight. Brochure writing, because you have to compress so much attractively and effectively into a small space, is very difficult – but very important. It will pay you to spend a lot of time on getting it right.

Business Cards

Make sure that you have plenty of smart business cards, incorporating your logo if you have one *and your telephone number*. They are very useful for pressing on anyone who shows the remotest interest in your wares, and are easy to carry and have with you at functions.

Leaflets and Handouts

It might pay you to at least design some cheap handouts or leaflets that give some idea of your services – a bit more than a business card but a lot less than a brochure. You never know when you might find yourself in a situation where they could be useful – trade fairs, for example, where everyone takes every bit of literature they are offered but most goes in the bin. You certainly do not want to waste your expensive brochures on these occasions, but it would be a pity to waste the opportunity to pick up a bit of business. If you have a master copy ready, you can get a couple of hundred copies run off very cheaply at a local photocopying shop.

Stationery

If you are going to communicate with your clients, you are obviously going to need a certain amount of stationery – in any case, as soon as you start up in business you are required to 'display prominently your own and your business name and address on any documents connected with the business'. Headed notepaper, compliment slips and business cards are usually quite sufficient, although I have always found postcards very useful as well.

In due course, you will also need invoices, on which should be displayed your terms of business – on receipt, 7 days, 30 days – and your VAT No., if and when you graduate to those heights. We have also always included a little note on our invoices to the effect that we hoped the client had been happy with the job but that if there were any complaints we were very anxious to hear about them. As you grow you may also decide on stationery for paying out money as well as receiving it. There are several very efficient accounting systems that include printed cheques and stationery, but I have gone into that in a little more detail in the accounting section.

Whatever stationery you do have should tone with your brochures and literature, although I don't think it necessary to include your logo, assuming you have one, unless you want to.

Franking machines are only worth the money if you have an enormous amount of post, but your own rubber stamp (they are easy and cheap to get made and can include your logo) to use on the outside of your letters can look quite fun.

Selling Yourself and Your Wares

No matter how wonderful a service you think you can provide, it will be no good at all without some clients to sell it to. How you get them is a different – and vitally important – matter. Incidentally, always remember to ask new clients – discreetly if possible – where they got your name; it will be a great help in monitoring the success of your promotional efforts. A note on your master order form will help to remind you.

Word of Mouth This is always the most successful way to get business, but it is less easy to organize than advertising or shoving handbills through people's doors. Obviously, if your service is good enough, it will do its own advertising –

there are always a proportion of people at any party who entertain themselves and who are therefore interested, at least in theory, in knowing about good caterers. Always be sure that there is a stock of small (and attractive) business cards available at any function you are doing and that all the staff know where to find them. If the host has no objection, these can also be scattered discreetly among the food and drink – I don't think you should go as far as shoving one in everyone's coat pocket! Business cards are usually quite sufficient as they will fit easily into a pocket or handbag and should provide their recipients with enough information to remind them of who you are and tell them where to find you. When you start up, these can also be thrust on all your friends and relatives in the hope that they will scatter them far and wide.

Some caterers actually fit their staff with lapel badges saying who they are – this does get the message across, but it can look too commercial for some more up-market functions. Again I would check with the client before I pinned them on.

Telephone Canvassing Very much the same applies to telephone canvassing except that it is much harder work and takes a pretty tough hide. Again, I would only recommend it if you are sure you have identified a market that is *really* going to be interested in your product.

Advertising This is a term that can cover everything from sticking a handbill through your neighbour's door to taking a double-page spread in a weekend colour supplement. Sticking handbills through doors and notes on the local newsagent's notice board are probably only useful when you are starting – although if you find that a newsagent's notice board brings you business, stick with it! They are also useful if you are specializing in one area and you can find a notice board read by people likely to want your specialization. For example, if you want to cater for children's parties, a monthly tour around all the toddler groups and nursery schools sticking handbills on their boards is going to pay you hands down.

Advertising in newspapers and magazines is a different matter as that will start to cost you 'real'

money. It is certainly not worth doing unless you can come up with a good and eye-catching advertisement – by no means easy to do! However, if you think you can, a relatively small investment in a couple of weeks or months worth of advertising (depending on the publication) might be worth making – as long, of course, as you monitor the results carefully. If it pays off, do more. We have never found advertisements a particularly fruitful source of business but I know others have.

Editorial Space 'Write ups' in any publication (or radio or television interviews, of course) are always *very* well worth having. Not only are they more or less free (if you were to squeeze yourself onto the radio or television, you might even get paid), but people read, watch or listen to them with a great deal more attention than they give to advertisements. The danger is that you have virtually no control over what is written or broadcast. You may, discreetly at least, tell the journalist or reporter what you want him or her to print, but there is no guarantee that is what will go out – it is not only actors who get nasty shocks when they read journalists' opinions of their efforts! However, on the principle that all advertising is good advertising and in the hope that the reporter concerned will actually like what you are doing and write a nice piece about you, editorial publicity is well worth pursuing.

You will, however, only get the media interested in you if you can provide them with a good story – so give this some thought. Incidentally, don't be too ambitious: it would, of course, be nice to get half a page in *The Times* but you will probably get a much better response from a column in your local newspaper – and you will stand far more chance of it being printed! Local papers, local radio stations and, to a lesser extent, local television networks, are always on the look out for stories of local interest and, particularly, good local services to tell their readers about – and local papers have a far higher readership than the nationals. And don't think that once you have got your write-up that is the end of it. No paper will print articles about you every week, but it is worth contacting them, and the local radio stations, whenever you have some function or idea that might be of interest. Like everyone else, journalists are lazy and, if they already know you and know that you gave them an interesting story last time, they are much more likely to look at what you send them second time around.

Directories and Referral Agencies Obviously, you should be listed in all the free directories. Whether or not you take a heavy print listing or a box is debatable and probably depends on the kind of business you are aiming for. Very up-market clients will not on the whole look for caterers or function organizers in the Yellow Pages, but an awful lot of other people will. It may well be worth the extra investment for a trial year – as long as you remember to monitor the response.

There are also innumerable televisual referral agencies whose 'books' you can go onto – for a price. These are relatively expensive and I am a bit dubious as to how effective they are – despite what they will all tell you! However, you may think that in your particular circumstances they would be worth a try.

No matter where you live, there are bound to be local chambers of commerce, tourist boards and various business (especially small business)

promoting agencies. It is worth contacting them all and talking to them – some may be of enormous use in providing you with clients; some may provide you with all kinds of general information and advice on running your business; some may be totally useless. A few of these may operate as trade associations and you would need to become a member of these. Do not dismiss this idea as trade associations exist to promote each other's business – and everyone needs to entertain at some time!

It is also worth sending details to other catering companies in the area, especially when you are starting. They may get enquiries that are either too small for them to want to handle or not in their line, but that would be ideal for you. They will probably be delighted to have someone to hand them on to.

Mail Shots Theoretically this is a relatively cheap way of getting your name in front of a large number of people's noses. The problem is that unless you have an efficient marketing organization behind you to target your market accurately you will waste a lot of money sticking the information in front of noses that have not now, nor are ever likely to have, the least desire to use your services. And that is assuming that it makes it to under their noses and does not get chucked in the waste bin first. For a small company, I think it is only an option worth considering if you think you have identified a certain small group who would genuinely be interested in your services and you think that you can get to them directly – ideally to the person concerned each time by name. If you do decide to try it, you can reckon that you will be lucky to get a 5–10 per cent response.

Entertaining and 'Chatting-Up' Potential Clients As we all know, many a deal is done with the brandy after a good lunch and there is no reason why caterers, just because they are in the food business themselves, should not attempt to secure business over a fillet steak and a glass of port. Whether you choose to do it on your own premises or in a restaurant will depend on your circumstances. However, it does seem to make more sense, if you are trying to convince potential

155

clients how wonderful a caterer you are, to entertain them yourself – it is also a great deal cheaper! This is, of course, easier said than done if you work from a scruffy kitchen in a back-street slum, so it might be worth borrowing or hiring an independent location in which you could display your own talents. Whether you choose to entertain all your potential clients together or separately will also depend on your circumstances and the clients'.

We normally hold one or two parties a year to which we invite both potential and existing clients. These are always joint productions between ourselves as caterers and suppliers of wine, one of our regularly-used locations, and a selection of our other subcontractors – florists, entertainers, calligraphers, etc. They all give their service free in return for which we supply

the food and drink, organize the event, send out the invitations, and make up a 'press pack' to be given to each guest in which all the participants can put their literature. This way they all get an excellent chance to impress very real potential clients with their skills at a minimal cost. We also include a reference 'cost sheet' for the evening, detailing what the party would have cost had the guests been paying for it, thereby giving them a very accurate picture of what they would get for their money. So far the parties have always been a rave success with a very high rate of acceptances and a good deal of business for us all resulting from them.

All of this, of course, only achieves the initial contact between the client and yourself – it does not guarantee that you will get the job. You still have a lot to do!

Handling Clients

Initial Telephone Call and Telephone Manner
Ninety-five per cent of all enquiries will start with a telephone call, so the impression you make during that first call is vitally important. You should always be polite, enthusiastic and sound as if you are enjoying what you are doing – even if you are feeling filthy, it is pouring with rain, and you have just burnt fifty fillet steaks – and you should always give the impression you know what you are talking about, even if you are bluffing like crazy. But that is not enough – you must also be able to judge very quickly what sort of person you have on the other end of the line. Are they formal and old-fashioned, young and trendy, joky, humourless, feeling put upon by having to organize this entertainment, nervous that they will get it all wrong...? The sooner you can slot into their mood or way of thinking, the better chance you have of pulling off the deal.

This may sound horrendously difficult, but you would be surprised how easy it is to improve your telephone manner once you start to think about it – and how improving it will repay you. Start by just listening to other people on the telephone – especially those trying to sell you something! Many of them do it *very* badly and it can be quite fun analysing exactly where they go wrong and in

what ways they fail to interest you in – or even actively put you off – whatever it is they are trying to sell you. Next, start to listen to yourself and notice where you may be guilty of the same mistakes. Remember that the person you are talking to on the telephone cannot see you (often a great relief), so you have to project the whole of your personality through your voice. It is no good saying something with a great smile on your face which they cannot see, that smile has to be heard in your voice. Again, this may sound very difficult, but listen to people's voices when they are really smiling with amusement (and listen to your own) and you will 'hear' the smile. Very simple vocal tricks, like keeping your voice up at the end of a sentence (so many people allow their voices to trail off) will make a surprising difference to the way you sound.

See if you can get someone else to work with. The chances are that they will never have thought about telephone manner either, but tell them what to watch out for and then experiment by trying to sell them an exotic dinner for two on a moonlit barge and see how you get on. Insist that they are critical. In fact, it would be good to do it both ways round as you may learn as much from criticizing them as from doing it yourself. But you must do it on the telephone – it is no good sitting in the same room and pretending.

I know I appear to be labouring this point, but it is incredible how useful a good telephone manner can be to you. Not only will it help you make deals, but it will help you throughout your negotiations. If your client is happy talking to you on the telephone, you may be able to cut down the number of actual meetings to a minimum – thus saving you a lot of time. It will also help you enormously if disasters occur, either to persuade someone to rescue you, or to pacify whoever you have offended.

However, the most persuasive telephone manner in the world will not be enough to ensure success unless you can follow up. During that first call, you need to discover what the client wants and whether you can provide it and then get as much information about the event as possible. Even if they are not ready to place an order, referring to a basic 'order form' (see page 146) will help to remind you of any vital questions you should ask. If the call does result in an order, you need only fill in the order form and get on with it. If, however, it is really a request for information, then you will have to provide it before you can go any further.

Estimates

Once you get beyond the initial enquiry, usually followed by sending a brochure, you will move on to the estimate stage. Here again, clarity and efficiency should always be your goals. A comprehensive and detailed estimate will not only be of great help to your client, it will also be extremely useful to you as a record of what you have suggested – and what you are proposing to charge. Even in this telephonic age, it always pays to have a written record of your arrangements.

You will find a lengthy sample estimate letter on pages 107–9, but a checklist of what every estimate should contain is always useful.

1 Date, time, location and numbers of proposed function.
2 Proposed menus and prices.
3 Proposed drinks and prices.
4 Any other suggested services – locations, flowers, entertainers, etc.
5 Costs of all suggested services, plus any extras – service, VAT, etc.
6 Your terms – a deposit if you want to take one, how soon you would like to be paid, etc.
7 You should also point out any problems that you anticipate with the running of the function, be it with food or anything else. Clients, especially inexperienced ones, will expect everything to run smoothly unless you warn them of possible hazards. For example, if they insist on a soufflé for a dinner party, you must warn them that if a guest is late the soufflé will be ruined. As long as you warn them, then if they want to go ahead the responsibility is theirs; if you don't, it is yours – even if it was their guest who was late!

Keeping Your Clients

The best way to keep them, of course, is to do their functions so well that they return to you next time. This is fine provided that they have regular functions and that their personnel do not change too much. However, if they are only occasional party or function organizers, they may easily forget about you; and if the personnel change, the next time they want to throw a party the new organizer may know nothing about you.

It therefore pays to keep old clients in touch with what you are doing. Send them new sets of menus, wine lists or price lists whenever you bring them out. Notify them if you add any new service to your stable – hire of puce-coloured limousines or bearded belly dancers! Send them greetings cards of some kind – I shy away from Christmas cards because so many people send them and yours will probably get buried under a heap of others. But how about a Happy Valentine, Burns Night, Hallowe'en or Midsummer Night card? Invite them to any promotional functions you may be holding, and if you get a write-up in a newspaper or magazine, send them a copy.

Dealing with Confirmed Client

Now that you have got your client hooked, you have only to keep him or her happy until the function has happened – for suggestions on how to do this, see page 105. Assuming that 'all goes right on the night', you can then sit back and graciously accept compliments, thanks and money! But what happens if it doesn't?

Dealing with Unhappy Clients

Each dissatisfied client has to be dealt with dispassionately on his or her own merits. First of all, you must decide whether the complaint is justified. You should, of course, be rigorous in your judgement of your own and your company's success and failure rate, but not every complaint is justified. However, even if you reckon you are in the clear, your attitude should always be apologetic and conciliatory – apologetic not because you were at fault, but because the function you had all hoped would be such a success was not. If you were at fault, then you must admit it immediately, unreservedly and with profound apologies.

Each complaint is different. Occasionally, it will pay you to be totally frank and admit that you completely forgot to do something – but you must be careful only to do this if you have already established a reputation for efficiency so that this peccadillo can be seen only as an odd and uncharacteristic lapse – it proves that even you are human. Such honesty usually only pays over relatively minor matters. Over more major disasters, it is better to have a good and convincing story (be it true or false) as to why whatever happened did happen. On the occasion on which our delivery van was held up by a bomb scare and finally arrived an hour late escorted by a flotilla of police motorbikes, the duck for the dinner was undercooked. We had been delayed for an hour by the bomb scare which set our timetable back. Of course, by the time the guests arrived the bomb scare was over so they were all on time and the dinner had to go ahead according to schedule despite our apprehensions about the readiness of our ducks. The client was unhappy about his pink ducks and complained loudly and bitterly. Obviously, we took full responsibility for the fact that the ducks were still pink, but everyone had to admit that it was really not our fault.

I am afraid for the sake of your reputation you may sometimes have to be somewhat 'economical' with the truth – or indeed blame some totally innocent, and hopefully fictional, third party for whatever the mishap may have been. But, however you 'talk your way out of the situation', you should always start with the attitude that 'the client is always right'. Even if you come to the conclusion that the complaint is completely unjustified and that the client is being totally unreasonable, stay cool and be polite but firm. Losing your temper will do nothing for your reputation – or your blood pressure!

Conclusion

It goes without saying that if you do manage to do all these things, and do them right, you are on your way to your first million – well your first half-million anyway. Even if you only manage some of them, as long as you realize that it will be hard work, you should still find yourself running a very successful catering business – but you should also enjoy it. Good luck.

Suggested Further Reading

Cooking for Cash by Jennifer Curry (David & Charles)
Catering for Functions by M. R. Small (Hutchinson Educational)

If you are thinking of going into large-scale catering, there are a number of excellent works on the subject of quantity catering to be found in most libraries or good bookshops.

INDEX